COGNITIVE BEHAVIOUR THERAPY IN THE REAL WORLD

COGNITIVE BEHAVIOUR THERAPY IN THE REAL WORLD

Back to Basics

Henck van Bilsen

Routledge
Taylor & Francis Group
LONDON AND NEW YORK

First published 2013 by Karnac Books Ltd.

2 Park Square, Milton Park, Abingdon, Oxfordshire OX14 4RN
52 Vanderbilt Avenue, New York, NY 10017

Routledge is an imprint of the Taylor & Francis Group, an informa business

First issued in hardback 2019

British Library Cataloguing in Publication Data

A C.I.P. for this book is available from the British Library

ISBN 978-1-78049-029-8 (pbk)
ISBN 978-0-367-32381-3 (hbk)

Edited, designed and produced by The Studio Publishing Services Ltd
www.publishingservicesuk.co.uk
e-mail: studio@publishingservicesuk.co.uk

CONTENTS

ACKNOWLEDGEMENTS

With thanks to: Mr Percy, the best co-therapist ever, Chris Struiksma, who taught me the wisdom of a scientific approach, Lies van Bilsen, from whom I learnt that reality is just one of many options, Albert van Bilsen, who instilled in me the belief that all will be all right in the end (and if it is not all right, it is not the end), and, most of all, Lynne, who understands. I would like to thank Nicky, Louise, Allison and Siobhan for their assistance in creating the verbatim examples.

ABOUT THE AUTHOR

Henck van Bilsen was born in Nederweert, a small village in the southern part of the Netherlands, wedged between Germany and Belgium. He completed his psychology studies at the University of Nymegen and did post-qualification studies in systems therapy at the 'Interaktie Akademie' in Antwerp and the Den Bosch 'Institute for Multidisciplinary Psychotherapy' before qualifying as a behaviour therapist. Behaviour therapy or cognitive behaviour therapy as it is known now became his psychotherapeutic focus with a health respect and scepticism for other innovative and evidence based psychotherapeutic modalities. Henck has worked in a variety of settings: addictions, adult mental health, problems of children and adolescents and personality disorders. A central theme in his clinical interest has been "making psychology and psychotherapy work in challenging circumstances" and his special interest is motivational interviewing. His writings on the application of motivational interviewing with addicted heroin users and the concept of controlled heroin use triggered interesting debates.

Although he has never shaken off the sandy Dutch soil from the southern Netherlands, he sees himself as a citizen of the world, having lived and worked in three countries over two continents.

Currently he leads the psychology department of St. Andrew's Healthcare in Essex and offers private consultations through the CBT-Partnership in Hertford.

Introduction

My interest in psychology was triggered by a book I picked up from the local library in my home town, Nederweert, in the Netherlands. The book was called *Diepte Psychologie,* which, freely translated, would mean "The Psychology of the Deeply Unconscious Mind". Sometimes, the Dutch can say a lot with few words. I was fifteen years old and the book opened up a new world of meaning for me. Inspired mainly by psychodynamic thinking, the author explained the phenomena of the mind in a clear and, at the same time, intriguing way. One author was referred to with a bit more reverence then any others, and I soon managed to borrow a book by this writer. I have to admit that the story that most intrigued me was that this psychiatrist would drink a glass of fine wine with his anxious patients in order to help them relax and be more open about their fears. The psychiatrist in question was Harry Stack Sullivan.

When I started reading his texts, difficult to get hold of in the Netherlands in the late 1960s and early 1970s, I felt as if I could see the world and the people in it for the first time as they truly were. The debate that I had been having with myself about which subject to study at university (computer technology, biochemistry, or psychology) was decided, and psychology it was.

Arriving at Nymegen University in 1972 as an utter convert to psychodynamic thinking, I was deeply disappointed that many classes and subjects were far removed from this. We were, however, blessed with a solid dose of philosophy, in which psychodynamic thinkers had a prominent place. There were also a few lecturers and professors who claimed to be behaviourists. These people had—in my view then—the crazy notion that the only thing that counts is behaviour and that behaviour is governed by scientific laws! How daft can you be? However, in a moment of wisdom, I opted to do a course on learning theory (the alternative would have been advanced statistics, so my choice was based on avoidance!). On this course, I met a lecturer who was a specialist in learning theory, and part of the work was that the students had to train a real living being to behave in certain ways. We had to use learning theory to get rats to do a series of tasks. At the end of the course I was convinced that these behaviourists, these learning theorists, had the future; no more psychoanalysis for me!

Learning theory has remained the foundation for all my clinical work until this day (now in 2012, it is forty years since I started my career as a psychologist). Cognitive additions have been inspirational and challenging, but, in the end, whether internal or external, it is all behaviour . . .

This book is meant to provide an inspirational and enthusiastic introduction to a fascinating field: human change. How can one person, who, until a short time ago, was a complete stranger, assist another person in changing? How is it possible that two people meet and discuss one person's challenges and difficulties and, after a series of meetings, the person's difficulties and challenges have lessened? We certainly occupy a privileged profession.

The book's concepts are illustrated throughout with examples of case material. It should be noted that these examples are based on problem scenarios developed during training and supervision, using role-plays and demonstrations that, while realistic, are not real. Any similarity with real people is purely accidental and unintended.

One of my (mild) disappointments in my professional life has been that I have not been able to follow Harry Stack Sullivan in enjoying a glass of wine with my patients. He did not know it at the time, but by doing this he created an environment that was optimally engineered to produce desirable behaviour (e.g., the mild relaxing effects of one glass of wine made it possible for anxious patients to discuss their deepest fears). Perhaps even then, as a sixteen-year-old, I was thinking in behaviouristic terms. I hope that the book will inspire readers to go back to first principles and use the richness of learning theory to inspire their work as clinicians.

CHAPTER ONE

Cognitive behaviour therapy in the front line

Introduction

The origins of cognitive behaviour therapy (CBT) can be traced back to some early attempts to apply learning theory to behaviour change (Watson & Rayner, 1920). Further theorising and laboratory experimentation on learning theory was done by Skinner (1938), Mowrer (1950) and Salter (1949). It took more than three decades between the first experimental studies on basic learning processes and the formal beginnings of the behavioural component of what we now know as CBT to emerge.

The development of CBT took place in three continents: Africa, Europe, and the Americas. Wolpe (1964), in South Africa, published the first structured treatment protocol: reciprocal inhibition to treat anxiety problems. Eysenck (1963) published accounts of treatment methods such as desensitisation, negative practice, and aversion therapy, all methods grounded in learning theory. Eysenck was the first to bring these various interventions together under the name behaviour therapy (BT) (Farmer & Chapman, 2007). The application of operant learning principles in therapeutic settings was developed in the USA in the application to children's problems and people with learning disabilities (Lovaas, 1987). The term coined here was behaviour modification. The behavioural wave was further developed by Ullman and Krasner (1975). Based on earlier work by Kelly (1955), Beck (1963), and Ellis (1958, 2004), it took until the 1980s before cognitive behaviour therapy as we know it today was firmly established. A further influence was Bandura's (1969, 1986) social learning theory.

A core element of cognitive behaviour therapy (at least, when I was trained in it) is a strong emphasis on the cognitive mediation of behaviour and the application of learning principles to bring about change. The focus of cognitive behaviour therapy is the application of these cognitive psychology principles and learning theory principles to the problems of the individual client. Cognitive behaviour therapists are like experienced chefs in a kitchen; they can follow the instructions of a cookbook, but they also can make a good meal without following a cookbook by using their knowledge about food, preparation of food and taste. Clark (2004) stresses the importance of the interplay between theories, experimental science, and clinical practice to produce clinical innovation.

Sometimes the development of CBT is described in waves (Öst, 2008). Hayes (2004) described the so-called third wave of BT:

> Grounded in an empirical, principle-focused approach, the third Cognitive wave of behavioural and cognitive therapy is particularly sensitive to the context and functions of psychological phenomena, not just their form, and thus tends to emphasize contextual and experiential change strategies in addition to more direct and didactic ones. These treatments tend to seek the construction of broad, flexible, and effective repertoires over an eliminative approach to narrowly defined problems, and to emphasize the relevance of the issues they examine for clinicians as well as clients. The third wave reformulates and synthesizes previous generations of behavioural and cognitive therapy and carries them forward into questions, issues, and domains previously addressed primarily by other traditions, in hope of improving both understanding and outcomes. (Hayes, 2004, p. 658)

The third wave consists of a range of creative and often inventive clinical applications, such as: dialectical behaviour therapy (Linehan, 1993); acceptance and commitment therapy (Hayes, 2004; Hayes, Barnes-Holmes, & Roche, 2001); mindfulness (Teasdale et al., 2000); schema focused therapy (Young, Arntz, & Giesen-Bloo, 2006; Young,

Klosko, & Weishaar, 2003). Many of these approaches are detailed descriptions of one specific technique, such as mindfulness or schema focused therapy, or a set of interventions packaged together as a comprehensive treatment for one identified disorder (dialectical behaviour therapy). I will not go into describing these new branches to the tree of CBT; what is striking, however, is the disparity in development of these various branches. Some are presented as therapeutic interventions after lengthy theoretical investigation, culminating in Randomised Controlled Trials (RCT's) demonstrating the effectiveness. Some interventions or treatments seem to follow the research strategy suggested by Clark (2004), which is that the final step is to make treatments more broadly available through dissemination studies. Acceptance and commitment therapy (ACT), which proposes a comprehensive additional perspective to the behavioural and the cognitive components in CBT and mindfulness, would fall in this group. At the other end of the spectrum, there is schema-focused therapy, which was disseminated through books, workshops, and conference presentations before any clinical trials had been concluded. Compare this with ACT, which only presented itself after a range of research trials had been completed. Dialectical behaviour therapy is somewhere in the middle. It is a serious and innovative attempt to design an effective intervention for a complex client group, but its initial claim to fame was one study with a specific client group and, subsequently, it was "advertised" as *the* treatment of choice for personality disorders. In comparison, mindfulness, which is based on a solid research tradition, has many clinical trials demonstrating its effectiveness in relapse prevention for depression (Segal, Williams, & Teasdale, 2001). It is, however, advertised as a panacea for many clinical problems and, as such, the advertising is ahead of the evidence.

The first wave of CBT was firmly founded in empirical research: therapy techniques and procedures were often directly derived from procedures that had been demonstrated to be effective in animal research (Clark, 2004). The second wave was based on Beck's clinical observations followed by the work of his clinical team (Beck, 1967; Beck, Rush, Shaw, & Emery, 1979), a model that was mirrored by the work of Ellis in New York. The theoretical underpinning of the work of these cognitive therapists was carried out later (Teasdale, 1977, 1983, 1988; Teasdale & Bancroft, 1977; Teasdale & Barnard, 1993). This demonstrates an interesting gap between the development of a clinically inspired theory of depression and the scientific evidence that supports it. The link between theory, evidence, and clinical practice in the third wave is even more variable. Let me make clear that third wave interventions are often very creative and examples of "outside the box" thinking, which should be admired. However, in some cases, the creative insights and practices are not followed up with enough rigorous research, as confirmed by Öst (2008).

Simultaneously with the third wave, another, and, dare I say, a less forward-moving, wave has been at work. The fourth wave of CBT is what I would call the protocolised medicalisation of CBT. It has been demonstrated (Kinderman, 2005; Kinderman & Tai, 2006) that a psychological model is far superior in explaining problems such as depression and anxiety. Within the field of CBT, it has also been argued that a focus on *DSM/ICD* diagnostic classifications is *not* helpful (Harvey, Watkins, Mansell, & Shafran, 2004). The development in mainstream cognitive behaviour therapy seems to have gone completely in the opposite direction, especially in the UK. Books focusing on CBT for specific disorders are published in abundance. CBT protocols for specific and identifiable *DSM/ICD* classifications are produced in vast numbers. The "Improving Access to Psychological Therapies" (IAPT) programme in the UK is a psychological therapy programme in name only, since the treatments are based on disorder-specific protocols and it is stressed that treatment needs to be preceded by having a *DSM-IV* or *ICD-10* classification. This is made clear in two pivotal documents relating to the IAPT programme: the *IAPT Implementation Plan: National Guidelines for Regional Delivery* (Department of Health, 2008) and *The Competences Required To Deliver Effective Cognitive and Behavioural Therapy for People with Depression and with Anxiety Disorders* (Roth & Pilling, 2007). Both documents focus strongly on disorder specific and protocol-driven CBT interventions. The assumption in these documents is that the specific disorders are real entities and that clients can be fitted into boxes of diagnostic categories. This fourth wave implies that many of the great achievements of cognitive behaviour therapy are ignored and that the clock is being turned back. The development of CBT had achieved a feasible alternative to the psychiatric/medical model of framing psychological problems: a psychological model (Kinderman, 2005). Another element of the fourth wave is the increasing protocolisation of "ordinary" CBT, as evidenced by the use of tick-box-type competence measurement instruments, such as the revised cognitive therapy scale (CTS-R) (Blackburn et al., 2001), as the yardstick for competent CBT.

Some critical thoughts about the current state of CBT

There are some problems with elements of the third and fourth wave. The inclusion of many interventions that have little or no theoretical link with the founding theories of CBT and had little or no backing from empirical research has stimulated the development of a range of interventions presented as part of CBT that do not have a solid evidence base. In itself, there is no harm in this; great things happen when clinicians try things out (as demonstrated by Beck and Ellis when they stopped following psychodynamically informed treatment models), report about it, and repeat the process until a new or better intervention is developed, which, subsequently, is tested with reputable research methods. However, what happened in the third wave is that some of the "inventions" were promoted, with little evidence to support the claim, as evidence-based interventions, and they were presented in the same light as CBT for depression. The firm connection of therapeutic techniques with the theories underpinning CBT was less well established and empirical support for some of these interventions is very thin (Öst, 2008). A prime example of an approach that was widely disseminated before any empirical studies had demonstrated its effectiveness is schema-focused therapy. The first randomised controlled trial (Giesen-Bloo et al., 2006) was published only a few years ago, yet schema-focused therapy had been introduced at many conferences and workshops as an effective intervention from the mid-1990s onward.

The fourth wave has given us many detailed and evidence-based interventions for specific and identifiable problems. The problem is that the specific problem categories are based on a classification system that is very much open to criticism (Grove, 1987; Helzer et al., 1977; Hyler, Williams, & Spitzer, 1982; Kirk & Kutchins, 1988, 1992).

This is also evidence of a further medicalisation of psychological therapies. As a clinical psychologist, I was trained to understand that a diagnosis is the idiosyncratic narrative or individualised holistic theory about *how* the client came to have these problems and *why* they still persist. In medical terminology, a diagnosis is allocating a *DSM* or *ICD* classification to the presentation of a client. In the field of psychological therapy, it seems that the word diagnosis is more and more based on this medical perspective. If we *have* the "diagnosis" (i.e., the *DSM/ICD* classification) we *know* which protocolised treatment to give.

Having treatment protocols for specific diagnostic categories assumes that clients in real life and in daily practice can be fitted into these distinct categories. Unfortunately, clients in real life often present us with a mixed bag of problems. A different perspective on mental health problems is the transdiagnostic perspective (Harvey, Watkins, Mansell, & Shafran, 2004). This approach debates the use of diagnostic categories as defined for clinical practice. In a categorical diagnostic model (whether it is based on *DSM* or *ICD*), a heterogenic group of people is captured under the umbrella of a diagnosis. No wonder that there are strong moves to focus more on dimensional models of mental health problems—for instance, with respect to personality disorders (Widiger, 1992). Harvey, Watkins, Mansell, and Shafran (2004) postulate that working with processes that are influential in many diagnostic categories might be a better approach for clinicians and researchers. They list important transdiagnostic processes responsible for human misery: attentional processes; memory processes; reasoning processes; thought processes; behavioural processes. Harvey and co-authors (2004) state that—for several reasons—a transdiagnostic process is the preferred model. First of all, thinking in diagnostic categories leads to easy "us and them" thinking. They also make the case that a classification–diagnostic approach is an impossible task for diagnosticians with, at the moment, 350+ disorders described in the *DSM* (no sane person is able to have this amount of information in their working memory). They further argue that, in a diagnostic approach, valuable personal and idiosyncratic information is in danger of getting lost. Furthermore, it becomes very difficult to deal with co-morbidity in a categorical model. I favour a transdiagnostic and problem-based approach: not the diagnostic category, but the processes involved in problem presentation and the identified problems are analysed in an idiosyncratic model to construct the basis of formulation and treatment.

Back to first principles

Nothing is as practical as a good theory! Kurt Lewin (1935, 1936, 1948) had it so very right when he said this. As cognitive behaviour therapists we operate in the real world as "scientist-practitioners". We cannot be practitioners alone; we have to use science to make sense of the phenomena we encounter. Science will also help us when "practice as usual" does not produce the expected results. As scientist-practitioners, we have to be able to use theory to think ourselves out of a practice problem. In other words, when we apply therapeutic interventions "as recommended" and they do not work "as predicted", we need to use our knowledge and understanding of theory to work our way out of this.

Readers who are sitting on the edge of their chairs, eagerly anticipating completely new insights and new theories on CBT, will be deeply disappointed. One of the current trends in CBT is the assumption that new theories and new intervention strategies are needed for each specific disorder. We would like to postulate that psychological difficulties are a human phenomenon and that theories that explain human behaviour can be applied to people with psychological difficulties. They are characterised by behaviours, emotions, and cognitions that have become problematic. Learning theory and cognitive theory, the underpinning theoretical frameworks of cognitive behaviour therapy, can be used to explain how problem behaviours, emotions, and cognitive processes emerge and how they are maintained. These theories apply to people with psychological difficulties just as they apply to other people.

A theory is like a map, and if you want to find your way with a map it is important to match where you are with the pages of your map book. If you want to find your way in Lisbon, it is a futile exercise to study the pages in the book of maps that has the street-plan of London. You will not find your way. Similarly, if one has the correct map and the situation is very complicated, it pays to be very careful and study the map and one's surroundings carefully. People with psychological difficulties present complicated situations for psychological therapists and, therefore, the available theories need to be applied with great care.

Positive deviancy as the starting point of CBT

The two founding fathers of cognitive therapy, Ellis and Beck, were both trained as psychoanalysts. Only through deviating from accepted (psychoanalytical) treatment protocols did they come to "discover" a theory and a practice that had more benefits for their patients than the therapeutic method that they were supposed to apply.

The greatest deviant ever (Best & Neuhauser, 2004) is, of course, Dr Ignaz Philipp Semmelweis (1 July 1818–13 August 1865). He was a Hungarian physician, described as the "saviour of mothers", who discovered that the incidence of childbed fever could be drastically cut by the use of hand disinfection (by means of hand washing with chlorinated lime solution) in maternity clinics. Doctors often went directly from doing an autopsy to attending to sick patients, often with only a cursory cleaning of the hands. Childbed fever was common in mid-nineteenth-century hospitals and often fatal, with mortality at 10–35%. Semmelweis postulated the theory of washing with "chlorinated lime solutions" in 1847, while working in Vienna General Hospital's First Obstetrical Clinic, where doctors' wards had three times the mortality of midwives' wards. He published a book of his findings on childbed fever, *Aetiology, Concept and Prophylaxis of Childbed Fever*. Despite various publications in which he demonstrated that hand washing reduced mortality to below 1%, Semmelweis's practice earned widespread acceptance only years after his death, when Louis Pasteur confirmed the germ theory. Semmelweis was fired from his position in the hospital, and banned from practising medicine because he had brought the profession of doctors into disrepute for suggesting that doctors could be responsible for the deaths of their patients. In 1865, a nervous breakdown landed him in an asylum, where, ironically, Semmelweis died of septicaemia, at the age of forty-seven.

Beck, Ellis, and Semmelweis were all positive deviants in the best possible way: they deviated from the norm and produced better results. When they started deviating, their reasons for doing so were similar and, at first, *not theory driven*. Semmelweis observed the different practice between doctors' wards and midwives' wards and made suggestions accordingly (without having a real theory to underpin these suggestions). Both Beck and Ellis were unhappy with the progress their depressed clients were making while undergoing traditional psychoanalysis. By listening to the content of what their patients were telling them, they came up with different intervention strategies, *at first without an explicitly formulated theory to support their intervention strategies*. Just as Semmelweis could argue on empirical grounds (fewer women died), so could Beck and Ellis put forward that what they did made sense (more patients recovered). Both are examples of scientist-practitioners in action. The scientist carefully observes the impact of the intervention and if the impact is wrong (in Semmelweis's case, women died) or does not produce good enough results, as in the case of Beck and Ellis, the practitioner tries a different approach. This different approach might not be completely theory driven; it might be purely intuitive, based on observations and correlations (Semmelweis) or based on incomplete theoretical notions linked with practical insights (Beck and Ellis).

In this chapter, I will highlight key features of cognitive behaviour therapy and outline briefly the core components underpinning CBT, in the hope of demonstrating that through the structure of CBT shines a highly innovative and creative therapy model that is more, much more, than merely following protocols.

Key elements of CBT

Few psychological therapy approaches have generated as much interest over the past decades as CBT. Based on the notion that learning and thinking play roles in how emotional and behavioural problems emerge and how they are maintained, this therapy aims to reduce distress by unlearning maladaptive habits, changing maladaptive beliefs, and providing new information-processing skills.

CBT can be seen as a huge tree with many "branches", such as rational emotive behaviour therapy (Ellis, 1970), dialectical behaviour therapy, ACT (acceptance and commitment therapy), mindfulness-based CBT, and compassionate-based CBT. Despite their commonalities, these approaches differ with respect to the processes that underpin change and the procedures to bring about change. All of these approaches have at least the following principles in common. They are:

- based on a cognitive and/or behavioural model of emotional disorders;
- brief and time limited;
- structured and directive;
- problem orientated;
- based on an educational model;
- based on a collaborative therapeutic relationship;

- using homework as an essential feature;
- using a holistic conceptualisation of the client and the client's problems;
- using problem-solving techniques.

All cognitive behavioural interventions attempt to achieve change by influencing thinking (Mahoney, 1977). Even primarily in behavioural techniques (exposure), the change in thinking facilitates effective processing. Cognitive behavioural approaches focus on the way in which an individual interprets the world in which they live. Thinking plays a role in determining subsequent affect and behaviour. Thinking itself is influenced by existing moods and the consequences of prior actions (Bandura, 1986). Thinking plays a strong facilitative role in how emotional and behavioural disorders start and are maintained. Therefore, changing thinking can serve to bring about therapeutic change.

Within the framework of cognitive behavioural approaches there is some variation with respect to both processes and procedure. Some approaches focus on the modification of behaviours through skills training (Falloon, 2003; Falloon et al., 2004; Linehan, 1993), while others focus on changing of distortions of existing beliefs. Others seek to compensate for perceived deficits in cognitive skills (Beck, 1963, 1976; Beck, Rush, Shaw, & Emery, 1979; Ellis, 1958, 1970, 2004; Kendall & Braswell, 1985). The approaches also differ in the extent to which they incorporate imagery strategies, behavioural components, and the variation of cognitive interventions.

Interventions are all based on a cognitive and/or behavioural model of human misery

An essential component of CBT is to understand as a therapist, and help the client to understand, that there is a link between one's misery on the one hand and one's beliefs and behaviours on the other hand. The behavioural element means that in CBT there is an acceptance that problem behaviours and emotions have been learnt. This learning process can be understood by applying learning principles of operant and respondent conditioning to human behaviour (Domjan, 2006).

An example is the CBT model of depression. Depression is a problem with low mood. The low mood is linked with ongoing negative appraisals of self (I am incompetent, weak, unlovable), others (other people are mean, unsupportive, critical), and the future (the future is hopeless, it will never get better). Depression is also linked with a change in activity pattern. Lowering of activities and avoiding engaging with other people reduces the chance that any of the negative appraisals is activated (negative reinforcement). A consequence of feeling depressed is often a reduction in satisfying and pleasurable activities; this reduction will subsequently result in a further lowering of mood. The low mood then fuels the negative appraisals further and, by doing so, creates a vicious circle.

Interventions are brief and time limited

CBT therapists work in a focused way and they aim for time limited and brief therapies. This means that therapies are not offered on a completely open-ended basis. All therapies are guided by identified problems and specific goals. This does *not* mean that therapy can only last a limited number of sessions; it means that therapist and client regularly evaluate progress and make a plan for the next period of sessions. It often makes sense to have agreements with clients for short sequences of sessions and not to leave therapy open-ended. With one depressed client, I made an agreement for four sessions of assessment and then came to an agreement of six therapy sessions, to be evaluated in the sixth session. In the end, we finished therapy at session nineteen, but evaluated progress at sessions ten, sixteen, and nineteen. Each time, we made an agreement for six or three more sessions, based on the progress made.

A sound collaborative therapeutic relationship is essential

The therapist is very empathic and rewarding when the client contributes to the therapy. The therapist is also focused on getting the client's input to the agenda; even when the client presents issues for the agenda in a "hidden" manner, the therapist brings them to the foreground and puts them on the agenda. In one of the case vignettes below (the first session with Abigail) the client is clearly reluctant to discuss her difficulties. By using empathic listening, the therapist gradually gets the client to talk about her difficulties.

Interventions are structured and directive

As can be seen from the case vignette detailed below, sessions start with the setting of an agenda and then follow the agenda. Setting the agenda is not always a straightforward process, but it is a very important one. It allows the therapist to be directive and allows for input from the client.

In the transcript of the beginning of a first session (below), the therapist demonstrates that with a sceptical client like Rachel, it is important *and productive* to stay firmly on track, while being careful not to alienate the client.

Therapy sessions are problem orientated

The therapist focuses the therapy on the problems the client wants to resolve. Complaints are translated into workable elements that can be changed in therapy. Identifying clear and specific problems and goals at the beginning of therapy is very important in CBT. The next case vignette occurred towards the end of the first session, where the therapist tried to establish some problems and goals for therapy.

Problems need to be established by getting clients to explore how certain things make them feel. Issues that cause negative and unwanted feelings result in a stronger motivation to work on them than issues for which this is not the case. In CBT, the therapist needs to identify issues that are connected with strong negative affect, and these need to be linked with the possibility of change.

Sessions are based on an educational model

The aim of the CB therapist is to educate the client so that she becomes knowledgeable about CBT and can make sense of her problems from a CBT perspective. In the case vignette, the therapist explains the basics of CBT and checks with the client whether he has understood it.

The style is educational, but not in the form of lengthy lectures. The client is invited to think with the therapist and to learn from the dialogue.

Homework is an essential feature of therapy

In CBT, the therapy sessions are important, but, equally, so are the "learning" tasks the therapist and client negotiate for the client to undertake between the therapy sessions; these can take different forms, but are often agreed as "behavioural experiments", intended to give the client the opportunity to try out and practise different or "new" behaviour. A CBT session is usually only one hour every week or fortnight. Therefore, for the therapy to have an impact, the client needs to work on therapeutic tasks between the sessions.

Therapy proceeds according to the therapist's holistic conceptualisation

The therapy itself and the in-between session tasks are structured upon the therapist's understanding of the client's problems. For clients with mild to moderate problems who present for the first time to a therapist, this understanding might be based on a brief assessment of the issues upon which the therapist decides to offer the client a structured (protocolised) CBT intervention. For clients who have received CBT or other treatments before without success, and for clients with severe problems, the therapist will opt for an in-depth and detailed assessment before deciding on an individualised treatment plan. A conceptualisation attempts to identify learning processes from the client's past and current maintenance factors.

The therapy uses problem solving techniques

CBT breaks down problems into manageable units, identifying the roadblocks which hinder problem-solving abilities. It does not perceive human change as an all-or-nothing phenomenon. The beginning of a change process involves careful identification of problems and goals. These are often broken down into smaller segments, thus making them much more achievable. Subsequently, these are addressed with a range of therapeutic interventions and, thus, break down the "problem wall" brick by brick and, thereby, assist the client to an optimal recovery step by step.

Here follows an example of a second session with a client having problems with feeling anxious. This is how Sarah talked about her experience of CBT after the first session.

> "My name is Sarah. I went to my GP about a month ago when I was quite worried that I had problems with my breath and my throat. I live in London and I've been working there for about three years and getting the Tube in with no problems. About six months ago, I went in rush hour on the Tube, which was unusual, and it was really crowded and I got jostled

and started feeling quite scared and trapped really, and I became aware that, if there was a problem, I wouldn't be able to get off the Tube. I started breathing really fast and everything started feeling like it was spinning and I just had to get off the Tube as soon as I could and get out of the station.

"Since then, I haven't really been on the Tube. I tried it again a couple more times and had the same experience, so I started getting the bus and that seemed much better, but then a couple of months ago the same thing started happening, so I started thinking that maybe it wasn't that there wasn't enough oxygen in the Tube, which was what I'd first thought, but maybe it's a problem with me and my breathing because it really feels, when this happens, that I'm going to suffocate and it's really quite scary. So I went to my GP just to try and get checked out and he did examine me, but he said that he thought it might be panic attacks, and he referred me for CBT.

"I have had one session, and so far it seems to make sense that this might be panic attacks or this might be anxiety, but, when I'm having these episodes, which are now happening whenever I go out really, it still feels that there's something wrong physically, that I'm going to suffocate. You know, I'm quite open-minded about it and I'm quite willing to do the work, but there's still a part of me that's quite scared that maybe I will suffocate and actually might die, so I've come along to the second session today and I've done some homework, which was to write down a couple of situations that I've been in where I've felt really anxious, and I think that we're going to be working through those today."

The dialogue that followed is given below, with comments describing what is happening in square brackets.

Therapist: Well, Sarah, thank you, and thanks for coming to the session again. We had a session a week ago and here you are again at our second meeting. Are there things that you would like to put on the agenda for today, things that you would like to talk about and address in this session? [Commenting on the fact that this is the second session, starting with "the agenda" and asking client to contribute to the agenda is evidence of the *structure and directiveness* of CBT and it emphasises *collaboration*.]

Client: Yes, something that's actually on the sheet that I did for homework about a situation at the supermarket recently.

Therapist: So I'll put "supermarket" down on the list. [Paraphrasing what client states and making a point of noting it down is, again, evidence of *collaboration*.]

Client: Yes, and it was just really uncomfortable and it would be quite useful to talk about that because of how to manage it really.

Therapist: So that's one situation that you also wrote about in your homework that you really would like to talk about? [Linking what the client says with homework given is evidence of *collaboration* and *structure*.]

Client: Yes, please.

Therapist: Excellent, so we will make sure that we prioritise that, so that's one. Is there anything else that you would like to put on the agenda? [Asking for other agenda points is evidence of *collaboration*.]

Client: Not specifically. I think that's the biggie for me.

Therapist: That's the biggie?

Client: Yes.

Therapist: So, to talk about the situation and perhaps get some tips on how to deal with the difficulties that you encountered there?

Client: Yes, it would be really helpful.

Therapist: Do you mind if I just say a few things that I would like to address in this session? [Asking permission before adding therapist's items to the agenda is a sign of good *collaboration*.]

Client: That's fine.

Therapist: There are just a couple of very basic things, checking with you whether you have any leftover questions from the last session, going through the homework, and I will make sure that we focus on this specific situation, which was also one of my plans, to focus on one specific situation, and perhaps to talk a bit more about that and see if we can use that situation to understand this anxiety problem a little bit better. Is it OK if we add this to the list of things to talk about? [The topics are all signs of the therapist *structuring* and *directing* the therapy process.]

Client: Yes.

Therapist: The other thing that I would like to talk about a bit more perhaps is to see if we can identify some specific problems we're going to work on and some goals for therapy. How does that sound as an agenda? [Introducing problems and goals means the therapist wants to make the therapy *problem focused*.]

Client: Yes, that sounds good.

Therapist: Any preferences for priorities? [Asking the client to prioritise is a sign of good *collaboration*.]

Client: I think the situation in the supermarket, it might be quite good to deal with that first because it's very big in my mind and I might struggle to think about other things. [The client selects that she wants to discuss a specific incident, this is not the "logical" order of the session that the therapist would have preferred (reviewing last session, homework review, etc.). By going along with the client's choice, the therapist demonstrates the *problem focus* of CBT and *good collaboration*.]

Therapist: So, the situation in the supermarket might be a good thing to start with, and then we might move on to perhaps things from the last session, whether there are any questions there, the homework, and problems and goals. That is what I have now, that we start with the situation in the supermarket, then we'll have a little check about the previous session, whether there are any leftover questions there, and then we might move to the homework and, last but not least, problems and goals. Is that OK?

Client: Yes.

Therapist: If anything else comes up, just interrupt me and we can add it to the list. Is that OK?

Client: That's fine, yes.

Therapist: The supermarket situation, can you tell me a bit more about that? [Open question to start the process of investigating the problem.]

Client: Yes, it was on Wednesday. I went in the morning because, you know, I was hoping that it wouldn't be too busy midweek in the morning. It was quite busy. I don't know why.

Therapist: So that was Wednesday morning? [The questioning will be based on a cognitive behavioural conceptualisation of the problems, trying to get the data so a CBT model of this client's problem experience can be built. In order to do so, the therapist will have in the back of his mind the conceptualisation models and frameworks he wants to use. In this case, the SORC model and the BASIC-ID elements (see Chapter Five).

Client: Yes.

Therapist: You were hoping it was not too busy?

Client: Yes, and I notice that I'm worse when there are more people around, definitely.

Therapist: When you say "worse", what do you mean?

Client: Well, when I start having these kind of strange episodes, I just feel really panicky and wanting to get out.

Therapist: So that would be worse when it's busy?

Client: Yes.

Therapist: And, when it's busy, you want more to get out and you feel more panicky? [Careful questioning, to really understand what the client's experience is: *collaboration*.]

Client: Yes, yes, very much.

Therapist: So you were hoping on Wednesday morning that it wouldn't be too busy? ["Hoping": therapist focuses on cognitions prior to the problem moment. This is evidence of paying attention to a transdiagnostic process: the "hope" creates an attentional focus on other people.]

Client: Yes, and I had quite a lot of shopping to do, so I didn't really, you know, I really needed to stay there and get it done.

Therapist: So when you say it was Wednesday morning, what time are we talking about?

Client: Late morning. I think it was 11 o'clock, as I've written down here.

Therapist: Just talk me through what happened. [Therapist varies specific and focused questions with open questions to give client an opportunity to tell her story.]

Client: Well, I kind of went in and noticed immediately that it was quite busy, so immediately I was, I suppose, uneasy really and I started thinking, "I need to get this done quickly and get out of here so that I don't have a panic", so I started getting on with the shopping and I had just become really aware of how noisy it was. There were kids crying and screaming and, you know, I could just hear all the noise all the time.

Therapist: So you heard the noise of the whole shop?

Client: Yes, yes.

Therapist: What kind of shop is it, may I ask? [This is not a trivial question, but aimed at really establishing the stimulus constellation (e.g., getting specific data to build a CBT model).]

Client: A supermarket.

Therapist: A small one, big one, massive one, supercentre?

Client: No, it was one of the larger Tesco's.

Therapist: So one of the super-Tesco's where you can you get—

Client: Clothes and everything, yes.

Therapist: Yes, I think they can host an army in them, very big! So it was very noisy?

Client: Yes. I've never really noticed the noise before, but it was really, really obvious, so I went round as quickly as possible. I'd sort of memorised the layout, when I wrote my shopping list, in the right order so that I can kind of go round the right way, so I was as prepared as I could be, I suppose. I did all right. I mean, I got everything I needed in my trolley and then I got to the tills and there weren't very many open, which is often the way, I guess, so I had to join this really big queue, and there was someone behind standing too close. You know when someone stands just that little bit uncomfortably too close behind you? [The client provides the therapist with a lot of invaluable information here with which an *idiosyncratic CBT model* of the client's problems can be built. The client has prepared her shopping trip like an army exercise, for example, it is not just a shopping trip any more but a series of success/failure tasks: do I remember the shopping lanes correctly, is my list correct, is the list in the correct order . . .]

Therapist: Hmm, hmm.

Client: She was kind of getting me in the leg with her shopping basket. I suppose I started feeling a bit like crowded in, a little bit like that time on the Tube when I'd felt trapped, and there was someone quite close in front and I suppose the gap at the till is quite narrow, so I started feeling, "If I need to get out of here, I'm not going to be able to."

Therapist: So, "If I need to get out of here, I won't be able to"? [Paraphrase = collaboration.]

Client: Yes, and then I started noticing I was breathing faster and I could feel my heart kind of thudding and, you know, I knew this was going to happen because it's always the same and then I start feeling tightness in my throat. [The therapist has noticed the client is in full flow and does not interrupt with his questions that can wait until later: evidence of collaboration.]

Therapist: So tightness in your throat, your heart thudding, breathing faster?

Client: Yes, and I started feeling dizzy and it feels really like I'm suffocating, but the more I'm breathing, as fast as I can breathe, I'm just not able to get enough oxygen in.

Therapist: So you're really trying to catch your breath?

Client: Yes, and I'm trying to breathe extra deep so I get more oxygen in.

Therapist: And that sense of suffocating didn't go on Wednesday?

Client: Not at all. I started feeling dizzy and, you know, I just felt worse really.

Therapist: What happened then?

Client: Well, nothing because I couldn't get out. I mean, I would've run away, but I had to stay.

Therapist: You had to stay?

Client: Yes.

Therapist: So what happened?

Client: I just tried to focus on my shopping. In fact, I was focusing on the "Next customer" sign on the conveyer belt and I just kept staring at that and saying to myself, "This will be over soon and just get home and, when you get home, you can have a cup of tea and it'll be fine", and I was just trying to reassure myself, I guess.

Therapist: And then what happened?

Client: Well, I paid for it and left.

Therapist: How long did it take from when you joined the queue and pushed your trolley through and left? How long did that take, do you think? [Ongoing questions to really get the picture what was happening.]

Client: God, I have no idea! It felt like ages. I'd say, realistically I suppose, probably ten or fifteen minutes. It felt like an hour.

Therapist: I want to go back over the story again and ask you a few more questions, if that's OK. In the morning when you woke up and you knew you had to do the shopping, how anxious did that thought of having to do the shopping make you? ["Going back over the story again" is a real sign of *structuring and directiveness*. Now the therapist will ask questions to fill the gaps in the model that he has been building up in his mind.]

Client: Quite anxious.

Therapist: How would you rate it on a scale from zero to 100?

Client: Maybe thirty or thirty-five, somewhere around there. I was still able to think straight, but I was quite uneasy.

Therapist: So, uneasy since "I've got to do this difficult thing that could potentially lead to a serious anxiety attack"?

Client: Yes.

Therapist: Then I gather from this that, at a certain point in time, you started to prepare yourself and write a shopping list in the order of the shopping aisles. Is that correct? [Here the therapist is again focused on how the client prepares for her shopping trip and the information collected confirms that it is a very well planned event!]

Client: Well, I'd done the list the night before, but then in the morning I actually rewrote the list in the right order.

Therapist: What would that do? Would it increase or reduce your anxiety? [This question has an interesting result. It gives insight in the client's reasoning regarding her preparations. An unstructured shopping trip, with no demands apart from "let's get everything in the shopping trolley that I have on my list" is an easier task to achieve than "I need to do the shopping in the most logical order so I will spend the absolute minimum of time in the shop. My list needs to be in the order of the shopping aisles". The client believes the opposite, and the therapist has uncovered a self-defeating behaviour and, thus, is building the *CBT model* of the problems.]

Client: I suppose temporarily it reduced it because I was thinking, "Well, at least I'm making it as easy as I can."

Therapist: So it reduced a little bit, but then it crept back up?

Client: Yes, yes.

Therapist: Do you have to get in the car to go to the shopping centre?

Client: Yes.

Therapist: So, when you got into the car before 11 o'clock to drive to Tesco's, how was your anxiety then?

Client: Yes, it had gone up, it was quite high, maybe fifty.

Therapist: So in the car to Tesco's, when you got in the car at your house, it crept up to around fifty?

Client: Yes.

Therapist: And, now you've arrived at Tesco's, what's happened to your anxiety? Is it still fifty, has it gone up a bit, gone down a bit?

Client: It's gone up, it's gone up. I'm feeling anxious now thinking about it.

Therapist: So you're at Tesco's, you've parked your car and you walk from the car to the entrance. What's happened to your anxiety? [Carefully monitoring client's anxiety development to improve the model.]

Client: I'm looking around the car park and thinking, "There are a lot of cars here" and, you know, it was obviously making me more anxious because I could see how busy it was going to be.

Therapist: That's very interesting, so lots of cars and, when you entered Tesco's, you walked in there and grabbed yourself a shopping trolley, how high was your anxiety then on that Wednesday?

Client: About sixty or sixty-five, something like that.

Therapist: So it's creeping up?

Client: Yes.

Therapist: So you had this thought when you were walking through the car park, "There are lots of cars here. It's busy in the shop"?

Client: Yes.

Therapist: That seems to be a problem for you, the busyness.

Client: Yes.

Therapist: Can you tell me a little bit more about that. Why is that a problem?

Client: Well, if you go in somewhere that's empty and you need to leave, you just leave because there's no one in your way. When places are busy, there's that sense of kind of having to find the way out and fight your way through a bit.

Therapist: So, when you were walking from your car to the entrance of Tesco's, you have noticed that it's busy. Is that just a thought? You described that very graphically, of fighting your way, so do you also have an image of that? [The therapist has picked up the word "fight", which is a rather strong word to use for a normal shopping trip, hence questions about imagery. Images are explicitly mentioned in the BASIC-ID (see Chapter Five) and can be very important elements in the maintenance of problems.]

Client: The image I've got actually, you know they've got that really enormous door and the image I've got when it's quiet is that it's really light and the image I've got of when it's busy is that I can't really see it and it's dark and I'm kind of obstructed, so the focus is on the door actually. That's quite interesting; I hadn't thought of it like that.

Therapist: So, when it's busy, you kind of feel obstructed by the crowd and the exit becomes almost like a big shutter that's closed and it's dark?

Client: Yes, yes.

Therapist: Was that image floating through your mind when you walked up to Tesco's?

Client: I don't know. It might well have been, but I can't really recall.

Therapist: So you're now in Tesco's and you were saying that you were doing your shopping really quickly. If you do your shopping quickly, how does that go?

Client: How do you mean?

Therapist: Well, do you push your trolley quickly and, if it's busy and you push your trolley quickly, how does that work with so many people in the shop? How does that go? [This question is focused on eliciting more information to build a CBT model and another self-defeating behaviour is identified: walking quickly with a trolley in a busy shop. Doing this will increase the chance of bumping into people with ensuing problems.

Client: Well, it's tricky because people keep getting in the way.

Therapist: So they block your way?

Client: Yes.

Therapist: So you are doing it very quickly and people are getting in the way and, when that happens, what happens in your mind?

Client: I'm just thinking, "Get out of the way!"

Therapist: "Get out of the way"?

Client: Yes, yes, which I wouldn't say!

Therapist: When you're shopping and you hold the trolley to push it forward, where do you look?

Client: I'm looking at the shelves to see where my items that I need are so that I can get them without having to stop for too long.

Therapist: So you look at the shelves and, when you're moving the trolley, do you still look at the shelves or do you look around you at the people?

Client: Well, I must be looking to some extent, otherwise I'd be bumping into people, I guess.

Therapist: Do you look at their faces; do you look at their feet? [This sounds like a trivial question, but it is not. If we rely on peripheral vision to alert us of potential "danger" then our startle response to these danger signs is much stronger than if we would really look at our surroundings. Again, the client engages in self-defeating behaviours.]

Client: No, no, I just have a sense of where there are people, I suppose, kind of out of my peripheral vision.

Therapist: Very precise, thank you.

Why CBT?

The research evidence for the effectiveness of cognitive behaviour therapy is abundant, from Roth and Fonagy (2004) to the Guidelines from the National Institute for Health and Clinical Excellence (during a search in the website of NICE with the term cognitive behaviour therapy, 217 hits came back), CBT is considered the treatment of choice for many mental health problems (Beck, 1976; Beck, Freeman, & Davis, 2007). The scientific evidence is very robust for a range of mental health problems, for example, depression and the anxiety disorders (with a few exceptions, such as body dysmorphic disorder and hoarding). With schizophrenia, there is evidence that CBT and family based CBT are effective in assisting clients to optimal recovery (Kingdon & Turkington, 1991), while for personality disorders there is indicative evidence (Giesen-Bloo et al., 2006; Linehan, 1993), but by no means is it as robust as for depression, anxiety, and schizophrenia.

Another consideration is that the bulk of evidence relates to standard CBT interventions, such as behavioural activation, cognitive restructuring, exposure, response prevention, and other standard techniques in CBT. The evidence becomes somewhat thinner for more recent additions to the range of CBT interventions.

Theoretical foundations

There are two theoretical elements to the cognitive behavioural understanding of human misery, cognitive and learning theory. If we accept that human misery consists of experiencing unhealthy negative feelings or behaving in an unhelpful way (drinking too much, violence, and avoidance), then we need to understand how both cognitive and learning theory contribute to the development of these factors.

Case history: "Try to be better tomorrow"

Abigail is a forty-year-old CEO of a finance company. Her world came crashing down when she collapsed at work some months ago. She describes herself as always having been very driven and hard-working. In the past ten years, she has never had a holiday apart from a few days around Christmas and New Year, and even then she would spend hours in front of the computer. Her "normal" working week consists of sixty hours at the office, around twelve hours travelling from home to work and at least twenty hours working from home. She looks rather puzzled when asked the question, "What do you do for fun?", and can only mention that when she was younger she played the piano and was a member of the local drama society.

About a year ago, she started to develop minor physical problems like never-ending colds, or throat infections. This gradually developed into feeling tired all the time, and finally resulted in her collapse at work. Abigail has explored medical explanations of her problems thoroughly and, although it is clear she has been very vulnerable to infections and colds, no evidence has been found of an underlying cause. She is now consulting with a psychologist, as one of her doctors told her that there might be a psychological root to her problems.

When asked to talk a little bit about her background, she mentions that her parents have taught her to strive for the best and that she would not have wanted it any other way. The goodnight message from both parents each evening was "And now try to be a better girl tomorrow." If she returned home with results of tests in which she had not scored 100%, her parents would question her as to why she had been so slack.

Learning theory

Learning theory encompasses a number of principles that explain how humans learn. The three most important of these are operant learning, respondent learning, and modelling.

Operant learning

Many scientists and psychologists have studied this type of learning, or "conditioning", particularly in animals. One of the most well known, arguably, is Skinner and his experiments with rats in the "Skinner box" (1938). This learning principle tells us that we learn as a result of the consequences of our actions. When we do things, our actions will produce a result. This could be an external event, for example, saying, "Good morning" with a smile to our neighbour results in a reply of "Good morning" from the neighbour. It can also be an internal event, for example, when we see a dog and become anxious, we can reduce or eliminate the anxiety by crossing the street and putting distance between the dog and ourselves. Behaviours that are followed by positive or enjoyable consequences are inclined to happen more often, while behaviours followed by unpleasant consequences tend to be suppressed.

Sounds simple and easy, doesn't it? In reality, it is far more complicated. For instance, the absence of something unpleasant happening seems to work as a reinforcer. This is, in fact, how many anxiety problems are maintained. If we take as an example the fear of failure (a predominant feature of our hard-working client, Abigail) triggers frantic attempts to prevent this from happening. As a result of this, the person will never really experience that failing at something is unpleasant, but not the end of the world. All the actions (overworking behaviour, demanding behaviour) to prevent failure result mostly in being successful and, as a consequence, *a predicted feared outcome* did not happen. We call this negative reinforcement: something unpleasant is taken away or is prevented from occurring.

In this form of learning, there are four alternatives; two result in an increase of the frequency of the behaviour, while two others have a reducing impact on the frequency of behaviours.

Positive reinforcement occurs when behaviour is followed by a positive event; in other words, the behaviour of the person "operates on the environment" in such a way that something positive is produced. Let's take the example of dad taking his little boy Johnny shopping on Saturday. As soon as Dad's shopping cart is half filled, Johnny starts to demand an ice cream in a loud and piercing voice that turns into a shriek when Dad postpones getting an ice cream. As soon as the ice cream is in Johnny's hand, he smiles and says, 'Thank you, Daddy." The giving of the ice cream is called positive reinforcement. Johnny's actions have produced this positive result from the environment.

Negative reinforcement occurs when behaviour is followed by the taking away of a negative/feared event. If we study the example of Johnny and his father, we see that Johnny is a born behaviourist: by stopping his shrieking and crying upon receiving the ice cream, he applies negative reinforcement to Dad's ice cream giving behaviour. And remember, reinforcement always leads to an increase in the frequency of the behaviour reinforced.

A word of warning: reinforcement is what happens, not what we say happens. Giving an ice cream and saying that this is the last time is by no means as powerful as the act of giving the ice cream. Deeds speak much louder than words!

Reinforcements can be very specific and are sometimes too specific for our own good. The father might believe he is reinforcing Johnny's good behaviour if he gives him the ice cream with a warning to behave nicely, but what is rewarded is the behaviour preceding the reinforcement. Punishments can be behaviour specific as well, but in a negative sense. They tell us what *not* to do, they do not tell us what to do instead.

Positive punishment occurs when the behaviour is followed by a negative event: a smack, a reprimand, or criticism. This results in the suppression of the behaviour involved, in the presence of the punisher (one reason why classrooms turn into chaos when the teacher leaves the room!).

Negative punishment is comparable to negative reinforcement: something positive is taken away from the environment following the behaviour. In the Johnny and father example, Johnny could have his ice cream taken away if he misbehaves. Negative punishment, when applied skilfully in educational and parental situations, only needs to happen a couple of times before the warning "If you do not do X, I will take away Y" becomes a powerful tool in controlling behaviour.

What does this learning theory have to do with psychological problems? Learning theory explains how certain very unhealthy behaviours are being maintained and triggered. For people with psychological problems, there is an abundant choice of self-defeating behaviours: self-harm, high risk behaviours, addictive behaviours, and oppositional behaviours. If we want to be able to help clients to change these, it is imperative that we understand the maintenance factors and can help clients to understand these as well.

How does operant learning play a role in Abigail's story?

First of all, Abigail learnt that doing things that displeased her parents was a bad thing. Her parents were not nasty or cruel, but they would let Abigail know when she had done something wrong. They would sigh, look despondent, become very quiet, and say their mantra: I hope you will be/will do better tomorrow. The feelings of guilt that this triggered in Abigail were something she desperately tried to escape from and to avoid. Working extremely hard and getting good results was the best chance of not disappointing the parents. This, of course, was not a guarantee of escaping/avoiding the parents' displeasure and only worked sometimes. We call this an intermittent reinforcement ratio, and the type of reinforcement is negative: something unpleasant is escaped from or is avoided. Abigail over-learnt this strategy and has continued to do this in her adult life, to the detriment of relaxing and battery-recharging activities.

Respondent learning

Respondent learning occurs when we make a connection between two events that originally were completely unconnected. The most famous example is, of course, Pavlov's experiments with his dogs. In this research, the dogs received food (which caused them to salivate) while, at the same time, a buzzer sounded. After a number of repeats of this exercise, setting the buzzer off without the presentation of food would lead to saliva production in the dogs. In humans, this mechanism operates in many anxiety problems where previous neutral events can trigger strong emotional reactions. (For example, after having been in a car accident, the sound of cars makes a person nervous.)

The importance of respondent learning cannot be underestimated for the development of human misery. Here, we learn reactions as a result of stimuli that have no reasonable connection with the manner in which we react. The example we frequently use in teaching about CBT is the following. Just imagine that a plane crashes on the building you are in now. Many people die a horrible death, you are in pain, and while you are suffering you are terrified of dying, and you hear other people's screams of agony. While you are experiencing that, your mind takes in everything from the surroundings: colours, smells, and sounds. In a rather trivial way, the mind can make connections between our fear of death and any of the elements of the environment that were observed. If you had been pinned to the floor on a bright red carpet, then the colour bright red might start to trigger feelings of anxiety. Reacting to these feelings of anxiety by avoiding situations with bright red activates the first learning principle (negative reinforcement).

How does respondent learning play a role in Abigail's story?

For Abigail, the combination between hard work and feeling good has become deeply entrenched (hard work and parental approval are frequently combined). As a result of that, being at work or being busy with work results in an almost immediate positive emotional response. What also has happened is that doing leisure activities, doing things for fun, has become associated with the parents' real and imagined disapproval and, therefore, putting her feet up at the end of hard day's work leads immediately to feelings of guilt that can only be removed by starting work again.

Modelling

The modelling paradigm means we also learn from seeing others do things (Bandura, 1969, 1986): for example, parents who smoke "teach" their children that smoking is an acceptable thing to do.

In summary, we learn to be miserable or behave badly as a result of how we interact with our environment. Consequences that are seen as positive will make the behaviours preceding them more likely. Negative feelings can be triggered by previously neutral events and stimuli when they have been combined once (for instance, in a traumatic event) or many times (for instance, being humiliated in a learning environment). Finally, we also learn to feel and do from what we see others feel and do.

Cognitive theory

What we do and feel is also influenced by our thinking. If we are on our way to an important meeting and we are running late, how we feel and behave will depend on what we think. For Abigail, running late for a meeting would trigger thoughts such as: "This is terrible. They will all think that I am incompetent." This would result in strong negative feelings of anxiety, guilt, and/or embarrassment. I was confronted with my own anxiety-producing thinking once when trying to catch a plane. This was in New Zealand, and the main road from central Auckland to the airport was just a two-lane road at that time and we (my ten-year-old son, Thomas, and I) were running a bit late. This must have been showing, as Thomas put his hand on my shoulder and said, "Don't worry Dad, if we miss the plane, there will be another one tomorrow." My first reaction was to list all the terrible things that would happen if we did miss the plane, but I could not really come up with anything terrible. Inconvenient yes, but terrible, no. We just made it in time.

We can identify various elements to our thinking: automatic thinking, deliberate thinking, and beliefs, core beliefs, and rules for living.

Automatic thinking

This is what it says on the package: thinking that occurs outside our willpower; it just happens. I like to illustrate this to my students with the following example. Between fifteen and thirty students are listening to the lecture and I ask them to close their eyes and just listen to my voice. I say the following: "I want you to listen carefully to my voice. Shortly, I will tap one of you on your right shoulder and that person needs to go to the front of the classroom and talk for five minutes about their first sexual experience." I repeat this instruction several times while walking around the classroom. Of course, no one ever gets tapped on the shoulder! There is always an abundance of automatic thoughts to choose from after the exercise. It is also immediately clear that most of the thoughts in the first instance are automatic thoughts. Not one of the students woke up in the morning thinking, "When I get asked today to talk for five minutes in front of the classroom about my first sexual experience, I will have these thoughts in my mind." What the students think upon hearing the instruction is purely automatic. A lot of our thinking is automatic like this, and we let it pass by without giving it too much attention, unless the thoughts cause strong negative feelings; then, we call these thoughts negative automatic thoughts (NATS). It is impossible to learn *not* to have NATS, but we can learn how we think about them. Popular NATS in the classroom exercise are:

- This is terrible, I will make a complete fool of myself.
- I can't stand this anxiety, it is intolerable.
- They shouldn't make us do this.
- It didn't even last two minutes, how am I supposed to talk for five minutes?

Crucial in how we feel about situations is not the NATS, but how we deal with our NATS. When the NAT "This is terrible, I will make a complete fool of myself" first appears in the mind, most people will have a brief anxiety startle response. Whether this feeling of anxiety remains or goes away depends on how we deal with these strong NATs. Do we dwell on them, do we repeat them over and over again?

Deliberate thinking (reasoning)

Once NATS are in our awareness, we can use our deliberate thinking to deal with them. Depending on our training in thinking about NATS, our learning history, and beliefs about the world and ourselves, we will either think in a way that promotes the validity of the NATS (and increases the negative feelings) or decreases the validity of the NATS and subsequently reduces the negative feelings (Table 1.1).

Beliefs, core beliefs, attitudes, and rules

Our NATS and deliberate thinking are guided by what we believe about ourselves, other people, and the future, as well as by the rules we apply to ourselves and others. Someone with a belief that "life should be easy" would be inclined to have NATS of the "it is intolerable" kind. Someone with a belief that others are potentially evil might produce a NAT of the "The bastards, they shouldn't make us do this" kind. In the literature, there is in general a distinction between beliefs and core beliefs. The latter are more fundamental and sound really unconditional and absolute, while beliefs are often conditional and less absolute. Unhelpful beliefs are often present in categories about the self, other people and/or the future (Table 1.2).

Table 1.1. NATS and their promotion or validity reduction.

NATS	NATS promotion	NATS validity reduction
This is terrible, I will make a complete fool of myself;	If I make a fool of myself,I will lose all respect, no one will like me any more.	Well, it might be unpleasant, but terrible, certainly not. We are all students together and if I make a complete fool of myself that might lead to some interesting discussions.
I can't stand this anxiety, it is intolerable.	This anxiety will kill me, I have to leave. It is unbearable.	Feeling anxious is not pleasant, but I have felt anxious in the past and survived it unscathed!
The bastards, they shouldn't make us do this.	It is imperative that lecturers do not put students in difficult situations.	Certain learning experiences might be unpleasant, but that doesn't mean the lecturers should not do it.

Table 1.2. Categories of beliefs and core beliefs and their effects.

	Belief	Core belief
Self	In order to be a good person I need to do things to perfection.	I have to be perfect or I am a reject.
Others	People will only accept me if I do things to perfection.	Others are mean spirited and never forgive me my mistakes.
Future	Things will get better in the future if I can only achieve perfection.	The future is hopeless.

With "rules", we mean rules for living. These are guiding principles about how the client demands that he/she should live, or demands about other people's behaviour. Examples are:

- I always have to be fair;
- people should treat me with respect;

- loyalty to the family above everything;
- people should give me what I want.

How we interpret what is happening to us dictates how we feel about a certain situation. Most of our interpretations are reasonably spot-on; we get it right. However, especially in situations where there is no real right or wrong interpretation, our minds might go into "thinking overdrive". In CBT, this is referred to as irrational thinking. This style of thinking is characterised by not being fact based, but on the person's opinion and/or preference. This irrational thinking also leads to feeling bad and/or doing bad things. In other words, irrational thinking is not helpful, because it is very "unscientific" and does not help us to get what we want out of life.

Irrationality can occur in automatic thinking, in deliberate thinking, and in beliefs and core beliefs.

In the following brief extract from a session, we outline how the therapist interviews the client in such a way as to gain an understanding of how the learning principles and thinking principles apply to the client's problems.

How does thinking play a role in the story of Abigail?

Abigail is prone to having automatic thoughts such as:

- I need to finish this.
- Don't be such a wimp, hard work never hurt anyone.
- I should have thought of that.
- I can't stand it (when something goes wrong).

Her deliberate thinking strategy is one of rumination and fault finding. Her rule for living is: if you cannot do something to perfection, there is no point in doing it at all. She has beliefs and core beliefs about not being good enough.

Irrational thinking

Irrational thinking is irrational because it

- is not based on accepted reality,
- defies logic,

- is unhelpful (leads to emotional, behavioural, and/or relationship problems).

Irrational thinking can be represented in all levels of thinking. NATs, deliberate thinking, beliefs, and core beliefs can all be irrational. When it comes to NATs and deliberate thinking, we need to make a distinction between inferences and evaluations (Ellis, 1970; Froggatt, 2001). Inferences are interpretations of reality that could be, or become, true:

- If I fail this test my career will go downhill.
- If I don't complete this task now, everyone will reject me.
- My colleague did not greet me this morning; he knows I am going to be fired.

Sometimes, inferences are far-fetched; sometimes, we can intuitively recognise them as plausible. Evaluations, on the other hand, are never true. When we evaluate a situation, or what we infer from a situation, it tells us what that situation/inference means to us (Table 1.3).

The events hypothesised under inferences are not pleasant or positive events and, although the evaluations sound understandable or even plausible, after a moment's reflection, we realise that being fired from a job is really not the end of the world.

Table 1.3. Inferences and their possible meanings.

Inferences	Possible meaning (evaluation)
If I fail this test my career will go downhill.	And that will be an absolute disaster.
If I don't complete this task now, everyone will reject me.	And that will be terrible.
My colleague did not greet me this morning; he knows I am going to be fired.	And that would be the end of the world.

Examples of thinking errors

Shoulding

This involves thinking in shoulds and musts: life should be fair, I must have what I want, people should be nice to me, and I have to be approved of by others. You infer from the facts that there is some law of the universe: shoulds and musts.

Catastrophising

This is making mountains out of molehills. In life, it is normal that things go wrong: we make mistakes, take a wrong turn, miss a train, arrive late for a meeting, are rejected for a job. Instead of seeing it as one of life's unfortunate and perhaps unpleasant/inconvenient or disappointing moments, we label it as a catastrophe, terrible or awful. You evaluate a situation or an inference as a catastrophe.

Self/other downing

We all make mistakes; we are all fallible human beings. When we apply the thinking error of self/other downing, we throw this fact of life out of the window. When noticing mistakes made by others, we are inclined to draw conclusions about them as a person: Joe was late for a meeting, what a bastard to show so little respect; I make some spelling mistakes, therefore I am a complete idiot. Based on the actual facts, we make inferences that go far beyond the facts.

Low frustration tolerance

Here, we overestimate the effect of events on us. We might say things such as: "I can't stand this any more", or words to that effect. We ignore the fact that if we still can say that we cannot stand something, we are still standing it! Based on the facts and/or the inferences, we evaluate that we will be obliterated by events.

All-or-nothing thinking

We see things in black and white categories. If our performance falls short of perfect, we see ourselves as total failures, or worthless. We might say things to ourselves such as this: "If I don't do it perfectly, there's no point in doing it at all." You infer from the facts that something is either good or bad. If we were to take this in numbers, it would mean that something is good when there is a score of 99% or higher and something is bad when the score is 98% or lower.

Over-generalisation

We see a single negative event as a never-ending pattern of defeat: for example, we use "always" or "never" words. An example of this might be: "I never get anything right." We make inferences about the facts that go far beyond the mere facts.

Mental filter

We tend to pick out single negative details and dwell on them exclusively, so that our vision of all reality becomes darkened, like the drop of ink that discolours the entire beaker of water. We say things such as: "I didn't have a moment's pleasure today." We make inferences about the facts that go far beyond the mere facts.

Disqualifying the positive

We reject positive experiences by insisting they "don't count" for some reason or other (e.g., we infer that anyone can do this task, that it was easy). In this way, we can maintain a negative belief even if that is contradicted by our everyday experiences.

Jumping to conclusions

We make a negative interpretation even though there is no evidence that convincingly supports that conclusion. This is an example of such an inference: "Everyone is fed up with me."

Magnification (catastrophising) or minimisation

We exaggerate the importance of things (such as our mistake or someone else's achievement), or we inappropriately shrink things until they appear tiny (our own desirable qualities or the other fellow's imperfections): "I always fail my exams, while other people always pass the first time" (inference).

Emotional/cognitive reasoning

We assume that our negative emotions necessarily reflect the way things really are: "I feel it, therefore it must be true." The same goes for our thinking: "I think it, therefore it must be true and important" (inference).

Personalisation

We see ourselves as the cause of some negative external event, which, in fact, we were not primarily responsible for. Self-blaming can lead to anger at ourselves and feeling much worse. Blame is only possible if one intends something, otherwise it is unfortunate, or regretful, but should not lead to self-downing or guilt. "If only I had paid more attention X would not have happened" (inference).

Thinking, behaving, and feeling

Thinking, behaving, and feeling are connected. What we think influences how we feel and guides our behaviour. How we feel affects what we think and influences what we do. Our behaviour has an impact on how we feel and what we think. These three elements of humanity are "loosely coupled systems": they influence each other in a reciprocal manner. Applying irrational thinking increases the likelihood of strong and unhealthy negative feelings and often promotes self-defeating behaviour.

Irrational thinking that does neither (no unhealthy negative feelings and no self-defeating behaviours) is of no interest to a cognitive behaviour therapist. We are not the thought police. It is people's right to think irrationally. If this irrational thinking leads to problem feelings and/or problem behaviours, then CBT can get involved.

This leads to the question of which feelings are unhealthy and which are healthy. The first principle here is that not all negative feelings are unhealthy, and neither are all positive feelings healthy in all circumstances.

To be grief-stricken when a loved one has died is a normal negative feeling in the first months and up to a year after the person has passed away. To be still completely grief-stricken after five years is an unhealthy negative emotion. To be overwhelmed with grief when visiting the grave of a loved one, even five years after the death, is a healthy reaction. However, to go into complete emotional meltdown each time the name of the loved one is mentioned after five years is, perhaps, an unhealthy emotional reaction.

To be irritated when a friend arrives late for an appointment is a healthy negative emotion; to be extremely angry is perhaps unhealthy.

In short, there are a couple of parameters to consider.

1. Does the situation warrant the *type* and *intensity* of the emotion? If we answer this with "No", then the emotion can be considered an unhealthy negative one.
2. Does the level, intensity, or frequency of the emotion have a negative impact on the person's life? If the answer is "Yes", then the emotion can be considered an unhealthy negative one.

We can put this in a table of unhealthy negative feelings and healthy negative feelings. It could be said that the aim of CBT is not to eradicate negative feelings, but to assist the client to put them in proportion: from unhealthy negative to healthy negative (Table 1.4).

In the following example, the therapist explores the client's thinking in a specific problem situation. The client is Ann, she is in her mid-thirties, married, and there are two children. She works part-time as a shop assistant in Harrods. She has come to therapy very reluctantly, believing that feeling depressed is just being indulgent. This is an

Table 1.4. Unhealthy negative feelings and healthy negative feelings.

Unhealthy negative feelings	Healthy negative feelings
Anxiety	Apprehension
Depression	Sadness
Anger	Irritation
Guilt	Remorse
Hurt	Disappointment
Shame/embarrassment	Concern

excerpt from the fifth session. Again, the therapist's explanatory comments are given in square brackets.

Therapist: Now, the problems that we highlighted last week were you were working so hard that it makes you sad, snappy, and aggressive with other people around you. Another problem that we identified was harsh self-criticism, which led you also to becoming kind of very sad and it also resulted in you becoming very snappy and nagging with other people. You also mentioned that you have this belief that you're not good enough, which makes you feel quite bad about yourself. Now, of these three problems, which of these happened in the last week?

[Explorations and challenging thinking always happen best when the focus is on a specific occurrence of these problems.]

Client: We were having people over for supper on Tuesday. Tuesday's not really a great day anyway because I have to pick the children up later on a Tuesday because it's choir, so I left work at half past two and I dashed home and then wanted to get the place clean, really properly, properly clean, and I got the duster and the stuff out.

Therapist: So you left work early and then you went home to give the place, say, a proper cleaning?

Client: Yes, and to try and get the supper ready, or started anyway. I managed to get all Hoovered through and everything and I started preparing the vegetables and things and then I just completely lost track of time and I ended up being half an hour late for school, picking the children up, for which I was so humiliated. They rang me on my mobile phone to find out where I was and, you know, I'm never late. Then I got the children in the car and got home.

Client: I gave them their tea and got them in the bath and, while they were in the bath, I was doing the supper. I put the supper in the oven, went upstairs and got the children out of the bath and I put them to bed. Then, John came home and the guests arrived and I served the dinner, which was OK, and they left, and I went upstairs at the end of the evening and, to my utter horror, I'd forgotten to let the children's bath out. There it was, grey, murky water where they'd had the soap in there and it just looked disgusting, all the toys and everything, and the guests had used the bathroom and they'd just seen it. I was mortified, so then I went downstairs to talk to John about it and he said it didn't matter, and clearly it did matter, I mean, it mattered to me, and then we had a row.

Therapist: So that was quite a big thing for you, and he said it didn't matter at all?

Client: He said that they probably didn't notice and, if they did notice, then they knew that we had children and, you know, they'd enjoyed the meal and that was what was important. Well, it wasn't all that was important. Anyway, he ended up sleeping on the sofa because I just went upstairs and shut the door. I didn't even want to look at him. I was so humiliated, I was utterly mortified and he had no understanding whatsoever of just how bad it was, and I'd been cross with the children, and I hadn't really enjoyed the supper anyway because I had this nagging feeling that I'd forgotten something and I couldn't think what it was that I'd forgotten. Everything was on the table and dinner was ready and I had got dessert there and everything, but—

Therapist: It sounds like it was a very hectic day in which you kind of had to do a lot of things. You had to do your own work in the morning, then you left work early to go home, clean up the house, get a meal, pick up the children from school, take care of them, prepare the meal, so it sounds like a day when you had to do a lot of things.

If you can go back to the bathwater incident, focus on that to see if we can make sense of that. You left the bathwater in the bath and your guests had seen this. When you noticed that, how did that make you feel? You used the word "mortified", but what kind of mortified? How did that make you feel?

Client: Just the pure horror of it. If you could have seen it! You know, when the children have been in a bath and they've had bubbles in the bath and then they've taken the soap and the soap's disappeared somewhere in the bottom of the bathwater, it goes grey and scummy, and there were ducks and Action Men and toys floating in it.

Therapist: So, when you've seen that, how did you feel? You say your guests have seen it, so what kind of a feeling does that give?

Client: I was disgusted with myself. I couldn't believe that I'd not—I always take the children out of the bath, wrap them in the towels, let the bath out, put the children to bed after I've dried them and then I go back to the bathroom and wash the bath out. I always do that, every night. Why, how can I? It's a habit; it's just what I do.

[Here the client is providing the therapist with lots of information about her reasoning: she is disgusted with herself for having made a terrible mistake (self-downing) and she infers from noticing a relatively small oversight that it is a terrible thing (catastrophising).]

Therapist: So you were disgusted with yourself. In the scheme of things, this event of dirty bathwater in the bath when there are guests in the house, how much would you give that as a kind of badness rating from nought to ten, when ten is as bad as it can get and zero is not bad at all? How bad would you rate this?

Client: Well, it could've been worse, I could've burnt the dinner as well. In terms of that particular evening, I don't know, seven or eight.

Therapist: So, in badness terms, it's seven or eight, and you felt disgusted with yourself?

Client: I just felt like I'm so stupid. I could just hear myself, you know, "How could you do that? How could you forget? For goodness sake, this is basic! What must those people have thought?" It was just going over and over in my mind. It just seemed so terrible and then, when I went downstairs, John laughed and trivialised it.

Therapist: So what was running through your mind was, "I'm stupid and this is terrible" and then you say, "What must those people have thought?" What did you think they thought?

[The therapist is a bit like "a dog with a bone", not letting go of further investigations of the client's thinking process.]

Client: I thought that they must think that I'm completely slovenly and totally incapable of organising anything, that I don't have an eye for detail. John said they would just think that I had been very busy and I'd forgotten to let the bath out and that I was making a disaster out of it, a complete crisis. I can tell you, it was a terrible argument.

Therapist: So, in your mind, you said, "Those people must've thought, 'Anne is completely slovenly, has no eye for detail—'"

Client: You nearly said it, a complete slut! That's exactly what I thought.

Therapist: That's what you thought?

Client: Yes.

Therapist: So you thought that they'd think, "Anne is a complete sloth"?

Client: Slut, totally incapable.

Therapist: So the things that were going through your mind were, "I'm stupid. This is terrible. They must have thought, 'Anne is a complete slut. She's totally incapable'"?

Client: I was angry with John for trivialising it.

Therapist: So that's something that happened later, that he just said it didn't matter and laughed.

Client: I wanted to just sit down and cry. I just felt like the whole thing had been a disaster. I had thought that it had been just about perfect. You know, I thought that I'd managed to recover from being half an hour late for the children; I'd managed to get them their tea and get them bathed and into bed, and I thought everything was OK, it was fine. They'd said that the supper was really nice. I mean, it wasn't the best that I'd cooked, but, you know, it was all right, and then I went upstairs and found that.

Therapist: So, because you found the bath filled with the murky bathwater that meant that everything was a disaster? Was that running through your mind, that the whole evening had been a complete disaster?

Client: That I'd failed. They were John's friends and I'd let him down.

[By repeatedly paraphrasing, the therapist delves deeper into the client's thinking and now the client comes up with a bottom line: having made a mistake like this means having failed.]

Therapist: "I have failed. I have let John down". That is quite a collection of thoughts that are running through your mind in a situation like this. Shall I read them out again?

Client: No.

Therapist: No? Why not?

Client: I don't want to hear them.

Therapist: One of the things in cognitive behaviour therapy that it is very important to realise is the thoughts that are running through our minds so that we can check whether these thoughts are kind of worthwhile having or not.

Let me go back to an example that we talked about in our previous session about your eldest, Sam. If she has to do a task at school and the tasks consists of ten things and then she makes one mistake in that task, for instance, she's writing with a pen and, all of a sudden, big blobs of ink drop out of the pen on to the paper and she's kind of a bit clumsy and she makes a complete mess of that bit of paper, but it's just one out of ten tasks that she had to do. If she had been saying, "This is terrible, mummy. I am so stupid. Everyone must think that I'm a complete idiot, that I'm completely incompetent. I have completely failed. I've let everyone down", what would you say to her?

Client: I would tell her that she'd done the work well and it wasn't her fault that the pen had blobbed and maybe we could write it out again so that it would look nice.

[The therapist is trying to get the client motivated to start thinking about her thinking. She clearly finds the experience so toxic that she avoids thinking about it completely, therefore continuing with the unhelpful thinking processes but also avoiding full experience and processing of the negative emotions. The therapist took as an example a similar experience of making a mistake by someone who is dear to the client and explored how the client thinks this person would need to evaluate this experience.]

Therapist: But you would agree with her that she is indeed very stupid for that to happen, that it is a terrible event and that she's completely incompetent? You would agree with her?

Client: No.

Therapist: You wouldn't? How would you talk to her about this experience?

Client: I'd tell her not to worry about it.

Therapist: How would you tell her not to worry about it?

Client: I'd tell her it wasn't her fault and we could find a new pen, that I could see that the rest of her writing was beautiful and that she'd been really trying very hard.

Therapist: So you would probably put across to her that, if there's one mistake, it doesn't mean that everything's a disaster?

[Therapist introduces the idea of fallibility.]

Client: Yes.

Therapist: How does that apply to your situation?

Client: Well, I don't think it does because she's only a little girl. I'm an adult and *I'm supposed to have everything under control.* I know you think it's a fuss over nothing, and that's what John said, but it was important to me.

Therapist: Do you think we have a choice about the things that are important to us? Do you think that the things that are important to us are inflexible, written in concrete, or do we have a choice?

[Therapist decides not to focus on the demand for control, but to introduce the concept of choice when it comes to finding issues important.]

Client: I don't know. Different things are important to different people, aren't they?

Therapist: Yes.

Client: I mean, it was important to me that I was doing my best for my husband.

Therapist: So you really wanted the best that you could do for your husband?

Client: And it wasn't good enough, not for me anyway.

Therapist: So you had all this stuff running through your mind: "I'm stupid. This is terrible. They must have thought, 'Anne is a complete slut, totally incompetent and incapable'. Everything's a disaster. I have failed. I have let John down and I am supposed to have everything under control at this age." That's all running through your mind. Which of these thoughts was really very powerful in making you think that you feel disgusted with yourself?

[This question is focused on highlighting the most influential thought in the whole array of negative and irrational thoughts.]

Client: I don't know really. They're all pretty strong. I hated the fact that I'd let John down.

Therapist: How much did you believe this thought (I have let John down and that is terrible) to be true?

Client: Well, I believe that 100%, I mean that I let him down. And that it is terrible letting him down, I believe that 80%.

Therapist: Excellent, so you believe these very strongly. Let's examine this thought a bit more, shall we? Would you call that a thought that's worthwhile having . . .

Client: Well, I think it is.

Therapist: Let's think for a moment what makes a thought worthwhile to have. Some people would say that thoughts are only worthwhile having if they're true and if they're helpful. True means that they're factual. Do you know what a fact is?

Client: Yes, I'm not stupid.

Therapist: Apologies, I did not mean to imply that. What I meant is, can you explain to me what a fact is?

Client: A fact is something that you can prove.

Therapist: That you can verify?

Client: Yes.

Therapist: That you can prove and that you can test whether it's true, whether it's factual?

Client: Yes.

Therapist: For instance, if I let go of this bit of paper, it will fall down. That's a fact, isn't it?

Client: Yes.

Therapist: OK, so it has to be factual. The other thing that makes thoughts worthwhile having is that they're helpful. It's helpful to make us feel better, helpful for us to get along with other people, or helpful to achieve our goals. Now, shall we test this belief (I have let John down) with these two criteria?

Client: All right.

Therapist: "I have let John down"; how could you test whether that's a fact?

Client: Ask him.

Therapist: OK.

Client: But he will just say no, and how do we know that he's telling the truth? I mean, he might think that I was letting him down, but, just to keep things calm and quiet, he'd say that I wasn't letting him down, except that that doesn't work because then I'd tell him that I was letting him down. How can we know?

Therapist: So you're telling me that John is in the habit of lying to you, that he's a kind of mischievous, lying—

[The therapist gently confronts client with her self-defeating thinking style. She has created an inescapable trap for herself. The only person who can tell her he does not feel let down will not tell the truth.]

Client: No, of course he's not!

Therapist: But you just told me that that's what he does, that, if you ask him something, he'll do anything to kind of keep the peace and not upset you and he kind of lies about that.

Client: No, that's stupid. No. He doesn't want to upset me, that's all, but no, he's very truthful.

Therapist: One of the other golden rules is that you can't have it both ways. It's a bit like things can't be black and white at the same time, things can't be dark and light at the same time. John's either truthful or he's a lying such-and-such. If he's a truthful person, then we have to go by his rules. If he's a lying such-and-such, let's be less trustful. But you know him, so you be the judge. If he tells you, "You have not let me down, Ann", should you be hearing, "Yes, you have let me down", or "No, you haven't let me down"? You decide.

Client: That's not fair because—

Therapist: I know it's not fair. You decide.

[The therapist is very directive here, attempting to focus the client on staying with the task of examining her thinking.]

Client: He doesn't lie, but then he's easy to please. You know, if I just stood there in my dressing gown and served beans on toast, he'd have probably been quite happy with it.

Therapist: So, even if you had done that, you wouldn't have let him down. This is your thought, "I have let John down", so what you are saying is that, if you left water in the bath, it was not something he would feel as a let down?

Client: No.

Therapist: So this thought, "I have let John down", in which category does it fall, is it a fact or is it a belief?

Client: I think I've let John down.

Therapist: That's what you think, but the question is, is it a fact or is it not a fact, it's not true. Let's go back for a moment to your little Sam. She has to do a test in school and she doesn't get the result that she really wants. She might say to you, "Oh mummy! This is the worst thing that ever could happen to me", and it's not true. You know that it's not true; it's just a small, little thing. How does this relate your bathwater situation and letting John down?

Client: John doesn't think that I let him down.

Therapist: And he's the judge of that, isn't he, because "I've let John down" means that he has to feel disappointment in order for this to be true? He has to feel disappointed and think, "Oh my God! My wife left the water in the bath! How could she do that?" and he didn't think that. He said, "It doesn't matter. They probably didn't notice and, if they noticed, they thought, 'They've got a family, a couple of small kids. No problem'".

Let's go for the next thing that we can check that our thoughts are worthwhile having, and that is: is this thought helpful? Does it help you to feel good about yourself?

Client: No.

Therapist: No. Is it helpful in getting along with other people? Does it help you to get along with John to have this thought?

Client: No.

Therapist: Is it helpful in achieving your goal to kind of work less in the house and perhaps to spend a bit more time on yourself?

Client: No.

Therapist: If you go back to your original thought: "I have let John down and that is terrible", which made you feel disgusted with yourself. How much do you believe these thoughts to be true now

Client: I don't know, it really feels as if it is completely true, but my mind also tells me that if John says he doesn't mind then I am not letting him down . . .

[This transcript aims to demonstrate how the therapist talks to the client about her thinking, highlighting how the client's thinking has an impact on her mood and behaviour. It also demonstrates how the therapist can assist the client to start doubting her automatic meaning-giving processes.]

Contemplating theory

We started off by saying that nothing is as practical as a good theory. Applying CBT as a psychological therapy in working with personality disorder is more than the application of a set of specific interventions. The complexity of psychological problems makes it beneficial that psychological therapists can understand the theoretical underpinnings of their actions (and of their clients' actions).

CHAPTER TWO

Structuring the process of CBT and structuring CBT sessions

Introduction

In this chapter, the reader is introduced to the overall structure of CBT and the structure within sessions in CBT. The importance of agenda setting, reviewing homework, and setting homework will be discussed. The importance of detailed information gathering, identifying problems and goals, having session plans that fit with the phase of treatment, and the role of the therapist as an active and initiating agent in therapy are discussed.

Explanations of the CBT way of structuring sessions, difficulties with structuring sessions, challenging moments in ending sessions, and other difficulties are further topics for this chapter and illustrated by way of the case examples.

Structuring therapy

As part of my university studies, I attended a seminar on organisational behavioural management. From this seminar, I remember one direct quote: "No communication without structure". As long as there is no structure in which communication can take place, most communication will be useless. It is my firm conviction that the same goes for therapy, especially cognitive behaviour therapy. A well-structured plan is the foundation for all good therapy. In conducting therapy, this means that the clinician needs to "hold" the line by structuring the therapy according to the evidence-based plan (sometimes against the preferences of clients who just want to chill out and not do the difficult work!).

Structuring therapy needs to be done along two lines: structuring the process of therapy and structuring the therapy sessions.

The process of CBT: from complaints to "smart" problems and goals, moving on to a "holistic theory", intervention, and evaluation.

Structuring the process of therapy

Cognitive behaviour therapy is, typically, a short-term treatment in which the therapist helps the client to learn more effective methods of dealing with troubling thoughts, feelings, and behaviours. It is also a problem-orientated therapy that addresses the situational difficulties that might have provoked anxious or depressive episodes and the underlying cognitive problems that might relate to the emergence and maintenance of emotional disorders. The phrase "short-term treatment" does not mean that the therapist has to be in a hurry and should act hastily. The current evidence indicates that CBT would require between twelve (anxiety problems) and twenty (depression) sessions in order to be effective. Unfortunately, most of the research at the foundation of such statements is based on clients with one predominant problem of moderate severity, while, in "normal" clinical practice, many clients will present with a conglomerate of problems and issues. I find that a better way of describing the "time-limited" aspect of CBT is to declare it a form of therapy that aims to be as brief as possible. Significant improvements can often be made between twelve and twenty sessions, but, for more complex problems of high severity or long duration, many more sessions might be needed in order to achieve lasting change. The chronology of treatment I suggest is that first there is a pre-therapy phase, in which the tasks of the therapist are to socialise the client to the CBT model, to identify SMART problems and set SMART goals, and to gather data with a view to interpretation. Then a treatment plan is negotiated, shared, and agreed upon. Once therapy begins, the tasks of the therapist are: symptom-focused interventions, interventions focused on underlying mechanisms, relapse prevention, and evaluation and ending.

Pre-therapy

The process of therapy begins with that first encounter between client and therapist. The client has a range of concerns. Will this person be able to help me? Will this person be kind and understanding? How much is it going to cost, in time, effort, and money? Likewise, the therapist will have thoughts about the client he or she is about to see. Will this be a pleasant client to work with? Will I be able to make sense of this client's problems? Will the problems be within my competence range? Both client and therapist might have information about each other before they meet. The therapist might have a referral letter or a summary from a colleague, while the client could have consulted the Internet about the therapist and/or service. And then the time is there; they meet.

I am often amazed by the implicit acceptance of many therapists that they *know* their clients have problems and, further, what kind of problems these are, as demonstrated by the following hypothetical dialogues. The implicit assumptions by the therapist are in square brackets.

> *Therapist*: So, Mr Smith, your GP tells me you suffer from depression. Could you please tell me when that started? [The GP is correct and the client suffers from depression.]
>
> *Mr Smith*: Well I don't know . . . depression . . . such a big word . . .
>
> *Therapist*: In CBT it is very important to understand how the problems started. It would be really helpful if you could tell me when you started to feel depressed? [Therapist does not listen to client's doubt and persists in pushing questions based on the assumption that the client is depressed.]
>
> *Mr Smith*: Well, it is more that, meeting people, I find that difficult, since college ten years ago, really difficult.

Therapist: So the first time you started to avoid people as a result of your depression was ten years ago? [Therapist does not listen to client's doubt and persists in pushing questions based on the assumption that the client is depressed.]

In the above example, the therapist is like the proverbial dog with a bone. Nothing will deter this therapist from finding depression as the problem of the poor client . . .

Here is another example.

Therapist: Thanks for coming in today, Mr Sorensen. What are the problems that brought you to therapy? [The assumption here is that the client has problems.]

Mr Sorensen: Well, I wouldn't call them problems, nothing to worry about really . . .

Therapist: So which problems would you like to resolve with CBT? [Again the therapist does not listen to the client and continues with the assumptions.]

Mr Sorensen: See, it is my wife . . .

Therapist: So your wife urged you to seek help for your problems? [Again the assumption is made that the client has problems.]

Mr Sorensen: Yes, she complains that I am too slow and take too much time to do things. She also thinks I clean too much, but she does not realise how dangerous germs are!

Therapist: So it seems that your problem is something called obsessive–compulsive disorder, and the therapy we do here is very effective for problems like this! What are your main concerns regarding your OCD? [Now that is a very quick diagnosis . . .].

Mr Sorensen: I didn't think it was that bad! I don't think I have a disorder. I am just here because my wife . . .

In the first example the therapist assumes that the client has a specific problem (depression) and misses the signs of disagreement from the client, while in the second example, the therapist takes for granted that the client is willing to see himself as having a disorder! Both actions will have a demotivating impact on clients.

I am astounded by the rights clinicians give themselves when interviewing clients. A typical process of therapy starts with the therapist bombarding the client with a tsunami of questions. It pays to have a think about this and to accept that there is a pre-therapy phase in which we have to elicit permission from the client to embark on an assessment process. In this eliciting phase (i.e., the phase in which the client either gives or withholds his agreement that he is interested in talking to the therapist about his issues), the therapist's goal is to make the clients curious about their situation, so curious that they want to embark on the assessment process in order to find out what it is that causes their misery. The pre-therapy/eliciting phase can be either very brief or last for several sessions. It all depends on client's perspective on their situation, the stages of change they find themselves in. For a client in the stage of precontemplation, the process might take longer than for a client ready for active change. In this pre-therapy phase, it is important that the therapist meets the client with an open and reflective mind. An open mind means having no preconceived ideas about the client (a letter indicating that the client suffers from depression might mean the client is depressed, but could also mean that the referring person sees depression everywhere). An open mind also means that when a client mentions the word problems, this does not mean that the client is ready to take action. Many people live with and "enjoy" their problems for a long time (as is the case for many habitual worriers). The reflective mind means that the therapist needs to be very reflective in this phase and not resort to series of questions. Instead, a more informal and almost chatty style can be adopted to assist the client in allowing the exploration of his internal world to occur.

Tasks of the therapist during the pre-therapy phase

- Retrieving information: asking questions and opening a dialogue (see Chapter Three for a more detailed description) with clients that allows the therapist to
  - assess client's suitability for CBT;
  - get sufficient information about client's problems to understand how the problem started, how it is maintained, and how it can be overcome.
- Giving information.
  - Therapist gives information about CBT as a form of psychotherapy.

 - Therapist provides information about the problems of the client with the aim of instilling realistic hope and increasing motivation.
- Change-directed interventions.
  - The therapist will deploy motivation enhancing strategies in case the client's level of motivation to change is too low.

Informing phase

During this phase, clients have become a bit curious about their personal situation ("Perhaps it is worthwhile to chat with this bloke, at least he doesn't preach to me!") or about the form of therapy the therapist has to offer ("This stuff about thinking and rational thinking sounds really interesting, so perhaps there is something in it for me"). The therapist needs to trigger clients' interest, so they will collaborate with an assessment that will provide information to allow the therapist to understand how the client developed the problem and how the problems are maintained. Both client and therapist need to be hungry for information. In situations where it is the therapist who is really interested in finding out about the issues, but not the client, things often do not work out that well. With the information that is collected, the client can decide whether there is reason to be concerned about his situation and take action, or whether there is nothing to worry about and things can stay as they are.

Based on the situation of the client and the expert knowledge of the therapist, a decision can be reached on whether the problem is real or imagined. I like to collect information on the following potential problem areas:

- Problem behaviours: encompasses all behavioural issues that could be problematic, of which these are some examples:
  - too much work;
  - not enough leisure; questions to ask would be:
    Is there any assertive behaviour?
    Is there evidence of too much checking?
- Affect: feeling issues that might be problematic:
  - too depressed;
  - too anxious;
  - never content/happy.

- Sensations: physical sensations that could be problematic, such as:
  - too often tired;
  - not being able to sleep.
- Interpersonal: includes issues involving interactions with other people:
  - problems in the family;
  - no friends.
- Cognitions: encompasses problems with thinking style:
  - imaging: issues relating to intrusive images: nightmares, etc.;
  - drugs and alcohol: excessive use of mind-altering substances.

Detailed questionnaires, base-line recordings of symptoms by the client, and problem-focused interviewing are all part of this "informing". This culminates in the therapist suggesting a formulation (also described as a conceptualisation, or holistic theory) about the causal and maintenance factors of the problems (see Chapter Three).

An important part of this formulation is a description of the problems in an objective manner, with the aim of increasing motivation for change. Most clients, when presenting for treatment, are motivated to have their symptoms removed, but not all are motivated to live life differently in order for that to happen. A written formulation is an opportunity for the clinician to link a client's symptoms with behaviours that need changing. In a written formulation, the symptoms of the client, problem behaviours, and the client's emotional reaction to his/her situation are objectively described. This might sound like redundant information, given that the client surely will be aware of this, but it is not unnecessary. Humans are not very observant and aware of their actions, thoughts, and feelings. Clients can say things such as: "I have the odd drink in the evening", and then the self-monitoring demonstrates that the client drinks two bottles of wine per day.

Informing the client about the extent of their problems, how their problems came to be, how they are maintained, and how change can be brought about if that is deemed to be desirable, occurs at the end of the information phase.

Negotiating phase

A third phase consists of the negotiation between therapist and client. By the end of the information phase, a client should have made a decision about the question: do I want to continue this way or do I want to change? This decision can best be made based on the formulation, and this is also when client and therapist identify specific problems to work on and goals that need to be achieved.

It is important that the therapist does not have strong and outspoken opinions on how the client should change. The client has to decide whether change is necessary, and how the change is going to be achieved. These are all clients' decisions, but they can only be made sensibly if the therapist provides the client with objective information about goals and treatment options. If a client has decided to change (for instance, to decrease his drinking a bottle of wine from seven times a week to once a week), it is the task of the therapist to give the client information on the possible treatment goals (pros and cons of abstinence and controlled use) and methods available. In doing this, the therapist takes care that the client gets the right information. The client can then choose a treatment goal and method, based on the information the therapist has provided.

Socialising to the CBT model

A step that the therapist needs to take at the beginning of therapy, before any change-directed interventions are attempted, is socialising the client to the CBT model of psychological problems. This can happen from the moment the therapist starts with the assessment, so that by the time the negotiation phase starts, the client has a pretty good idea about what CBT is all about.

The client needs to become a gifted amateur in cognitive behaviour therapy. It is essential, therefore, that the client learns that:

- problems are the result of an often long learning process;
- problems are influenced by unhelpful/irrational thinking;
- The brain sometimes learns to have a mind of its own.

A therapist can often make a start with this during the first session and then, while conducting the assessment, develop the client's understanding of CBT even further.

It is very tempting for inexperienced therapists to skip this step, since junior therapists often are in a hurry and believe that "fast is good". As a result of this haste, teaching the client about the CBT model of psychological problems is seen as a deviation and getting in the way of achieving the change. Nothing is further from the truth; teaching the client about how psychological problems come to be and how they are maintained is a wise investment of time, as it is the first step in getting the client to become their own best therapist.

Problems are the result of a learning process

It is helpful for clients to understand that their current situation and problems are the result of a learning and adaptation process. Depression and avoidance did not suddenly appear yesterday; excessive drinking did not suddenly start on a specific date. More often than not, a long learning process preceded the emergence of the problem. Human beings are like creative learning machines. When we are confronted with situations that we find difficult, we try to find a way to deal with this. Many psychological problems are the result of this. A beloved family member dies, which results in natural grief, and in order to cope with the pain, the person develops feelings of extreme sadness and depression (and will report feeling numb, not feeling the grief any more). To feel alive again, they develop a gambling habit. It is important for the therapist to realise that clients do not go out of their way to deliberately engage in this kind of learning: "Oh, goodness, I am grieving, that is a bit painful so let's get depressed, which after a while really sucks, so let's liven things up and go to the casino . . ." This learning develops in a trial and error manner. People use their existing skills, and learn from models in their environment and informational feedback from their environment.

Problems are influenced by irrational thinking

Clients need to understand that what they say to themselves plays an enormous role in how they will feel. Clients need to be weaned off the idea that it is what happens to us that makes us feel our feelings. It will be important to teach clients that the meaning we give to what happens to us dictates how we will feel in any given situation. Clients need to learn that because they are human, they are very much prone to irrational thinking (i.e., the therapist needs to take away the implicit belief that only stupid people think irrationally). It is very easy to get into a mode of just paying lip service to this concept in therapy. In particular, clinicians who have not received a thorough training will go along with clients that there are certain beliefs that really are true (you have to be respectful, life should be fair, I should not make mistakes, other people should approve of me, etc.). If the client does not buy into this model, then cognitive restructuring interventions later on will be difficult.

What I typically try to teach clients is that their thinking develops along various lines. First, there is the automatic thinking. Thoughts and images that pop into our mind without us doing anything for it; they just happen. If these thoughts are the trigger of strong negative feelings we call them NATS (negative automatic thoughts). Everyone has them and will continue to have them. Whether we have problems as a result of these negative automatic thoughts depends on how much attention we give them. Just imagine what would happen if the depressed person reacts to her negative automatic thoughts (life is hopeless, I am hopeless, my future is dark and grim) by simply ignoring them and getting on with life and focusing on her goal-directed *deliberate thinking*. Well, in all likelihood, the depression would be a considerably diminished, because it is the deliberate engagement with the NATS that causes trouble. Yes, the first burst of NATS might result in a sense of depression and sadness, but that will lift sooner rather than later if the person does not engage with these thoughts. So, using will-powered thoughts to engage with the NATS can be along rational lines (this is just a thought, no need to give it too much attention) or along an irrational path (oh my god, there I go again, can't get rid of this depression, I will not be able to cope with the day). This deliberate thinking is strongly influenced by the *beliefs* the client holds on to as well as his/her *core beliefs* and *rules for living*.

Beliefs are ideas about how one's self, life, and other people should be. Examples of beliefs are:

- If I don't score 100% on this test I am a loser.
- Life shouldn't be as difficult as this.
- If I ask for help, people will take advantage of me.

Core beliefs have a more absolute character to them (some authors would call them schemas):

- I have to be perfect.
- I am bad.
- Other people are out to do me harm.
- The world is a cesspit of misery.

A good metaphor to use with clients is to compare the whole thinking process with the workings of a computer. The NATS are the images you see on a computer screen. The beliefs can be compared with the software, while the core beliefs are like the hardware. The computer user pounding away on the keyboard can be seen as the deliberate thinking. If one reacts to the wrong message on the screen all might go wrong . . .

The brain has a mind of its own

Clients have to learn that they sometimes are the "victim" of automatic processes in the brain. The emotional processing centre of the brain might send out an all-points alarm bulletin before the thinking part of the brain has had a chance to look it over.

This plays a role in post traumatic stress disorder and panic disorder. Clients with problems like this frequently report noticing their body being in a full state of arousal, followed by their catastrophic thinking. Therapists might have a hard time identifying thoughts that triggered the physiological arousal, because there might have been none. The emotional regulation centre of the brain has, with a mind of its own, decided to signal to the body that danger is approaching. This signalling occurs much faster than the processing of the cortex. Consequently, the person experiences physical signs of anxiety without really knowing why. The *post hoc* meaning-giving process (my heart is racing, I must be having a heart attack) subsequently leads to anxiety, which further activates the arousal system.

And what CBT is all about . . .

The therapist needs to prepare the client for the style and structure of cognitive behaviour therapy. The client needs to appreciate a form of psychological therapy that has the following characteristics.

- It is based on the cognitive model of emotional disorders.
- It is brief and time limited.
- It perceives a sound collaborative therapeutic relationship as essential.
- It is structured and directive.
- It is problem orientated.
- It is based on an educational model.
- Homework is an essential feature.

Clients who prefer to have unstructured sessions in which they express their emotional incontinence are perhaps best referred to another therapist.

Let the change begin . . .

Therapist and client have completed the assessment process, the formulation has provided both client and therapist with insight as to how the problems started and how they are maintained, the client has identified specific problems and goals, and has a basic understanding of the CBT model. If all these tasks have been completed, now is the time to propose a treatment plan and elicit the client's approval of this. Treatment in CBT often occurs from the "outside inwards". This means that the first focus of treatment is rarely the underlying cause of the client's difficulties, but the unpleasant symptoms the client is bothered by.

Symptom-focused interventions

Assessment is done, the formulation completed and shared with the client, the CBT model has been explained to the client, and the problems and goals fine-tuned. Now the therapist and client can design an intervention plan and start working on reducing symptoms and problems.

As discussed before, the first port of call might be problems and symptoms that are not really central to the presentation, but might result in quick symptom relief and, as a result, increase motivation for change.

Typical symptom-focused interventions are:

- Behavioural (re)activation to get the client active and experiencing some pleasure and satisfaction (an example of modifying emotion-driven behaviours and preventing emotional avoidance, see Chapter Four).
- Self-control training to give the client an increased sense of having some control over their behaviour (an example of modifying emotion-driven behaviours, see Chapter Four).
- Cognitive restructuring to reduce negative feelings that block goal-directed behaviour (an example of altering antecedent cognitive appraisals, see Chapter Four).
- Psycho-education to enlighten the client about how their feelings, behaviours, and thoughts are connected.

The impact of these interventions is often that client's immediate suffering is vastly reduced. The next step in therapy can be to focus on the underlying mechanisms (or vulnerabilities) that make the client vulnerable to problems like this. I explicitly state "can be". There is no law in the universe, and not even one in the field of psychology, that dictates that clients have to address their underlying vulnerabilities. We, as clinicians, can clearly see how client's core beliefs of self-sacrifice play a role in the depression; this does not mean, however, that the client *has* to agree with us or that it is 100% certain that the client's depression will come back if the issue is not therapeutically addressed. It is very important to go back to a phase of negotiating with the client and to weigh up whether the cost (time, effort, money, and emotional upheaval) of continued therapy is worth the further changes that are going to be made. Sometimes clients decide that the cost is too high.

Interventions focused on underlying vulnerabilities and mechanisms

Underlying vulnerabilities are self-defeating habits or life-styles; cognitive structures and belief systems that lead to trouble.

For example, the belief that one never ever should put one's personal needs first might result in never assertively standing up for personal needs, always volunteering to do extra tasks, and could give rise to depression and over-tiredness. By using behavioural reactivation, focused on increasing pleasurable activities and cognitive restructuring, the depression was dealt with. In order to minimise the risk for relapse, the underlying mechanism of self-sacrifice and the skills deficit of lacking assertion needed to be dealt with.

Typical interventions are:

- Belief and core belief change (an example of altering antecedent cognitive appraisals, see Chapter Four).
- Skills training (an example of modifying emotion-driven behaviours, see Chapter Four).
- Reorganising reinforcement structure (self/other).

Relapse prevention

Once the client has made changes in his life and has achieved the goals set for therapy, then the big task starts to maintain the changes made in therapy and to prevent a relapse into the old problem behaviours. Psychological therapies are just like going on a diet, they are only effective when the client continues to follow the guidelines. A formerly depressed client who returns to the old habit of overworking and over-investing in others and, therefore, experiences no pleasure, will become depressed again. Marlatt and Gordon (1985) developed a relapse prevention model based on social–cognitive psychology and incorporates both a conceptual model of relapse and a set of cognitive and behavioural strategies to prevent or limit relapse episodes (for a detailed description of the development, theoretical underpinnings, and treatment components of this model, see Dimeff & Marlatt, 1998; Marlatt & Gordon, 1985). A central aspect of the model is the detailed functional analysis of factors that can contribute to a relapse in the old problem behaviour. In other words, what makes a former depressed client give up a healthy life-style; what makes him/her say yes to an offer of working 100 hours a week? It will be very important to incorporate high-risk situations, a person's coping skills, outcome expectancies (what does the person expect of engaging in the problem behaviour), the effect of all-or-nothing thinking ("OK, I have given in once to work overtime, can't say no when asked again"), lifestyle imbalances and physiological triggers. Relapse prevention (illustrated in Table 2.1) involves making a detailed plan of action to counter these relapse pushers!

Table 2.1. Relapse prevention model based on Marlatt and Gordon (1985).

Relapse prevention strategies	Self-monitoring & behavioural assessment	Stress management training, HRS coping skills training, skills training, self-efficacy training	Behavioural contracting	Cognitive restructuring	
Steps in the relapse cycle	High risk situation (HRS)	No coping response to deal with HRS	Decreased sense of self-efficacy & increased anticipation of engagement with problem behaviour (PB)	Initial onset of PB lapse	Perceived guilt, shame, anger with self and loss of control = new HRS
	Mental images of PB in the past				

Evaluation and ending

Before client and therapist say their final goodbyes, it is important to evaluate treatment. There are various ways to do this. The therapist can use a set of measures at the start of treatment and give them to the client again at treatment completion. There is an abundance of measures for anxiety, depression, and other psychological problems available. Most of these are sensitive to the impact of treatment.

A more personalised way to evaluate treatment is to focus on the problems and goals the client identified. This method is borrowed from "goal attainment scaling" (Kiresuk & Sherman, 1968; Stolee, Rockwood, Fox, & Streiner, 1992).

Client and therapist really look at the problems and try to ascertain how severe the client thinks this problem is: how much does this problem interfere with the client's daily functioning, what would the client like to achieve with respect to this problem, and how far away is the client now from achieving this goal? These questions can be asked and discussed at the beginning of treatment and again at the end of treatment. It is of vital importance that both problems and goals are written up very specifically, in sufficient detail, and in a measurable way.

All being well, therapist and client would have completed the following problem and goals form.

Problem	How severe do you rate this problem 0= not a problem 10= extremely severe	How much does this problem interfere with your daily functioning? 0= not at all 10 = it makes life impossible	What would you like to achieve with respect to this problem?

An example could be the following. It concerns a young woman, Louise, in her mid-thirties, working as a sales representative for a large company. She had come to therapy as a result of a general malaise, feeling depressed and generally unhappy.

Problem	How severe do you rate this problem 0= not a problem 10= extremely severe	How much does this problem interfere with your daily functioning? 0= not at all 10 = it makes life impossible	What would you like to achieve with respect to this problem?
I find it very difficult to interact with people, I feel anxious most of the time with other people, I can't speak up for myself for fear of making mistakes.	8	8	I would like to speak up for myself, I would like to interact with others with minimal anxiety. Evidence of success will be when I offer to do the monthly presentation to the sales team *and* actually do it!

In evaluating treatment, client and therapist would use the following form.

Problem	Severity rating before treatment 0= not a problem 10= extremely severe	Interference rating with daily life before treatment 0= not at all 10 = it makes life impossible	Severity rating post treatment	Interference rating with daily life post treatment	Goals set with respect to this problem	How far away from goal attainment now

We really like to look back with the client at the end of therapy, to see how they perceive the problems they had at the beginning of therapy. This is important as clients may have forgotten the seriousness of their problems.

This is how Louise's evaluation looked at the end of treatment.

Problem	Severity rating before treatment 0 = not a problem 10 = extremely severe	Interference rating with daily life before treatment 0 = not at all 10 = it makes life impossible	Severity rating post treatment	Interference rating with daily life post treatment	Goals set with respect to this problem	How far away from goal attainment now
I find it very difficult to interact with people, I feel anxious most of the time with other people, I can't speak up for myself for fear of making mistakes	8	7	4	3	I would like to interact with others with minimal anxiety. Evidence of success will be when I offer to do the monthly present-ation to the sales team *and* actually do it!	Well, I do speak up for myself and interact with others a lot more, I still do feel some anxiety, especially when I think that others are criticising me, my anxiety can creep up.

(*continued*)

	So would give me a 4 for this, have made progress, but need to keep working at it. I have done the presentation!

Severity rating before treatment

Here, the client indicates how severe they perceived the problem to be at the beginning of treatment (before column) and they indicate how severe they now thought their problem is at the beginning of treatment (now column). This takes into account any incorrect (exaggerated or minimising) perception of their problems by the client at the beginning of treatment. For instance, a problem drinker might evaluate his drinking problem as 5 at the beginning of treatment, but, looking back, might increase this to 9. A person with a worry problem might evaluate this as 10 at the beginning, but, looking back, might think that 6 would be a better rating.

Interference rating with daily life before treatment

Here, the client rates how much the problem interferes with daily life, and again the client is asked to do two ratings. One was done at the beginning of treatment and one is done now, looking back.

Severity rating post treatment and interference rating with daily life post treatment

Here, the client gives a rating how he/she perceives the severity of this problem at the end of treatment. It becomes immediately clear why it was necessary for the client to re-evaluate the severity of the problem at beginning of treatment. The problem drinker who rated his drinking as a 5 problem would not have made progress if he rated his problem at the end of treatment also with a 5. But, by getting him to re-evaluate the problem with the benefit of hindsight, we get a more realistic evaluation.

Goals set with respect to this problem

Client and therapist revisit the goals that were set regarding this problem and include goals that were added during the course of treatment.

Structuring sessions: from agenda setting to homework

Cognitive behaviour therapy is not only highly structured in its overall process, but also in how the individual sessions are organised. Sessions are planned according to pre-set structures. The structure during the assessment phase is different from the structure during the treatment phase.

After an agenda has been set and the homework from the previous session is reviewed, the therapist and the client proceed to discuss the other issues on the agenda in order of importance. Generally, it is possible to make progress on one to three problem areas in a particular session.

In addressing a typical issue, the therapist usually begins by asking the client a series of questions in order to clarify the nature of the difficulty. For example, is the client misinterpreting events? To what extent is the problem "real"? Are the client's expectations realistic? Are there alternative explanations or solutions? If the problem is symptomatic or behavioural (e.g., insomnia, problems with eating, low mood, or "overwhelming" chores or tasks), more specific history taking and behavioural analysis might be necessary. At the end of this questioning process, the therapist suggests focusing on one or two key thoughts, assumptions, images, or behaviours during the session. Once such targets are selected, the therapist recommends a cognitive or behavioural intervention and explains the rationale for use of the technique to the client. These procedures might include actions such as setting up an experiment, role playing or cognitive rehearsal, generating alternatives, weighing advantages and disadvantages, and activity scheduling (Beck, Rush, Shaw, & Emery, 1979).

Towards the end of the session, the therapist again asks the client for feedback. It is generally useful to encourage questions about potential areas of confusion and to ask the client to summarise the major points of the session. Finally, the therapist suggests a relevant homework assignment. The homework is tailored to help the client apply what is being learned in CBT during the interval between sessions.

Although the structure of the cognitive behaviour therapy session illustrated above does not change substantially as treatment progresses, the content does. The initial sessions are generally concerned with setting priorities, building empathy and rapport, reducing hopelessness, demonstrating the relationship between thoughts and feelings, identifying errors in thinking, and making rapid progress on readily solvable problems.

There are a few strategies that I have found helpful to improve a client's learning and to facilitate progressing further. The first one is to make audio recordings of the sessions, ask the client to listen to these recordings between sessions, and, if possible, to identify their key learning points in this session. This ensures that the client gets two therapy sessions for the "price" of one! Many clients report that they hear certain things for the first time when they listen to the recording. The second strategy (if recordings are not possible) is to ask client to think about the session and to formulate their "take-home message" from that session and bring that to the subsequent session. The third strategy involves session preparation on the part of the client. Here, the client is asked to think about the therapy session beforehand and write down any unfinished business from the previous session, reflections on the homework, and topics for this session.

Session structure during assessment

Session 1

The minutes behind the topics are indicative. Using an empathic and business-like style, therapists will be able to stick to an agenda like this with clients who present with an average suitability for CBT. Clients with very serious communication problems (schizophrenia) or serious interpersonal issues (personality disorders) might cause the therapist to deviate from this.

Setting the agenda

Agenda setting is a crucial element of each session. In a first session, it is perhaps better to start by saying something like, "You have made an appointment to see me. I am sure we have lots of things to discuss. Let's make a list of the things we want to talk about in this first session. What are the issues you would like to talk about today? And after the client gives a few topics, "Now, what I would like to discuss are the following points. Are there any more things you would like to raise in this (first) session?"

Explain process

In this first session, it is important to explain that the therapist is going to do an assessment, which will last between two and four sessions. At completion, the therapist will present the client with an overview of the results. Based on these, a treatment plan will be set up. The client's views on issues will be welcomed and, together, client and therapist will establish an intervention plan that suits the client.

Ascertain presenting symptoms and complaints

Now it is time to ask the client what it is that he/she has come to see a therapist about. The previous steps outlined need not take longer than about five minutes. The therapist should keep in mind that an empathic but business-like style of discussion and enquiry is the optimal approach. Too often, inexperienced (and not so inexperienced) therapists fritter time away by talking about non-relevant issues in the name of rapport building. It is my view that time is valuable and needs to be used in a focused way.

In this section, the therapist wants to know which symptoms the client is concerned about. It is important to get to the bottom of things and get a comprehensive overview, hence

- enquire regarding all of the complaints;
- establish whether you have heard all the client's concerns. "Is there anything else?" brings sometimes surprising results! At this point

the therapist just lists the concerns. When the list is fairly complete, it is perhaps time to summarise and categorise the issues.

An example of a list of concerns: sleep badly, cannot get out of bed in the morning, stopped enjoying things, feel miserable, do not like eating any more, and cannot concentrate.

From complaints to problems: the provisional problem list

Complaints are the things the client mentions that are bothering him or her. Translating complaints into a problem list means that we have to look beyond the presentation and ask ourselves, and the client, what the problem is with having this symptom. Problems need to be defined very specifically and focused on changeable entities.

Good problems:

- I don't do anything enjoyable because I am depressed.
- I feel depressed and don't have fun with my family any more.
- My partner and I have frequent arguments and then I become too angry.
- I can't speak up for myself because I am too shy.

Bad problems:

- Life sucks.
- People are so unfair.
- My parents abused me.

Provisional goals list

Based on the provisional problems list, client and therapist now create a list of goals. The therapist asks the client to state what he/she wants to achieve for each identified problem. Just as with the problem list, the aim is *not* to create an exhaustive, detailed list of SMART goals, but to get client and therapist to think in terms of goals and to check how realistic these goals are.

Questions that will assist clients to be specific and concrete are:

- How would your life be different if you would achieve that goal?
- What would be different in your life after having achieved that goal?
- How would I be able to see that you had achieved your goal?

First explanation of CBT

Once the goals have been established, the therapist moves into explaining cognitive behaviour therapy. It cannot be emphasised too much that this explanation should be tailored to the needs of the client. For a client who impresses the therapist as being psychologically minded, the explanation will have to be different than it would be with a client who finds it difficult to grasp that thinking and feeling play a role in doing. In other words, the therapist has to use the first part of the session to "assess" the client with respect to his/her need regarding a CBT explanation. Sometimes, we need to supply clients with a detailed and sophisticated explanation of how thinking facilitates feelings and how feelings influence behaviours, followed by explaining how our thinking goes haywire, etc. At other times, we just need to explain that problems emerge because we have learnt to react in an unhelpful manner and we need to train ourselves to react in more helpful ways.

Application of CBT to symptoms and problems

At this point, it is important to apply your explanation to the problems and goals of the client. Your job is now to use the "theory" with which you have provided the client to explain the practical problems and/or goals the client presents you with. In other words, you explain how learning about thinking and changing thinking might be beneficial for example 1, and how learning skills might be beneficial for example 2.

Understanding check

This should become a standard element in the repertoire of each CBT therapist. Once a concept is explained to the client, check whether the client has understood it. The best way to do this is to ask the client to explain it back to the therapist: ". . . as if you are explaining to a good friend what you have learnt today . . ."

Homework discussion

Homework is an important feature of CBT. The homework assignments at completion of the first session can be: monitoring the frequency, intensity, and duration of problem(s), completing standard questionnaires, and perhaps some reading about a CBT perspective on the client's symptoms. Remember to give homework that will assist in the assessment. Completed homework in this phase should be helpful in completing the conceptualisation.

Evaluation

Take time at the completion of each session to check how the client has experienced the session. Topics to check for are: did I do things you did not like and what were they; did I do things that were helpful and what were they; what did you learn today—any tips for the next session?

Therapist's work

The therapist cannot be idle between sessions. As soon as possible after the session, it is important to evaluate what has been said in it. How do the symptoms fit together; what kind of hypothesis regarding diagnoses can be formulated? What is the plan for the next sessions? In CBT, doing therapy is a process whereby the therapist constantly tries to give meaning and understanding to the presentation of the client. Why does the client have these problems? How did they emerge and how are they currently maintained?

Session 2

Setting the agenda

- Discuss and evaluate homework.

Homework is an important and integral part of cognitive behaviour therapy. The therapist should give homework the attention it deserves and go through it with the client, drawing conclusions from it with the client and using it in the planning of the therapy.

- Assess for history of the problems.

At this point, the therapist investigates the history of the problems: when did the problems start, what happened in that period, etc. The aim of this is to gain an understanding from a learning perspective: how did life teach the client to choose these problems as coping strategies?

- Assess for cognitive, affective, behavioural, and interpersonal issues.

Apart from the problems the client has identified, are there other cognitive, behavioural, affective, and / or interpersonal issues in the client's life that are of importance? Simple open questions are often the best strategy in getting this information: any other concerns, how do you feel in general, what do you do for fun, how often do have fun with other people, etc. Another helpful tool can be found in Lazarus (1989).

- Discuss specific problem examples using the SORCC format.

The crunch here is to ask the client for a specific occurrence of a problem and either analyse it from a reinforcement perspective or from a cognitive perspective. Or both!

What you need to know is how the problem is linked with antecedents (things that occurred before the problem) and consequences (things that happened after the problem occurred). Now, a problem can be a behaviour engaged in by the client (drinking, working, shouting, self-harm) or behaviour the client did not engage in (avoiding social contact, not standing up for himself, not getting up, not going for some exercise) or a feeling such as anxiety, depression, etc. Be careful not to accept other people's behaviour (unless we are doing parent skills training) or circumstances as a problem. Also be careful not to take thoughts as a problem, unless they have an impact on behaviours and / or feelings that are unwanted.

By careful questioning of the client about the problem occurrence and investigating what happened in the client's environment (finding external stimuli that might act as prompts or triggers), you should find out a good deal that will be helpful. A good model to follow is the SORCC model (Borg-Laufs, 2011; Hillenbrand, 2006; Kanfer, Reinecker, & Schmelzer, 2000) combined with the BASIC-ID template.

S = External stimuli: what happened in the client's environment when the problem occurred.
O = What occurs inside the organism: feelings, thoughts, and physical sensations and how these interconnect.
R = The person's behavioural reaction: what did he / she do.
C = The consequences, both internal and external, after the behavioural response.

C = The contingency or relationship between the behaviour and the consequences. In other words, what is the correlation between behaviour and consequences?

The BASIC-ID template (Lazarus, 1989) can function as a reminder to include all elements of life in the picture: (B = overt behaviour; A = affect, S = sensations, I = interpersonal, C = cognitions, I = imagery and D = drugs and alcohol). The aim of the interview here is to develop an understanding of which meaning-giving processes contribute to the problems and which signalling and reinforcement processes contribute.

Second explanation of CBT

Based on the problem example, it might be necessary to review the explanation of the CBT model again and focus on an idiosyncratic application of CBT to symptoms and problems.

Understanding check

Now might be a good time to check whether our first and second explanations of CBT made any sense to the client. A very good way to check this is by getting the client to recount back to you what their understanding is of the CBT model. The can pretend that they are explaining what CBT is all about to a good friend.

Homework discussion

Both therapist and client have learnt from the first homework. The new homework depends on how the client coped with the first set of homework. A natural tendency for therapists is to "double up" if a client has not managed to complete all tasks, but this is wrong, for obvious reasons. It is much better to focus on getting client to complete small tasks successfully rather than bigger tasks unsuccessfully.

Evaluation

It is very important to evaluate the sessions and therapists need to learn not to skip this for "more important topics". Questions such as:

- What was helpful in this session?

- What was most/least helpful today?
- Did I (therapist) do or say things that were not helpful.

A more structured way of getting feedback is to use the following form.

Client's Evaluation of Therapy Session

Client's initials ____ Date of session ______ Therapist's name __________

Please put a tick on the appropriate spot on the line

Your thoughts about the session you just completed

This was a very good session

No____Yes

I made progress during this session

No____Yes

I got out of this session what I wanted to get out of it

No____Yes

The session was very well organised

No____Yes

I was really engaged in the session

No____Yes

Your thoughts about the therapist during the session

My therapist was helpful to me

No____Yes

My therapist moved me on when I needed encouragement

No____Yes

My therapist was patient and understanding

No____Yes

(*continued*)

Your thoughts about your progress in today's session

I achieved better insight into, and understanding of, my problems.

No____Yes

I learned methods or techniques for better dealing with people.

No____Yes

I learned techniques in defining and solving my everyday problems.

No____Yes

Greater ability to express myself.

No____Yes

I increased my confidence.

No____Yes

I achieved a greater ability to cope with negative feelings.

No____Yes

I gained better control over my actions.

No____Yes

I achieved a greater ability to recognise my irrational and unhealthy thoughts.

No____Yes

I achieved better ways of scheduling my time.

No____Yes

I increased my motivation to do something about my problems.

No____Yes

Session structure during treatment

Once the client and therapist have discussed the implications of the assessment a treatment programme can be started. Session structure does not change much; the content, however, now comprises more and more therapeutic interventions that are tried out or practised in the sessions, after which the client will try them out between sessions. The discussion of homework is filled with the client reporting back on their success and/or difficulties regarding these therapeutic tasks.

Setting the agenda

Agenda setting remains important. The temptation might be to skip it ("we—client and therapist—know what we want to talk about, no need to check"). This assumption has resulted in trouble for many therapists.

Discuss and evaluate homework

Homework now consists of therapeutic tasks. This could be behavioural experiments, exposure tasks, thought records, etc. It is important to ensure maximum preparation before giving a client a therapeutic task to complete. For instance, complete a thought record *in* a session before asking client to apply it to a difficult situation between sessions.

Further socialising to the CBT model

A common mistake of inexperienced therapists is to assume that clients will be able to apply the CBT model after the few explanations they have received. Good therapy means that the therapist uses every opportunity to highlight and explain the CBT model, using examples based on what the client brings to therapy.

Discuss specific problem examples using the SORCC format

During agenda setting, clients will often mention issues and problems that they have encountered in the previous period. A good collaborative way to review these problem issues is to discuss them while using the SORCC format (topographical analysis). In doing so, the therapist and client will rapidly find out what kind of problem in CBT terms we are dealing with and which interventions might be useful.

Understanding client's problems from an SORCC perspective provides useful information with respect to

- which situations (S) are involved in triggering problem moments;
- which internal stimuli (everything the "O" contains: thoughts, feelings, and sensations) trigger problem moments;
- which behaviours are involved in the problem (R);
- which consequences follow on from the behaviour, and how these consequences connect to the behaviour.

This understanding can then result in further discussion and exploration regarding specific interventions:

- which skills does the client need to learn to deal with the situations (S) to prevent the problem from occurring;
- which feelings and/or sensations does the client need to learn to tolerate, so the problem does not occur again;
- which thoughts need to be addressed and changed in order for the problem not to happen again;
- does the client need to learn behavioural skills as alternatives to the problem behaviours;
- is it necessary to re-arrange environmental contingencies to stop the problem behaviour from being reinforced and the desirable behaviour from being punished.

Several examples of agenda setting

Agenda setting without difficulty

An excerpt of a first session with Gemma. As before, the therapist's comments are presented within square brackets.

> *Therapist*: Well, thanks for coming. We have just under an hour today to talk and I have it that your name is Gemma. Is that correct?
>
> *Client*: Yes.
>
> *Therapist*: In this first meeting that we have, are there things that you really would like to talk about, that you would like to put on to the agenda, so to speak?
> [The client is invited to put issues on the agenda.]
>
> *Client*: I guess really just to focus on how I'm feeling and why and really to discuss any ways that I might be able to improve how I'm feeling.
>
> *Therapist*: So how you're feeling, why you're feeling the way you're feeling and ways to improve the way you feel?
>
> *Client*: Yes.
>
> *Therapist*: Anything else, apart from these three things?
> [Inviting the client to add to the agenda.]
>
> *Client*: I think that mainly covers it.

Therapist: Let's also talk about the things that I would like to focus on, like what is the problem basically that you've come here to seek help for, and I also would like to talk a bit about the type of therapy that we do here so that you have an idea of what you're in for, so to speak, and we will have time for questions if you have any questions. Is that okay?

Client: That's great.

Therapist: So you started off by saying, "I've come here to talk about how I'm feeling" and why you're feeling like this and what I can do to improve it. Can you tell me a bit more about that?

[A more elegant approach would have been briefly to list the points and ask the client where she would like to start.]

Client: Well, I think I have always been a bit of a worrier.

Therapist: A worrier?

Agenda setting with difficulty (Ann)

This is an excerpt of the second session with Ann. She is a rather reluctant client . . .

Therapist: Thanks, Anne, for coming back today. Our last session was a week ago and, in that session, if I can briefly recap, you decided that you might want to give cognitive behaviour therapy a go to see if that might be helpful to overcome some of the obstacles you had in feeling happy within yourself. Is that still the case?
[The therapist knows that the client was reluctant to come to therapy and checks how her interest in therapy is now.]

Client: I don't know. I mean, it's going to take a lot of time, isn't it?

Therapist: So you're saying you're wondering whether it's going to take a lot of time?
[Paraphrase, could have been followed by "Could you tell me a bit more about that?"]

Client: Yes.

Therapist: Well, that might be an issue that we might want to talk a little bit about today. One of the ways in which we try to work when we do cognitive behaviour therapy is that, at the beginning of each meeting, we make what we call an "agenda", which is a list of things to talk about to make sure that all the things that you're worried and concerned about get discussed and all the issues that I would like to talk about get discussed, so this sounds like one of the things we might want to put on the agenda. Is that OK?

[Therapist starts teaching the client about the structure of CBT.]

Client: OK.

Therapist: So you said, "Is it going to take a lot of time?" Are there any other things that you would like to put on the agenda?

Client: It still seems very odd, doesn't it, coming and talking to a stranger about things. You know, it's not exactly getting on with it, is it?

[Therapist notices the defensiveness of the client and sticks to paraphrasing.]

Therapist: So it is odd talking to a stranger.

Client: "You just have to kind of get your head down, stiff upper lip", I suppose that's what people would say, "and just deal with it. That's what life's like, isn't it?"

Therapist: So stiff upper lip, and that is what life is like. So we've got three things so far that we might want to put on the agenda: is it going to take a lot time; it's kind of odd talking to a stranger about these things; and wouldn't it be better just to have a stiff upper lip and to get on with life and ignore the fact that you're unhappy. Any other things?

[Therapist "rolls with resistance"; each issue the client mentions as potentially problematic is countered by suggesting putting it on the agenda.]

Client: I don't know. I mean, I don't know what I'm supposed to do here, do I? It's not something I've ever done before, so I don't know how I'm supposed to behave.

Therapist: I think you're doing quite well, meaning you're talking about the things that seem to be of concern to you and you're listing them as issues that we can talk about, but this is also a very good point, how to do therapy.

Client: I've spent the first six sessions having lessons in how to do therapy!

Therapist: If we look at these four things that we have now: is it going to take a long time; it's kind of odd talking to a stranger; isn't it much better to have a stiff upper lip and to ignore the fact that you're unhappy; and then another question is how to do therapy, how does it work, this cognitive behaviour therapy. They are good points on the agenda. Is there anything else that you would like to talk about today?

[Therapist decides to ignore the client's sceptical tone, for the moment, and stays on task.]

Client: I don't know. You said that you would be putting things on the agenda.

[The client is collaborating and invites the therapist to contribute to the agenda.]

Therapist: That's very good and thank you very much for reminding me of that. Yes, what I would like to talk about is perhaps to make a list of problems you would like to resolve with therapy and what your goals would be around these problems.

Client: Well, I don't know. If I don't know how it works, I don't know what I can expect from it really, do I?

Therapist: That's a good point.

Client: It's not like you're going to come and help me do all my work or get on with things in the house or anything, is it? I mean, it's still me that's going to be going back home and doing everything I have to do, so I don't know how I can make a list.

Therapist: I think you just did. What sounds like a real problem for you is the overwhelming amount of tasks that rest on your shoulders. Would that be correct, that that's a problem for you?

[Paraphrasing client's words to create discussion points.]

Client: It's just what has to be done. I don't see how talking to somebody can take that away. It's not going to change the fact that those jobs are there, is it?

Therapist: I'm not saying that it will change the amount of jobs, I'm just enquiring whether, from where you're sitting, the enormous amount of tasks that you have to do where you're feeling overwhelmed by that is a problem for you, or whether you're happy with being overwhelmed.

[Therapist "holds" the line and "forces" client to think about the issue. Is it a problem or not?]

Client: It's not a question of being happy or not, is it? I mean, it's just a question that it has to be done and, if I can't cope with it, then that's my problem, isn't it?

Therapist: So you say that quite clearly, that, if you can't cope with it, that is indeed your problem, so shall we put that on the problem list then, not coping with the amount of tasks that you have to do?

[By paraphrasing the therapist can include an issue on the problem list.]

Client: I didn't say I'm not coping, did I? I mean, I'm getting them done, I'm getting everything done. If you've put me down as not coping, it means that I'm a failure, doesn't it?

Therapist: So, if you don't cope with something, that means in your own terms that you're a failure?

Client: Of course it does. What else does it mean? If you don't get things done, then you've failed, haven't you?

Therapist: I'm just going to write down a few things there.

Client: I'm not sure about this, you know. I feel worse now than when I came in.

Therapist: So what you're saying is that talking about these issues makes you feel worse?

Client: Being called a failure makes me feel worse; being told I can't cope with things makes me feel worse.

Therapist: So what exactly did I say that implied that I thought you were a failure?
[The client clearly distorts what the therapist has said and the therapist gently confronts her with this.]

Client: I don't know, I can't remember. You said something about, if I can't cope with things or something, I'm overwhelmed. I don't remember.

Therapist: I kind of reflected on what you said yourself about the enormous amount of tasks that you seem to have to do when you're at home, and I reflected on what you said about these tasks, that you felt overwhelmed by them.

Client: I don't want to let anybody down.

Therapist: Can I just write that down as a topic that I would like to discuss with you, that you don't want to let anybody down? That really sounds like, if you let anybody down, that would be terrible for you. Can I go back, deviating a little from the agenda? You asked me, the therapist, what I could put on the agenda, and I said I would like to talk about the problems and the goals of therapy and then we started to talk about them. What I would also like to do in this session, and it's also one of your points, is explain how this therapy works and that coincides with one of your points, so that overlaps quite nicely.

[The therapist structures the session back to the agenda.]

Towards the end of the session, I would like to hear from you what you thought of this session, what were the good bits and the less good bits, and how I could improve the way I do therapy in order to help you.

Client: You want my advice?

Therapist: Yes.

Client: I don't know anything about therapy, so I don't know.

Therapist: Well, towards the end, when I ask you what you thought about the session, you will probably realise that you know a lot more about therapy than you think. We have the following things on the agenda: is it going to take a lot of time, the therapy; it's odd to talk to a stranger; wouldn't it be much better to have a stiff upper lip, to get on with life and to ignore one's personal unhappiness; how does therapy work, looking at problems and goals. In there we've identified already three things, that the amount of tasks that you have to do sometimes feel overwhelming, but, if it feels overwhelming, it means that you get a sense that you're a failure and that is very upsetting for you, and it also means that you might let people down, which is also very upsetting for you, so we've already got some problems there that you've identified. I would like now to explain what this type of therapy is, and that's on the list already, and I would like your feedback on the session towards the end, so that's all on the agenda. Do you have anything to add to that?

Client: It seems like quite a lot.

Therapist: Well, we'll just see how we get along. We've got another fifty minutes left, so we've got probably a bit of time to explore some of these things. Where shall we start out of what I've put down? [Shows list of points.]

Client: You mean I have to choose?

Therapist: You can choose if you want to.

Client: Well, I really want to know how much time I've got to spend doing this, and then I suppose that's linked with how to do it.

Therapist: Good choice, so in order to answer the time question, I might need to explain a bit more about how CBT works. Is that OK?

Client: Whatever you think.

Therapist: Then that might lead into how much time you need to invest in it. This type of therapy, cognitive behaviour therapy, is a therapy that is based on the idea that human beings don't need to be unhappy. (*The client laughs.*) I am glad to make you laugh.

Client: Don't need to be unhappy?

Therapist: Don't need to be unhappy.

Client: You say that like it's a choice.

Therapist: Well, it's not a choice, but it's what we have learnt from life. Cognitive behaviour therapy looks at human misery, human unhappiness as the end result of a long learning process. I'm sure you know of people who have a bad back or something like that and they have to go to a physiotherapist who then teaches them to walk slightly differently, to sit slightly differently because, throughout their life, they have acquired a way of walking and sitting that's detrimental for their back, and they didn't do that wilfully, they didn't do that on purpose, but they just did that because that's how they learnt to sit, walk, stand, sleep. With happiness, depression, anxiety, feeling miserable, it's the same; we have learnt a way of doing life. For some people, they learn to do life and they feel OK, sometimes happy, sometimes less happy, but in general they feel OK. Other people learn to do life and they feel very bad, and it doesn't mean that they wilfully do that, that they wake up in the morning and think, "What am I going to do today that will make me feel miserable?", but it is just like the person with the bad back; it is the way they've learnt to do life.

Now, what cognitive behaviour therapy does is it analyses how that came about, how this person, who is clearly intelligent, can think about him or herself, has a number of talents and skills, how they have come to be this person and lead a life that results in feeling miserable. In that analysis, in that kind of making sense of it, we have to look at what that person is doing, how that person thinks about what they do, thinks about life, thinks about themselves, and how that person feels about things. In cognitive therapy, we often use feeling as a thermometer, just like in medicine, where they use a thermometer to decide whether there's a fever. We say that a feeling, especially a bad feeling, is a signal that something's wrong. What kind of bad feelings have you had in the last couple of days?

Client: Being worried.

Therapist: Worried?

Client: Yes, really, really worried.

Therapist: If you wanted to give that feeling a name, what kind of a feeling would go with that? Is that a feeling of anxiety, depression, fear, despair?

CHAPTER THREE

Assessment, engagement, and formulation in cognitive behaviour therapy

Introduction

This chapter starts with a more elaborate explanation of the importance of a formulation for effective and efficient CBT. All assessment efforts should serve this one goal: develop a pocket-sized theory on the emergence and maintenance of the problems. The concept of establishing baselines is introduced, identifying SMART (specific, measurable, achievable, realistic, and time-framed) problems and goals and how to use the results of the assessment to assist the clients in gaining insight into the connections that maintain their problems.

Engagement problems will be discussed in the context of Prochaska, Diclemente, and Norcross's transtheoretical model (1992) and Miller's (van Bilsen, 1995) motivational interviewing. Examples of assessment-focused interviewing strategies will be shown.

*Understanding/*verstehen *the client*

Although we say that, in technical terms, the aim of the assessment is to develop a pocket-sized theory on the emergence and maintenance of the problem, the real goal, of course, is to understand the client. We need to understand why this person, with this learning history, developed these problems. The best description of really understanding the client is encompassed in the word *verstehen*. This is a German word with exactly the same meaning as the English word "understand". However, since the late nineteenth century, in German philosophy and social sciences, it has also been used in the meaning of "interpretative or participatory examination" of social phenomena. The term is particularly associated with Max Weber (1926), a German sociologist. In anthropology, *verstehen* has come to mean a systematic interpretative process in which an outside observer of a culture attempts to relate to it and to understand others. It describes very well what the task of a cognitive behaviour therapist is when working with clients.

A good and detailed assessment resulting in an individualised formulation and treatment plan will pay off. It might seem as if quite a bit of time is spent on this before actually offering treatment to the client, but it is time very well spent. It is a bit like making a route plan before embarking on a journey. If it is a very familiar journey, then the planning might not take that long, but if it is a complex journey that we are not familiar with, the planning will take longer and that will pay off when we are confronted with unexpected situations during the journey. It is very rare that a client will present with a simple problem, leading to a clear-cut problem definition indicating that it could be treated by strictly adhering to one of the existing treatment protocols. I have found that, in real life, it is very important to use the disorder specific models and treatment protocols as inspiration and *not* as procedures that need to be followed as if they were *cordon bleu* recipes.

Power-up CBT with values

One of the great tragedies of the human race is its susceptibility to adopting corrupt values. My own childhood in the Netherlands during the 1950s and 1960s was filled with reminders of the madness of the Second World War. Between 1933 and 1945, a normally rational people that brought forth Goethe, Einstein, Heine, Mozart, Lang, Dietrich, and many others became hypnotised by the values of National Socialism. Could any of the excesses have been committed without the link to values? Values energise, they motivate for action and are—in the context of psychotherapy—a precondition of meaningful lasting change. Any change that is achieved through psychotherapy that goes against important values of the person involved will be doomed to be short-lived: values always win.

A traditional and "normal" part of CBT assessment is to get an idea of the client's habitual patterns of negative automatic thoughts, his maladaptive beliefs, core beliefs, and rules for living. In general, these are linked with the presenting problems and symptoms. For example, a client complaining of feeling depressed might have the profile shown in Table 3.1.

The cognitive processes and cognitive content uncovered in the assessment have a negative connotation, which is logical, since they promote the problems and symptoms. If we examine the rules for living and core beliefs more closely, we can see two things: there is always a positive intention at the basis of them and at the core these rules and beliefs have a strong positive element. These core elements of core beliefs often represent important values that good CBT can be built on, as shown in Table 3.2.

Take a moment to compare the elements of the cognitive profile with the values column in Table 3.2 and you will see how the values are, in fact, a core element of the cognitive profile, or a milder and less dogmatic description of the same issue. Behavioural activation

Table 3.1. Example of profile of a depressed client.

Elements	Cognitive profile	Result
Negative automatic thoughts	This is not good enough. There is no point in trying. Life is just too difficult.	Depression
Beliefs	I have got to give it my best. I am a failure if I don't achieve perfection.	
Rules for living	You can do things perfectly or not at all. No point in starting if you can't you can't finish it to perfection. No rest before the work is done.	
Core beliefs	I am not good enough; I am incompetent.	

Table 3.2. How CBT can be built on a client's values.

Elements	Cognitive profile	Pro-social core values
Negative automatic thoughts	This is not good enough. There is no point in trying. Life is just too difficult.	*I appreciate good work.* *It is important to persist and not give up easily.* *It is important that life is balanced: doing difficult things and less difficult things.*
Beliefs	I have got to give it my best. I am a failure if I don't achieve perfection.	*I appreciate hard work.* *Doing a good job is important.*
Rules for living	You can do things perfectly or not at all. No point in starting if you can't finish it to perfection. No rest before the work is done.	*Doing a good job is important.*
Core beliefs	I am not good enough; I am incompetent.	*It is important to me to think positively about myself.*

treatment for depression (Veale, 2008) and acceptance commitment therapy (ACT) (Hayes, Strosahl, & Wilson, 1999) suggest that it is important to review values in the following domains: relationships, education and career, recreation and interests, mind–body–spirituality, and daily responsibilities. At the beginning of treatment, a client's values are often one-sided (in the example above, all focused on good performance) while other areas are neglected (in the example above, no values identified with self-care). In order to power-up CBT with values it is important to use the assessment process to identify the values that are important for the client and to ensure that a balanced value system forms the basis of the CBT process. A balanced value system consists of values in most of these five domains *and* the values are a healthy mix of duty (for example, good work is important) and pleasure (for example, appreciating the beauty of nature is good).

Once values have been identified, it is important to pinpoint activities that could underpin these values.

Towards the completion of the assessment phase, therapist and client might end up with a value system like that shown in Table 3.3.

Table 3.3. Potential value system at the end of an assessment phase.

Cognitive profile	Pro-social core values	Activities
This is not good enough. There is no point in trying. Life is just too difficult.	*I appreciate good work. It is important to persist and not give up easily. It is important that life is balanced: doing difficult things and less difficult things.*	*When working, planning it carefully and taking the appropriate time to complete a task. Learn a new and unfamiliar skill (a new language!) and persist despite difficulties. Set up a daily half hour of doing whatever I like to do as long as it is not work.*
I have got to give it my best. I am a failure if I don't achieve perfection.	*I appreciate hard work. Doing a good job is important.*	*When I have been working hard at a task for 2 hours, I deserve a pat on the back (coffee break).*
You can do things perfectly or not at all. No point in starting if you can't finish it to perfection. No rest before the work is done.	*Doing a good job is important*	*Saying no to people who want me to take on more work that would overwhelm me and make me stressed: stick to the workload that I can manage well!*
I am not good enough; I am incompetent.	*It is important to me to think positively about myself*	*I will stop trying to please the friends and family who constantly criticise me and make sure I meet up with supportive and kind people on a regular basis.*

The therapist conducts a "flanking" exercise by establishing a value system with the client that is supported by specific activities. There is no direct "attack" on the problems, but, by making client's existing value system more explicit and more balanced, one of the pillars of client's problems is being eroded.

Information phase and assessment

The assessment consists of three steps, step one to retrieve information from the client, step two is for the clinician to make sense of the information and compose a formulation, while step three is the feeding back of the information and formulation to the client, leading to an agreed treatment plan.

The information to retrieve from the client depends on the presenting complaint of the client. For instance, if the client is a young man still living at home who is complaining of depression but explaining that whatever he does, the family will always support him, then part of the informational quest is to find out whether the family over-supports the client (by asking the client to monitor his activities and monitor offers of help that are effective). A good starting point for collecting information is to get a helicopter overview of the problem. A good question to ask, for instance, is "What would be the issues you would like to resolve with this therapy?" This often results in a list of issues or symptoms that the therapist, through careful listening and questioning, can "translate" into problem statements.

The therapist needs an overview of client's present engagement in the problem behaviour: how often, how much, how intense, etc. The therapist needs to use the four Ws to structure the process of information gathering, as explained below.

What is the problem? Just listing symptoms is not sufficient to understand why this symptom is a problem for the client. It is important to understand exactly what it is that the client finds problematic. For example, one client who came to the clinic complaining about blushing all the time defined as the problem: "When I am with other people, I get a sensation of being very hot in my face. I then think I blush and also think that the other people will reject me for it. I then hide my face, or make an excuse and leave."

Where does the problem occur? It is important to know whether situations make a difference to the frequency and intensity of the problem. Some problems are situation specific, while others are not. The only way to find out is to ask. Our client's blushing problem was not situation specific, but people specific.

With whom is the problem better or worse? Here, it is important to check if the problem is influenced by the presence of people and if certain people make a difference. For our blusher, it seemed that the problem was very much worsened by the presence of people and even further increased if these people's attention was focused on him.

When does the problem happen? The time of day makes a difference for some problems: sometimes it is not the time of day *per se*, but the end of a working day, the beginning of a weekend, etc. For our blusher, the later in the day, the more likely it was that the problem would occur and there was increased likelihood that he would experience the problem as more severe. This was not a time issue, however, but more an activity issue. The client had a stressful job, and by the end of the day he would have experienced a whole series of stressful events, which meant that his autonomic nervous system had been activated, making it more likely that he would feel hot in the face or blush.

What makes the "problem" a problem? This is an important component of the assessment. This is where the therapist finds out what motivates the client to seek help. For our blushing client, it was not the blushing as such that was a problem for him. (This was evidenced by the client's answer to the following question: "If you are standing alone in your bathroom and you notice that you were blushing, how much of a problem would that be for you?" The client's answer was "Well, I would worry whether the blushing would go away quickly so that no one would see me blush upon leaving the bathroom.") For our blushing client, the problem was not blushing, but the hypothesised negative opinion of others.

The assessment in cognitive behaviour therapy focuses on finding out how the client learns to have these problems and how these problems are, at the moment, still maintained. This means that the therapist needs to start a process of persistent enquiry. The therapist needs to find out exactly what the client sees as the problem, how frequently the problem occurs, where the problem occurs, with whom the problem occurs, at what times the problem occurs, how intense the problem is, and how much does this problem interfere with the general well-being of the client.

The four Ws can easily be investigated with the assistance of the client. The client can be given homework to monitor the frequency, intensity, and duration of problem occurrences. Ideally, the therapist will ask the client to keep a record of some of these after the first session. The simplest form of monitoring and establishing a baseline is to ask the client to record the occurrence of behaviours/feelings in relation to the time of day. More elaborate baseline recordings would include information about the "where" and "with whom".

What the client sees as the problem (e.g., I am depressed) needs to be reshaped into a problem definition that the therapist can work with. A good problem definition would include emotional, behavioural, and cognitive components (e.g., I am depressed and, as a result of that, I have stopped doing the things I enjoy and I persistently see the negative side of things). In order to get the necessary information about the issues, it will be necessary to ask the client to keep some records regarding the problem. For instance, with the depressed clients, it is often a good idea to ask them to keep a record of what they actually do during the day. With anxious clients, it is sometimes good to ask them to monitor their levels of anxiety during the day. By collecting this type of information, therapist and patient gradually get a good overview of what exactly the problem is, the intensity of the problem, how it interferes with life, and which people are involved in the problem. Asking the client to do tasks between the sessions has the added benefit that the therapist has an opportunity to see how motivated the client is to work with psychological therapy. In the assessment process the therapist can also make use of information gathering that combines events in client's life. For instance, if the client complains of feeling anxious in social situations, the therapist could ask the client not only to monitor their level of anxiety, but also to provide information as to how many people were present each time their anxiety flared up. In general, it is a good idea to agree with the client a ten-point rating scale regarding the levels of negative feelings. In doing so, we make it easier for the client to complete his homework. It is easier to write down that the anxiety level was seven than to describe the level of one's anxiety in words.

Problems

From a CBT perspective, problems can be seen in various ways. The problem could be that you experience a negative emotion too frequently or too strongly (e.g., depression, anxiety); it could be that you behave in certain ways too frequently or too intensely (e.g., aggressive behaviour, drinking alcohol); it could be that you think certain things too frequently (worrying ruminations). Of course, the problem could also be the opposite: the client does not behave in certain ways often enough (expressing positive feelings, expressing negative feelings, doing nice things). The task of the therapist is to come to an understanding of how the problem fits into a cognitive behavioural model. This will help us understand the mechanisms involved and assist us in creating a good treatment plan.

An example of the type of monitoring we can ask clients to do is demonstrated in the following exercise.

John identified feeling really depressed as one of his issues and, as a result of this, not doing things he normally needed or liked to do. John also mentioned drinking too much and, at times, getting very angry and aggressive towards family members.

First, the therapist interviews the client to get a retrospective diary of last week's problem behaviour. A good way to do this is to use a flip-chart, with the format shown in Table 3.4 as a guideline, starting either with yesterday or with yesterday a week ago, and working day

Table 3.4. Example of monitoring through a retrospective diary.

Day	Morning	Afternoon	Evening/night
Monday	Depression: 8 out of 10. Avoidance: did not go to work.	Depression: 8 out of 10. Avoidance: did not go to work. Drinking: three cans of beer.	Depression: 6 out of 10 Avoidance: did not do anything, watched TV. Drinking: bottle of wine. Aggression: shouted at children.
Tuesday	Depression: 8 out of 10	Depression: 3 out of 10	Depression: 4 out of 10. Avoidance: did not do anything. Drinking: 2 cans of beer and a bottle of wine.

by day through a week. As shown, the therapist splits every day into three parts and begins by asking the question "How often/much did you feel/do it on Monday morning", and so on, trying to ensure that the client is specific. If the client cannot remember, then the therapist can mention a very low figure and a very high figure. The client will then feel that he or she can safely mention his or her best guess.

Monitoring of frequency, duration, and intensity of problems is something that the therapist can ask the client to do as homework after a first session. It can be followed in the second session by focusing on one or more problem incidents that the client or the therapist would like to focus on in the form of a topographical analysis. This is a detailed analysis of one problem occurrence. The aim is to uncover specific triggers (internal or external) for the problem and the relevant consequences (internal or external).

Example of interviewing for problems with Ann

This is an excerpt of my second session with Ann; we are about ten minutes into the session. As before, the therapist's comments are given in square brackets.

Therapist: If you wanted to give that a feeling a name, what kind of a feeling would go with that? Is that a feeling of anxiety, depression, fear, despair?

Client: Maybe anxiety.

Therapist: So you're feeling really worried and feeling anxious?

Client: Yes.

Therapist: That's a very good example, because anxiety is a real signal that something's not right. Anxiety is a good feeling to have when we're in a really dangerous situation. When an unpleasant person with a big gun stands in front of you and threatens to shoot you, then it's very appropriate to feel anxious, isn't it?
[Therapist slips in some psycho-education about negative feelings.]

Client: Yes.

Therapist: But, in your situation, when certain tasks in the house aren't done, when certain things aren't as clean as other people might want them to be, to feel anxious about that is perhaps—

Client: You see, I know you're going to say it's silly and it's about what people think about you, isn't it? It's about how people see you and you just think it's silly because it's not a gun. Well, it's like a gun to me.

Therapist: So that's very good, your saying that, excellent. So what you're saying is that an unclean house feels like someone is holding a gun to your head?
[Therapist decides to ignore client's emotional outburst and compliment her for collaboration, which leads to a fine-tuning of understanding.]

Client: No, not an unclean house, what people think about you.

Therapist: What people think about you, it feels like there's a gun held against your head. That's a very good example of how anxiety can really be a very unpleasant problem. I assume it feels horrible to feel anxious about what people might think about you all the time. What cognitive behaviour therapy tries to do is to teach you about this anxiety and what the foundation of that anxiety is. For instance, is a loaded gun in the hands of a madman just as dangerous as the negative opinion of your neighbours? I'm not wanting you to answer that now, but what cognitive behaviour therapy does is talk about that and to look at how the beliefs we have, like people talking critically about me is terrible, if my patients see me as a bad psychologist, oh my God, that would be the end of the road, are they true? It is investigating whether the beliefs we have and that we hold on to very strongly, whether these beliefs are really helpful and beneficial to us.
[Explanation about anxiety as a false alarm.]

Client: And make sure that you keep the house clean.

Therapist: So this explanation that I just gave you of what CBT is, did it make any sense to you?

Client: A bit.

Therapist: If I were to ask you to kind of summarise back to me what I just explained, would you be able to do that?
[Understanding check.]

Client: I don't know.

Therapist: Just give it a go. I'll help you when you get stuck.

Client: I think maybe what you're trying to say is that—you see, I used to do ballet when I was little and the ballet teacher always used to say, "You shouldn't get into bad habits with your posture", and it's like what you said about someone with a bad back, that you should always stand tall and walk properly. I think maybe what you're saying is sometimes you can get into bad habits with the way you think about things.

Therapist: That is an excellent summary!

Client: Then you're not exactly walking tall any more. You kind of feel a bit slumped over and constricted. Is that right?

Therapist: I think that's a very good explanation. That's a very good way of summarising what I just said, yes, excellent. A ballerina who walks slumped over, how do you think she feels?

Client: She can't do what she has to do because you can't do ballet hunched over, you have to stand tall and you have to place your body properly, your arms and everything in relation to each other, and you just couldn't do it.

Therapist: A ballerina who has been doing ballet for many years and is slumped over, do you think it will be easy for that ballerina to learn to stand tall again?

Client: Well, if she was really slumped over, she wouldn't be dancing, would she?

Therapist: But, if she wants to go back to dancing, she wants to shine again and dance?

Client: She'd have to learn how to walk properly again.

Therapist: So it will be a step-by-step process is what you're saying? You wouldn't start her dancing, but you would start her walking properly?

Client: Yes.

Therapist: That's exactly how cognitive behaviour therapy works. It doesn't start with the most difficult things to do, it starts with small things, small, do-able things to gradually kind of, what I would say, hack away at the problems and reduce them. In answer to your question, is it going to take a lot of time, well, it'll take some time. Your issues have been with you for a long time, so therapy will not be something that we will be able to fix in a couple of sessions, but the harder you work at it, the faster the therapy will go. The harder you work at it, the quicker you will have results.

Client: I'm just worried about the time because, while I'm here, I'm not doing things. It's not just an hour here, it's getting here and getting home and fitting it in and not doing the things I should be doing. It's like it just feels terribly self-indulgent.

Therapist: And doing something self-indulgent is good or bad?
[The therapist deviates here from the agenda as he picks up on a strong countertherapeutic belief of the client.]

Client: I don't know.

Therapist: You don't know?

Client: The whole world seems to be pursuing the 'me' agenda, you know, "If I concentrate on me, everything will be all right", but that's not true.

Therapist: So, doing a bit of self-indulgence, is that walking slumped over or is that walking tall?

Client: I don't know.

Therapist: We're not talking about self-indulgence 24 hours per day, 365 days per year. We are talking about therapy costing you at most four hours per week. Would dedicating four hours per week mean that you are excessively self-indulgent?

Client: I don't know, it feels just wrong to spend time on me, but four hours per week does not sound too much. My husband spends that amount of time on one of his hobbies and he has three hobbies: golf, model trains, and gym. So perhaps you are right and it is not self-indulgent . . .

Therapist: So is it OK if we move on to the next point on the agenda, which was looking at problems and perhaps whether we can identify some goals for therapy, things that you would like to achieve. Now, there are a couple of things that I wrote down, but I'm not quite sure if I wrote them down correctly.

Problems are things that are going on in your life at the moment where you're unhappy about the way that you deal with these issues, so that's what we could identify as problems.
[It seems the client and therapist are now again on the same wavelength and the therapist can structure the session back to the agenda.]

What you identified so far at the beginning of our discussion, if you remember, is that there is an enormous amount of tasks and, at times, you feel completely overwhelmed by the amount of tasks. Then, you think, "I'm not coping", you have that thought, and then you think, "I'm a failure", and being a failure is something that's terrible.

The other problem that you identified was that you're very much worried about what other people think of you and, if you have an idea that other people might have critical thoughts about you, then you do your utmost to avoid that and you get very worried and anxious about that.

The third problem that you identified was that you're very concerned about letting other people down and, if that happened, that would make you very, very anxious and upset.

If we look at the first one, the sense that there is an enormous amount of work that you have to do and you're feeling overwhelmed by that, is that a problem or did I misunderstand that?

Client: Yes, because I feel like I'm always snapping at people and am short-tempered because I can't get things done and, even if I do manage to get everything in order, then everybody comes home and the whole place is a mess again. That's what it's like.

Therapist: If your family comes home and creates a mess in the house, how do you react to that?
[This is *not* a clever move by the therapist. It would have been much better to focus on the problem (short tempered and snapping).]

Client: I get cross and I shout. I feel like I'm constantly nagging people to put things away and I feel like they don't understand, they don't appreciate just how long it takes to get the place looking good. Do you know, I used to be—

Therapist: You used to be?

Client: I was going to say "a fun person", but I don't suppose I've ever really been that, but I just feel, well, I look at myself now and I wonder why anybody would—it's like I'm giving 500 per cent the whole time and yet I still look at myself and wonder why anybody would want to spend their life with me.

Therapist: So you're saying you used to be more of a fun person than you are now and you are giving 500 per cent of yourself, but you're still wondering whether someone would want to be with you. The way that sounds is it sounds like you're working very hard to do a lot of household tasks to keep things in order and, at the same time, always this hard work does not result in your being pleased with yourself and being proud of yourself, so it seems that all the hard work goes into some kind of bottomless pit and it doesn't lead to you feeling OK and proud of yourself.

Client: It's like a black hole. It just all disappears as soon as everybody comes into the house. I have a friend, she's an elderly lady, and she always says that no matter how much she did during the day, and she always reminds me that they didn't have washing machines and things like that then, she always used to do her hair and put her lipstick on and take her pinny off before her husband came home. I mean, I don't wear a pinny, you know, but—

Therapist: I also sense from the way you talk that you don't have time to look after yourself, to do things that are good for you. How does that make you feel that you don't have time to look after yourself?
[The therapist takes a risk here and interprets what he thinks is behind client's spoken words, and it works out well.]

Client: I feel like part of the furniture. I feel like I'm just there when everybody gets home, just like the sofa and the curtains. Bizarrely, I was going to say I feel very grey and colourless.

Therapist: Is that a good feeling? Is that the way you want to feel?

Client: I feel like an overcast day. No, it's not the way I want to feel. I don't feel as if the sun's ever going to break through again.

Therapist: So, to try and make sense of the issues you brought forward, it sounds like a problem is the enormous amount of tasks that you feel you have to do and the self-criticism that you have when you do not complete these tasks. Would I be correct?

Client: Yes.

Therapist: The other problem we have is the enormous amount of tasks that you sense you have to do and the kind of criticism you expect other people might give you if you do not complete them, and you really worry a lot about that?

Client: Yes.

Therapist: The third problem you identify is that you don't take time to look after yourself and to do things that are good for Ann, which makes you feel like part of the furniture, which is not a very good feeling and which is not how you would like to feel. Another problem you mentioned is that all the good work you do in the house, you have a sense that that's not appreciated by your family.

Client: I just feel really disloyal in now saying that about them.

Therapist: Now, your words were: "Others do not appreciate how much energy it takes." How does that make you feel, that the family doesn't appreciate your effort and your 500 per cent energy that you invest in them? How does that make you feel?

Client: I shouldn't have said anything.

Therapist: Well, if we put that aside for a second, how does it make you feel that your family doesn't really appreciate how much energy you invest in the household?
[Selective ignoring here on the part of the therapist.]

Client: Like I'm nothing really.

Therapist: So that makes you think that you're nothing, and how does that make you feel when you think, "I'm nothing"?

Client: No, I don't think, "I'm nothing"; that's how I feel.

Therapist: Is that a good feeling, or is that a bad feeling?

Client: It's not a good feeling.

Therapist: OK, not a good feeling. Well, it seems as if there's a lot of things in your life that promote not a good feeling. One is not doing good things for yourself. The other things that I heard you say are: having to do household tasks to perfection; no recognition from family; harsh self-criticism; and five is worried about people's opinions. Now, if I get it right, these are things that are happening to you or that you do and they lead to this. Not doing positive things that are good for you, anyone who would do that would have these feelings, so it's not something especially for you, but anyone who would do so little positive for themselves would start to feel worried, sad, anxious and not worthwhile.

Client: Can I put something else?
[Therapist is on a winning streak now; the client is volunteering more information and suggesting problems.]

Therapist: You can.

Client: Boring. I feel really boring.

Therapist: That's so good that you added that, not that you feel really boring, but that you've come up with this. That's really very good because that's of a different quality from things that we've written down already because there's what you do, but this is about a belief you have about yourself, so that's number six, "I am boring". There's no recognition from your family for all the hard work you do and, if you do things that are not up to a certain standard, you criticise yourself very harshly and you expect other people to criticise you harshly as well, and then you have a belief that you're very boring.

Topographical analysis

If we want to know how problem behaviours, emotions, thoughts, problematic environmental reactions, and physiological responses interact together, then we need to construct several topographical analyses. A topographical analysis (TA) is a detailed description of what actually happens during a problem moment (Table 3.5). This is mapping out a specific problem occurrence. The most basic way of doing this is in the format of an A-B-C description: antecedents (A), behaviour (B), and consequences (C). A more detailed method (SORCC/BASIC-ID) will be discussed later on.

A topographical analysis is helpful in uncovering trends that warrant further investigations that result in a functional analysis.

Specific examples are shown in Table 3.6.

From the topographical analysis depicted in Table 3.6, the therapist can hypothesise that for the problem of depression and avoidance the client finds it impossible to resist the thought "I can't cope" and/or the sensation of tiredness. For the "shouting" problem, the therapist can hypothesise that the client can only reduce his frustration/irritation by raising his voice and acting aggressively. If these hypotheses are confirmed by further topographical analyses and self-observations, the therapy goals become obvious: cognitive restructuring of the "toxic" thoughts, learning to ignore "toxic" thoughts as guidance for behaviour, and learning stress/irritation reduction by non-aggressive means.

The second step is that the client keeps a diary regarding the problem behaviour and the triggers and consequences involved. In this diary, the client keeps track of his/her behaviour and in which situations it occurs. This will help in confirming or disconfirming

Table 3.5. An example of the format of topographical analysis.

Antecedents	Problem behaviour	Consequences
Internal: thoughts, feelings, sensations.	What the client did to go from antecedents to consequences.	Internal: thoughts, feelings, sensations.
Personal behaviour. External: situations, times, people		Personal behaviour. External: situations, times, people

Table 3.6. Specific examples of the A-B-C format in topographical analysis.

Antecedents	Problem behaviour	Consequences
Feelings: lethargic, tired; thinking: 'I can't cope' Personal behaviour: lying in bed at 8 a.m. External: in the morning, having to go to work.	Depressed and avoiding going to work	Internal: Thoughts: "At least nothing can go wrong here"; feelings: relief, lethargy, tiredness. Personal behaviour: lying in bed. External: still in bed.
Antecedents	**Problem behaviour**	**Consequences**
Internal: Thoughts: I can't stand it any longer; feelings: irritation; sensations: tense. Personal behaviour: watching TV on the couch External: situations: in the lounge at home, times: late afternoon, evenings; people: children asking me to play a game with them.	Shouting at the children.	Internal: Thoughts: they should not have done that; I am a bad person for shouting at them; feelings: briefly reduced frustration; sensations: bit energetic. Personal behaviour: walking away to my room with a drink. External: situations: alone, no one bothering me.

hypotheses about triggers and relevant consequences that the therapist has put forward.

The next step is putting everything together. What the therapist and the client need is a clear understanding of the client's problem behaviours and the process he uses to deal with the problems. Forming a conceptualisation of this person's problem behaviour is like mapping out a particular route to drive. If you do not do this before your journey starts, you might get hopelessly lost. The client needs to know how serious his/her problem behaviour problem is. How big is the change that is needed? In which life areas is it necessary to make changes? Which situations will elicit excessive problem behaviour? Which thoughts and emotions elicit excess? How does the problem behaviour help the person to cope with life?

When the therapist has a number of monitoring and diary sheets of the client, when the notes of the session with the client are organised, and when the answers are known to the questions of historical interest, then the therapist can start creating a functional analysis of the client's problem behaviour. Subsequently, these functional analyses can be put together in a comprehensive formulation.

Functional analysis

A functional analysis aims to uncover the *function* of the problem behaviour. Functions can be defined as enabling someone to achieve something or avoid something. In other words, a function of behaviour can be

- Avoiding negative feelings (when feeling depressed, staying in the warm and cosy bedroom); aversive thoughts and feelings (self-harming to avoid feeling very depressed and thoughts about being bad); situations, people, etc.
- Having access to positive feelings (drinking alcohol to relax); behaviours that are seen as positive (drinking alcohol to be able to socialise); access to situations, people, etc.

The function of problem behaviours can be understood by carefully examining what triggers the behaviour and what is the result of the behaviour.

A functional analysis will explain which antecedents are too difficult for the client to handle without the problem behaviour, and establish for which feelings or behaviours the client needs the problem behaviour.

The first quest is to find out what usually happens before the problem behaviour. By scanning carefully a number of occasions in which the client engaged in problem behaviour, the therapist might be able to locate "eliciting factors" of the problem behaviour. These factors are situations, places, people, emotions, thoughts, and so on which, through a learning process, have become powerful enough to elicit certain behaviours: in this case, the problem behaviour.

In which situations (places, people, or combinations) does the problem behaviour occur? In some situations the problem behaviour might be appropriate (drinking two glasses of wine during a meal), but in other situations the same behaviour might be inappropriate (drinking two glasses of wine in the morning before going to work). The therapist has to find out what in the situation makes the client decide to engage in the problem behaviour. By doing so, the therapist prepares for the next step. By "forcing" the client to explain why he/she did drink, smoke, or whatever, the client has to expand on the thoughts and feelings that were involved.

Traditionally, it was thought that people engaging in problem behaviours did so as a result of negative emotions: for example, the client experiences negative feelings and engages in the problem behaviour to reduce those feelings or to get rid of them completely. Clients use the problem behaviour to rid themselves of a negative emotion or to improve on a positive emotion in order to feel even better. By analysing the problem behaviour diaries, the therapist can compile a list of emotions that the client deals with by "indulging" in the problem behaviour. The implication for treatment is that the client needs to learn different strategies for dealing with these emotions than through the problem behaviour.

Emotions and thoughts are linked. We know that certain types of irrational thinking styles lead to certain negative emotions. Emotions such as anger, guilt, anxiety, shame, embarrassment, and depression are all the result of an irrational thinking style. The therapist needs to be able to understand how the client's thinking contributes to the emergence and maintenance of the problems.

Four examples of irrational thinking are listed below.

- Dogmatic demands: the person thinks in musts and shoulds. Our blushing client was often thinking: "I should not blush". Of course, repeating this demand in a very strong manner leads to focusing the mind on blushing. It also makes the client very sensitive to all signs related to blushing.
- Catastrophising: negative and unpleasant events are evaluated as terrible, awful, out of proportion.

"If I blush, that will be terrible." This thought really exacerbates things in all situations connected to blushing. It elevates blushing to a very high threat level.

- Low-frustration tolerance: the person is convinced that he/she cannot stand these feelings or this situation any longer.
  "If I blush in this meeting today, I won't be able to stand it" is what our client predicted. Frequently people will make this prediction of not being able to tolerate something.
- Self/other downing: the person puts him/herself and/or other people down; people are not evaluated as whole persons, but on the basis of one aspect of their personality.
  "I am *soooo* stupid for blushing all the time." The client gives himself an all-encompassing negative label as a consequence of something that is only a very small part of their life/personality.

We can also recognise thinking strategies that are "problem behaviour inhibitors" and thinking styles that are of the "permission-to-do-it" kind. The kind of thoughts that inhibit problem solving are: "This is going to be very difficult"; "I am not sure if it is even worth trying to solve the problem". Permission-giving thoughts are of the kind (for a problem drinker) "I'll just go to the pub to have a chat with my mates . . .".

In analysing the client's diaries, the therapist has to scrutinise the client's thinking and identify any signs of irrational and permission-to-do-it thinking styles.

The therapist has to make an analysis of the actual problem behaviour. If, for example, the problem behaviour is drinking too much, then the following questions are important. How does the client drink? Is he drinking alone, in his room, from the bottle, as quickly as he can gulp it down? The importance of doing this is that the therapist learns all there is to learn about the client's actual problem behaviour. This knowledge will certainly be helpful later on when the therapist and client are designing a change plan.

It is important to talk to the client about their problem behaviour, based on the diary form the client has filled out, and to check whether the behaviour itself makes it possible for the client to avoid negative things. For example: a man who works eighty hours a week avoids a very unpleasant home atmosphere in doing so. Important questions to ask are: what has to be done at the same time as the behaviour, what do other people do at this time, what would the person do when he/she was not indulging in the behaviour?

What does the person expect to achieve through the problem behaviour and what is actually achieved? People engage in certain behaviours because they make decisions that engaging in this behaviour will bring them something they want or believe they need. The expected result of certain behaviours is not always what does happen. For instance, problem drinkers might drink in the expectation of becoming less depressed. Drinking alcohol, however, increases feelings of depression. The drinker experiences this effect, but does not conclude that his/her expectancy is wrong, but concludes instead that more alcohol is needed to achieve the desired effect. The client concludes that he/she has not been drinking enough alcohol and that, given persistence, the depression will go. Expectancies of effects and actual effects of the problem behaviour are extremely important. Behaviour is controlled by its reinforcing consequences. In the case of problem behaviours, we see that behaviours are controlled by the expected positive consequences even when they they do not occur in reality.

In examining the problem behaviour diaries, the therapist has to differentiate between the expected consequences and the actual consequences. Expected consequences can be very powerful in controlling behaviour. This explains the fact that people continue with the problem behaviour despite the fact that, in reality, short-term and long-term consequences are negative, but the expectancy of short-term consequences is positive. Which behavioural, cognitive, and/or emotional goals can be achieved with the problem behaviour? The therapist has to analyse the diaries very carefully to check for this factor. The behaviour might have become a coping strategy for the client in dealing with certain difficult situations. Using the problem behaviour to achieve this (either in reality or as an expected achievement) is using a sort of short-cut. For example, if using cocaine provides the energy and courage to play the stock-market and be successful as an investment broker, then this is using a short-cut. Sufficient rest and thinking one's feelings of anxiety through would achieve the same result, but would take longer and require more effort.

Sometimes other people in the client's environment provide the client with a desirable or reinforcing consequence. The problem behaviour elicits responses from a spouse, a friend, or a parent which reinforces the addiction.

Problem behaviour: history

Part of the functional analysis is to put the problem behaviour in a historical context. The following questions might need answering.

- When did the client start engaging in the problem behaviour?
- Which rules and regulations were connected to the problem behaviour?
- Which models did the client have for the behaviour?
- When did the behaviour become problematic?
- Are there difficult circumstances connected with the period in which the behaviour became problematic?

It might be helpful also to make a chronological timeline of the behaviour and a retrospective overview of the past couple of years with regard to the problem behaviour.

Functional analysis form

A functional analysis will enable the therapist to complete the relevant form and compose an account to accompany it. This account would need to explain the connections between the six loosely coupled systems (Figure 3.1).

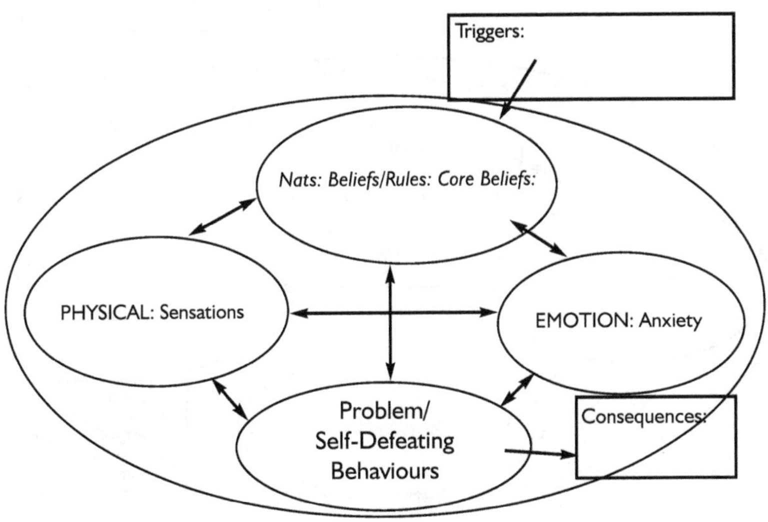

Figure 3.1. The connections between systems explored in functional analysis.

An example of a functional analysis could be that a client, Alex, presented with overwhelming feelings of tiredness and depression (Figure 3.2).

The narrative would be that Alex's beliefs prompt him to work very hard and to see time off for relaxing as a waste of time. This results in overworking and tiredness, which results in increasing uncertainty about whether he has done a good job ("I could have done it better"). The reinforcement for the hard work is the brief sense of having completed some work.

Formulation

A functional analysis focuses on one problem area, while a formulation is a holistic theory about the emergence of the problems and the interaction and maintenance of all of these. In the above example, we can imagine that Alex, in order to "escape" his depression and irritation, develops a gambling habit, which results in marital conflict. The marital conflict increases the depression and irritation and lead to Alex finding solace in alcohol and anxiety-reducing medication. It is important to make a functional analysis of each of the problems and

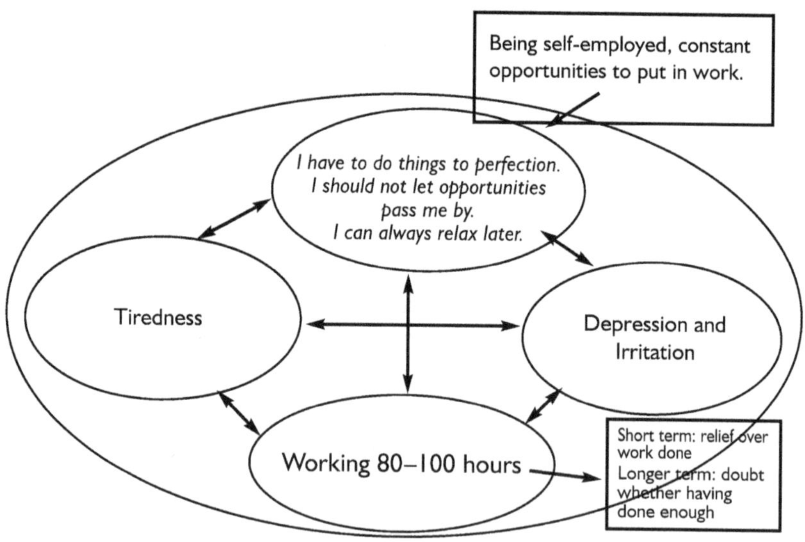

Figure 3.2. An example of a completed functional analysis.

ultimately find the connection points between the various functional analyses.

In a formulation, the therapist links the various problems and defines their relationships (Figure 3.3). At the same time, each problem needs to be understood within the context of a functional analysis.

A formulation comprises the main problems that make life difficult and explains how they are linked together. It helps to understand which problem issues are more or less central, that is, which problems are causing the others and which are more peripheral. As can be seen from Figure 3.3, there are four arrows emerging from "tension" and four from "irritation". A treatment would need to teach the client to reduce tension and irritation *and* learn to tolerate these feelings without engaging in the self-defeating behaviours.

The formulation will indicate what the client will need to learn in order to overcome the problems and, as a consequence, points in the direction of specific therapeutic interventions. I find it useful first of all to link the problems with skills deficits. Following this, a treatment plan logically consists of steps the client needs to take in order to learn the missing skills (Table 3.7).

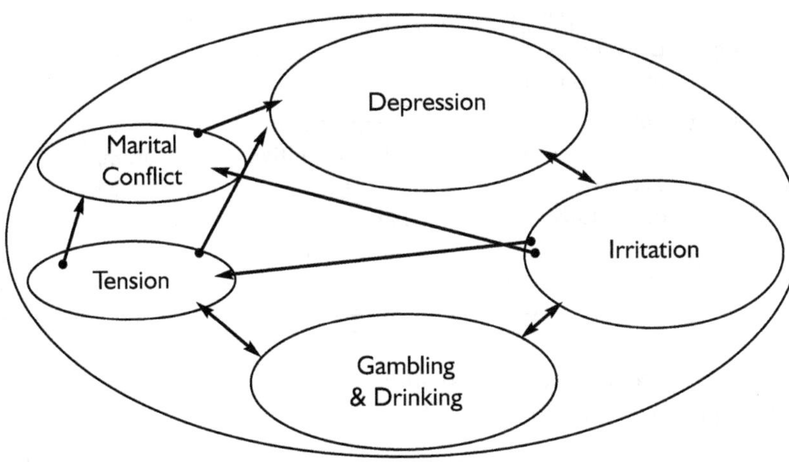

Figure 3.3. Diagrammatic example of a formulation.

Table 3.7. Problems, skills deficit, and what the client needs to learn.

Problem area	Type of skills deficit	Domains	Skills client needs to learn in order to alleviate the problem
Tension	Inability to engage in helpful tension reduction behaviours; inability to reduce intensity of negative feelings to a manageable level.	Changing antecedent cognitive appraisals, changing emotion-driven behaviours.	Cognitive restructuring, behavioural activation.
Irritation	Behavioural and emotional excesses.		Cognitive restructuring, behavioural activation.
Marital conflict	Lacking communication and problem-solving skills.	Modifying - emotion-driven behaviours, and preventing emotional avoidance.	Psycho-education and behavioural training, role-plays.
Gambling	Lacking self-regulation skills.		Self-control. training.
Drinking	Lacking self-regulation skills.		Self-control training.
Depression	Low level of satisfaction due to a restricted range of reinforcers. Behavioural and emotional excesses.	Changing antecedent cognitive appraisals, changing emotion-driven behaviours.	Behavioural activation, cognitive restructuring.

Assessment: feeding back information or introducing client to the formulation

When the therapist has completed the assessment, this needs to be shared with the client. An assessment takes as long as it needs to take.

However, in general, it needs to be remembered that the formulation is a *hypothesis*, which will be tested by the therapy. If the therapy is successful, then the formulation was correct. If, on the other hand, the therapy does not produce the required results, then the formulation needs to be revisited. In general, most therapists take between two and five sessions to complete an assessment. The exact number of sessions needed depends on the complexity of the pathology.

Sharing the results of the assessment and the formulation with the client is another strategy that helps clients to become their own best therapist. Sharing the formulation with the client is the first test of the formulation. If it cannot be explained to the client, if the formulation does not "stand up" to the client's feedback, then it perhaps needs some more work.

Fine-tuning problems and goals

Based on the shared formulation, client and therapist review the initial problems and goals and decide on fine-tuning and prioritising these. Now is the time to define the goals into specific and definable terms. Here is a list of questions that the therapist can ask that will assist the client to define the goals more specifically.

- What would you do more of/less of if your problem was no longer bothering you?
- What would have changed in your life if the problem was no longer a problem?
- What are you not doing now as a result of your problems?

It is important to define goals as specifically as possible in terms within the client's control. So, instead of defining a goal as "losing weight", it should be framed as "going to the gym three times a week"; not as "getting rid of my depression", but as "getting up each day and going for a brisk walk for thirty minutes".

In this stage of therapy, client and therapist are left with a list of problems (things that are currently happening which bother the client) and goals (things the client would like to happen, but cannot put into effect). The therapist has come up with a hypothesis (the formulation) as to how this discrepancy between the current situation and the client's ambition came to be. Based on the formulation and the redefined problems and goals, a detailed therapy plan is now discussed with the client.

Criteria for target selection

The client decides on which problems and goals therapy should focus, but the therapist can provide guidance. Although it is impossible to develop a list of criteria that would be appropriate for each case, some general rules can be stated that help clinicians to take into account technical and professional realities as well as basic theory in selecting possible therapy targets. The following list presents a few of the items to be considered in this regard (see also Gambrill, 1977).

- Does the behaviour threaten the life of the client or others? Does it seriously interfere with the client's minimal function? Does it have potentially dangerous economic, social, or physical consequences?
- Is the target behaviour most amenable to treatment by the clinician, some other mental health worker, or another professional?
- What is the likelihood that the target behaviour is amenable to change with the available methods and within the limits of the clinician's competence, the resources of the client, and the tolerance of the social environment?
- To what extent and in what way would the client's present life improve if the treatment goal were attained?
- Are there any negative side effects, for the client or others, of selecting this target?
- Is the proposed change in the target behaviour or situation consistent with the client's goals and values?
- To what extent is the client motivated toward attainment of this goal in relation to other goals?
- What is the cost–benefit ratio with regard to investment of energy, money, and other resources by client and therapist? What would happen if the client did not change?
- Does the selected target behaviour have any catalytic effects on the therapy process by preparing the ground for later interventions on other targets of higher priority?
- Will the goal be maintained by the client or the natural environment for long post-therapy effectiveness?
- Are the behaviour targets and means to achieve them ethically acceptable by the client's milieu and the therapist's professional standards?

- Is there a basis in clinical experience or research to support the effectiveness of the chosen technique in attaining the desired outcome?
- Is the desired end-state sufficiently clear to yield criteria for stopping the intervention process?

Prioritising interventions: moving from outside in

In prioritising what to start working on, there are two types of guidelines. The first guideline is set out in the thirteen points listed above. A problem that threatens the life of client or others obviously will need to be prioritised. A second guideline is the centrality of the problem. Intuitively, most clinicians would want to start the therapy process with problems that are central to the formulation, that is, problems that are considered to be the cause of other problems. I would counsel against that. It is much better to work from the "outside inwards". This, in a way, feels counter-intuitive: it is more likely that there will be a feeling that all will be well if we can get rid of the cause of the problem. The metaphor of a high-rise building might be helpful. Let's assume you have to demolish a twenty-storey building and you need to do it by hand, without making it crash on nearby buildings. Which floors would be easiest to demolish: the ground floor, floor twenty, or the foundations . . . yes, if one could destroy the foundations the whole thing would come crashing down, but that might result in some collateral damage. Clearly, it would be best to start at the top and carefully bring all the demolition rubbish down. The same goes for psychological problems. Peripheral problems are often easier dealt with than more central problems (and, consequently, this approach gives the client a greater sense of competence and success). It is also a way of gradually removing the problems that underpin the central problem.

Motivation for change

People with psychological problems are often not very motivated to change. This could be because their problem behaviours result in too many rewards, or because of the familiarity of the current situation, or it might be connected with being afraid of the unknown that change will bring. These clients are a challenge for psychological therapists.

In this section, I describe a strategy that will enable psychological therapists to understand the mechanisms underpinning the lack of motivation (the stages of change model). The building blocks of motivation for change are discussed, together with methods describing how to engage with clients in ways that allow these building blocks to be strengthened rather than dismantled.

Stages of change

Prochaska, DiClemente, and Norcross (1992) describe a stages of change model. The model describes the journey of a person from being unmotivated to a stage where changes have been made and are now maintained. They postulate that different stages of change demand different engagement strategies (Figure 3.4).

Pre-contemplation

During this stage, people are not aware that they have problems and, therefore, do not think of change; there is a lack of integrated and

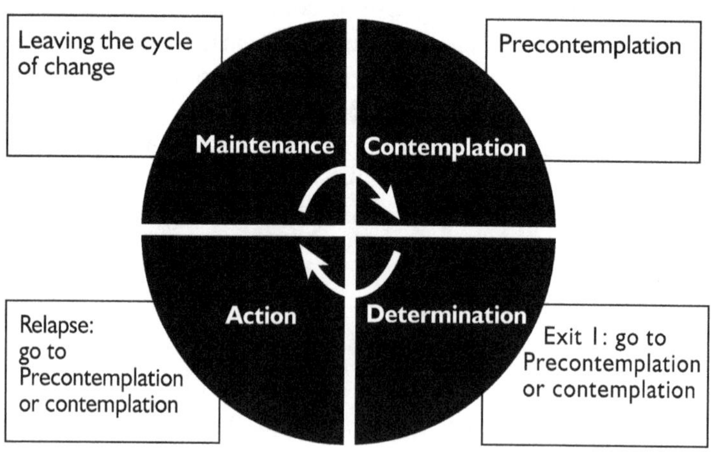

Figure 3.4. Stages of change (Prochaska, DiClemente, & Norcross, 1992).

accepted personal knowledge of the problems. They might have some form of abstract knowledge that the behaviours they engage in are not all right for people generally, but for some reason this does not apply to them. Realising that one engages in problematic behaviour does not feel good. It often is accompanied by a temporary loss of self-esteem and self-efficacy. This implies that people are likely to defend themselves against the idea of having problems. People tend to have a certain built-in defence mechanism against a decrease in self-esteem and self-efficacy. This defence is stating that nothing is wrong, or, if there is something that is wrong, it does not matter.

If a person in pre-contemplation wanted to change anything, this would not be their own behaviour, but the behaviour of others.

Obstacles in progressing from pre-contemplation to contemplation are as listed below.

- No integrated and personally accepted *knowledge* about the problems: there is knowledge and then there is KNOWLEDGE. For knowledge to become relevant in influencing attitudes and behaviour, it has to be personalised. There is a difference between academic knowledge (drinking too much is bad for people) and the personal knowledge that the way I drink is bad for *me*.
  This knowledge goes beyond abstract knowledge ("People who are angry all the time will have no friends") and needs to be personalised ("I don't have any friends because I am angry and critical with everyone around me").
- Too low a level of self-efficacy and *self-esteem* (accepting the knowledge that something is wrong brings the sense of self-esteem and self-efficacy to a critical low threshold). If you are in a problematic situation (e.g., feeling lonely and having no friends), that might be a problem to you if you see yourself as deserving better (e.g., being worthwhile enough to have friends). If, on the other hand, you see yourself as undeserving and worthless (in other words, you do not appreciate the value of your good self), then having no friends is just what you deserve. Knowledge about the problems is only effective in stimulating motivation for change if it is combined with a sense that one is worthwhile enough to not have these problems.

Meet a pre-contemplator: Ann

Ann is a typical example of a pre-contemplator. She experiences problems, but does not link them with how she lives life. She sees her unhappiness as "just the way life is" and she fully believes that this is as good as it gets! Here are some quotes from Ann that are indicative of being a pre-contemplator:

- it is going to take a lot of time;
- it is strange to come and talk to someone about problems;
- my problem is that there is simply too much housework;
- I am not sure about this, I feel worse now than when I came in.

Contemplation

In this stage, the client realises there are personal problems. He/she starts thinking about possible ways to get rid of the problems, but has not yet made the decision to change.

The main worry in this stage is the fear of losing something pleasant and the fear of not being able to solve the problems adequately. The person's mind works like an old-fashioned weighing scale. On the one side, there are arguments for change, and on the other, there are arguments favouring no change.

Obstacles that impede progress from contemplation to determination are:

- a lack of concern about the problems (knowing that something is not all right does not automatically lead to concern over these facts); a fear that the pleasurable aspects of the present status quo will diminish and that no other positives will be returned;
- fear of not being able to change (lack of competence).

So, in order to be able to make a decision whether personal change is needed, we need to know that we are involved in the problem, we need to be concerned about that, we need to see ourselves as worthwhile, and as competent enough to resolve the problems.

Meet some contemplators

John states, after a few sessions of motivation-focused CBT, "This drinking gets me into trouble; I will lose my licence this time for certain. But giving up hanging out with my mates and getting completely plastered, not so sure about that."

Belinda can see a (slightly) different perspective after a few sessions: "Vandalizing someone's car after they have hurt your feelings—perhaps I am a bit too self-centred and sensitive, but you can't let people get away with treating you like a doormat!"

Determination/decision

This is the transition from contemplation to active change. It is also possible to decide not to change, dropping out of the circle of change by way of Exit 1. The main obstacle that could prevent clients from reaching a decision is a lack of knowledge regarding change methods, and, therefore, not being aware of a change method that would fit clients' preferences.

This is the crux of motivational interviewing: getting the client involved in wise decision making. Too often, we make decisions based on our beliefs and not on the available facts.

Knowing the facts is not enough; we have to apply the facts to ourselves as well.

Facts are known ("I don't take any leisure/relaxation time"), but the person cannot see how this behaviour links with problem issues (being very tired all the time).

Developing motivation for change is a decision-making process in which the person needs to learn to be objective about all the issues and accept the facts as they are presented. On a personal level, one can see how challenging this is. Accepting that one has been engaging in self (or other)-damaging behaviours for years is not an easy task and it might be easier just to distort the information ("it is not that bad"). It also involves being able to objectively assess one's personal strengths. Sometimes people have "forgotten" or distorted previous experiences of competence and endurance ("That was just luck").

Active change

In this stage, people alter their overt behaviour and this is where traditional change-directed psychological therapy comes in with all its strategies.

Maintenance

The client tries to stabilise the changes he has made. He tries to prevent a relapse into the old unwanted behaviour (for instance, drinking too much alcohol). Clients might seek professional help in this stage, too, because they are afraid of a relapse. Clients might remain in this stage for up to six months. However, if preoccupation with a possible relapse vanishes and the client does not identify himself any longer with his former problems, he "steps out" of the circle of change by way of the permanent exit.

Relapse

Relapsing means returning to the old problematic ways of living life. A relapse mostly results in going back to the stage of contemplation.

Clients will become increasingly sceptical about the possibilities of change after experiencing relapses.

In summary, motivation for change consists of five elements, listed below.

- The client needs to be aware of the fact that his behaviour has an impact on the problematic situation he finds himself in (knowledge).
- The client needs to have sufficient self-appreciation (or self-esteem) to see hinself as worthwhile enough to be without the problems (self-worth);
- The client needs to be concerned about the problems he experiences (concern);
- The client needs to have some confidence in his own ability to bring about change (felt competence);
- The client needs to know about change methods that he believes can work for him (trust in the change process).

A bit more about the last point, trust in the change process: in order to make the necessary steps towards change, the client needs to believe in the change methods that are offered. The felt competence is about the client's self-perception, while this element is about the change methods that are on offer. Clients might believe that they will be able to change, but they lose faith when informed about the change methods available. (For example: the message "The only way to overcome your psychological problem is by going into a therapeutic community for three years" might have a discouraging effect on some clients.)

Decision making

Becoming motivated for change is a decision-making process in which all five elements mentioned above are processed. In many of life's decisions, we process these in an implicit manner, often without really being aware of the process. As a result of this, we often make decisions that are based only on part of the complete picture.

- Dedicated smokers seldom think of all the consequences of their habit before lighting up.
- When buying that dream house and signing the mortgage paperwork, we might "forget" certain financial facts that would have put our loan application in jeopardy.
- When declining to board a plane because we are terrified of flying, we forget the statistics (flying is safer than driving) and our own competence (in the past, we have flown successfully).

In a therapeutic context, we have to make this process explicit (and bring elements to the foreground that the client finds difficult to acknowledge).

Cognitive dissonance

The end result of a successful motivation enhancement process is "cognitive dissonance" (Festinger, 1956, 1957). A state of cognitive dissonance is experienced by clients as unpleasant, and, therefore, most people try to avoid it or, once in it, try to escape from it. *Cognitive dissonance* is an uncomfortable feeling caused by holding two contradictory ideas simultaneously. The theory of cognitive dissonance proposes that people have a motivational drive to reduce dissonance (because it feels unpleasant) by changing one or more of the following: attitudes, beliefs, and behaviours. Dissonance occurs when people perceive a logical inconsistency in their beliefs, when one idea implies the opposite of another. The emotional consequence of the dissonance might be guilt, anger, frustration, or embarrassment. Examples of opposing ideas in practice are:

- I am a healthy person/My drinking has cause irreparable damage;
- I am a very important person/People treat me as just anyone;
- I am an honest person/I have told lies and stolen to cover up personal mistakes.

Ways to resolve cognitive dissonance are:

- behaviour change: stop drinking; stop being dishonest;
- attitudinal change: being healthy is widely overrated, let's have fun; what other people think is unimportant; I am not an honest person.

A very elegant example of changing preferences as a result of challenging circumstances is told in the fable *The Fox and the Grapes*, by Aesop (ca. 620–564 BCE), where the fox decides that the grapes he is unable to reach are probably not ripe enough to eat anyway: desiring something, then criticising it because it proves unattainable. We see this phenomenon in clinical practice often, when a client embarks on a change process that proves more difficult then envisaged: "This therapy is not for me, all the problems were exaggerated anyway, no real need to change".

It is clear that, in practice, the aim would be to promote behaviour change in a healthy direction: stop drinking, behave more honestly, and/or develop more realistic attitudes: "I am just as important as everyone else and don't deserve special treatment".

Engagement strategies

Let's go back for a moment to the characteristics that are typical of people with psychological difficulties. Rigid and inflexible patterns of behaviour and thinking; negative consequences of behaviour are often ignored and the "instinctive" reaction is that improvement can come through the change of others. This means that the therapist who works with clients with psychological difficulties has to be prepared to apply specific strategies to get these clients ready for therapy, ready for change, and motivated to work towards change. It sometimes feels a bit like trying to sell something to people who do not want to buy anything.

I suggest that there is a distinct set of techniques that can be used to this effect: motivational interviewing (Denisen & van Bilsen, 1987; van Bilsen, 1985, 1986a,b, 1991, 1995, van Bilsen & van Emst, 1989; van Bilsen & Wilke, 1998).

Motivational interviewing (MI)

MI is a set of techniques of talking to people about difficult topics without alienating them. Therapists working with psychological disorders are, after all, often talking to people who do not want to change and who might feel quite antagonistic towards the therapist and everything he/she represents. So, the first port of call is to talk to clients without increasing their antagonism. I like to think that motivational interviewing is Socratic dialogue with a twist, the twist being that it is based on the stages of change model and that it incorporates a few new techniques (for example. overshooting and undershooting).

Motivation for change is based on knowledge, concern, self-appreciation, felt competence, and trust in the change process. MI makes these elements of motivation a target and is exclusively focused on enhancing these within the client. In other words, MI is specifically focused on creating cognitive dissonance:

- I am a worthwhile person and I am destroying this person;
- I am concerned about my situation and could change it for the better if I wanted to.

Traditionally (Hettema, Steele, & Miller, 2005; Miller & Rollnick, 2002), the perspective was that in order to motivate people, the best strategies were to tell people what to think and do and to threaten them with negative consequences if they did not comply.

Unfortunately, these traditional motivational strategies seem to work only in a very limited way and then only with people who are ready to change (e.g., are in the stage of Action). These strategies trigger resistance and opposition in clients in other stages. Imposing insight on people will result in them starting a debate, giving people knowledge will result in that knowledge being disputed; try to teach skills to people in the stage of contemplation and you will have very reluctant participants.

Key assumptions of MI

The first assumption is that motivation is the end product of a complex interaction between person/client elements and environmental influences. This means that motivation is not something that grows within clients without any connection to what happens around them. Motivation to change fluctuates as a result of a person's experiences with life, with other people, and how things go for them in general. Let's be honest: would you, the reader, be motivated to change if you were in a very problematic situation but were convinced that you could only make things worse? If you know that your experience is that whatever you try to improve things, it will fail, then you are bound to be very sceptical about new attempts at improvement.

The second assumption is that motivation is interpersonal: motivation for change is influenced by interpersonal relationships and interactions. Specific interactions in specific situations can make us deny and lie. Take, for example, a situation in which you are discussing your tax return with the tax office and you notice that you claimed as an expense a workshop on MI for which you had been compensated by your employer. The taxman asks whether you were indeed compensated for this by your employer. You know that if you say yes, in all likelihood he will scrutinise your whole tax file with a lot more care and might find other inconsistencies. If you say that you did not receive any compensation, it will be highly unlikely that he will find out you lied and the whole inspection will be over in five minutes. It would take an extremely moral person to admit the mistake and suffer the consequences in a situation like this. Most people try to avoid "punishment" in interpersonal situations. As a consequence of this, we also have to admit that resistance to change is interpersonal. The lie told to the taxman is a form of resistance, triggered by the specific circumstances. With clients, the specific circumstances are that they can discover that there is a serious problem and that they might have to bring about some change. People are inclined to protect themselves from potential bad news: if it seems as if the therapist could bring bad news, the client will go into defensive/denial mode.

The third assumption is that our behaviours as therapists matter: what we do is important. This follows logically from the first two assumptions, but is important to iterate, as many clinicians seem to forget this. Too often, we hear clinicians state that they just want the best for their clients when they have been trying to convince clients of their problems, and are stunned by the clients' denial of problems that are very obvious to everyone else. Good intentions are the basic standard, but they need to be translated into clinician behaviours that promote motivation for change. Lecturing, explaining, and arguing do not produce motivated clients; they will produce clients who are very well versed in debating with therapists why they should not change. This is especially so for clients with psychological problems. These clients have often been engaging in extreme self-defeating behaviour that has resulted in many hospital admissions, serious medical problems, and, sometimes, incarceration in prisons or forensic institutions. Many clinicians tell us, "I just wanted them to know how self-defeating their behaviours are". Persuasion is usually not an effective method to increase motivation and change; it leads to counterarguments, especially if agreeing with the other person would mean accepting something that is perceived to be unpleasant.

MI: how it all works

I shall address this in three steps. First, I will review the spirit of MI, followed by the basic principles of MI (Miller & Rollnick, 2002), and, finally, we will review what we see as the main MI techniques (Miller & Rollnick, 2002; van Bilsen, 1986a,b). I want to stress here that MI is not merely a set of techniques. Just applying it in that way is like playing a beautiful piece of music by playing each note to perfection but forgetting the whole. It will sound like music, but its beauty will be vastly reduced. Applying MI works similarly: applying the techniques described needs to be based on understanding the spirit and principles of MI.

The spirit of MI

MI is based on *acceptance* instead of demands. In working with complex clients with long-standing problems, psychological therapy services often impose demands upon the clients that counteract the development of motivation for change (remember, demands create resistance). Examples of these demands are: stop drinking alcohol, stop self-harming, stop stealing, and stop lying. The most creative demand I have ever seen being imposed on clients was in a family therapy service in the Netherlands. Here, families were taken into therapy only when they had stopped having arguments for two weeks. I am sure you all know of similar demands in the addiction services or in working with clients with psychological difficulties. MI is accepting what is, instead of demanding what should be.

In line with one of the cornerstones of CBT, motivational interviewing focuses on *collaboration* instead of confrontation. This makes MI a *de facto* Socratic process *à l'extrème*. The building blocks of motivation are not imposed upon the client, but are jointly discovered by client and therapist in what, on the surface, looks like a casual chat, but is, in fact, a detailed and specific way of talking to clients.

Education is one of the core strategies in CBT. When doing motivational work, it is important to restrain this. MI focuses much more on *evocation*. In evocation, the clinician focuses on eliciting issues from the client that are going to be the focus of the discussions. This is opposed to education, whereby the clinician imparts his/her wisdom to the client. There is, of course, a need for educational activities in CBT, but to apply education within a motivation enhancement strategy is often self-defeating. Giving the client space to talk and focusing on specific MI techniques, that conversation will be much more helpful.

Basic MI principles

Develop discrepancy

MI is focused on developing a discrepancy between where clients are now and where they would like to be. For this, two things are needed. First of all, clients need to develop a clear and objective perspective of where they are now. In working with clients with psychological difficulties, many clinicians are so impressed by the problems and suffering of their clients that they move immediately to goal setting, without having investigated the current circumstances of the client in clear and objective detail. In these situations, we often see clients making some haphazard attempts at changing, but, upon encountering the first challenge, go back to the status quo. This is possibly because the therapist has not allowed the negative aspects of the status quo to come to the fore. Hence, the client can easily believe that avoiding the difficulty of the change process will result in going back to a less problematic status quo. The second element of this is, of course, "hope and vision". The therapist has to assist the client to develop a vision of a less problematic future and instil hope in the client that this future is attainable.

Here is an example of "developing discrepancy" in a first session with Ann. As before, the therapist's comments are given in square brackets.

Therapist: The way you describe your situation, it sounds like you feel very tired, run down. Can you tell me a bit more about that?
[Open question, inviting the client to explain her perspective.]

Ann: Yes, there is a lot to do during the day, go to work, be nice to everybody, even difficult customers, spending more on three shirts then I spend on my mortgage, looking after the children . . .

Therapist: It sounds like there is a heavy burden on your shoulders and this heavy burden makes you tired. Your husband and GP have called this tiredness depression, but you see this differently.
[Empathising with the client *and* bringing in a reality check from the GP and husband about client's situation.]

Ann: There is nothing wrong with me, I am not crazy you know!

Therapist: So, on the one hand you say there is nothing wrong with you, on the other hand, the way you describe the tiredness, it does not sound like a nice restful . . .
[Empathising *and* bringing in facts the client has disclosed.]

Ann: No, it is dreadful, I feel completely exhausted, worn out, but still can't relax because I can't stop worrying about stuff.
[This results in more self-motivational statements.]

Therapist: The way you say this, it sounds like the worrying is in the same corner as the tiredness: you don't like it and would be a happier person if you could get rid of it?
[Empathising and structuring.]

Ann: Oh yes, but how can I there is so much to do . . .

Therapist: Tiredness, can't stop worrying about stuff . . . do I understand it correctly that your husband and GP recommended you come and see me because they think that you could do something about this tiredness and these worries?

Ann: Yes, but like I said, there is so much to do, I have no control over what I have to do during a day, have I?

Therapist: So, on the one hand, you have a sense that you have no control over the amount of tasks to do, and, on the other hand, this seems to have a negative impact on your life to such an extent that your husband and GP think it is not good for you. How would you like things to be, as they are now or would you like a change?
[Empathising and asking client how she would like things to be.]

Ann: Well, it would be nice if I was not so dog tired all the time and was less snappy with the children and my husband. It would be nice if we could go out for a meal once in a while . . .
[Resulting in the client stating a discrepancy between how things are now and how she would like things to be.]

Roll with resistance

Resistance can be defined as disagreeing with the therapist ("I don't need any time for myself, hard work is the best way to overcome problems") or denying obvious facts ("Hard work always improves my mood" when from the data collection by the client it is clear that she feels more and more depressed after hard work). In a traditional approach, the therapist might try to convince clients of the therapist's perspective. Within an MI approach, the strategy is to "roll with the resistance" by asking clients to explain their perspective a bit more. This is based on martial arts' principles. If you want to create movement, it is pointless if you do the same thing as your opponent. When both push or pull at the same time, there will be a standstill and a battle of strength. However, when one pulls and the other reacts by pushing, there is movement and movement opens up the potential for change.

Express empathy

Developing motivation for change can be a painful process for the client. It is a journey of discovery in which what is unearthed might be negative and unpleasant. In order for the client to be able to tolerate this, the therapist needs to be very empathic and respectful of the client's emotional responses to the process. Expressing empathy is making it clear to the client that we understand their perspective; we understand their pain and discomfort. Please note, just saying to the client, "I know how you feel", is bound to backfire, as, in all honesty, we do not *know* how the client feels; we can only attempt to reflect back to the client how we understand they are feeling and how we understand their thinking.

Support self-efficacy

MI is focused on client's self-efficacy and self-determination. Often, clients with longstanding and enduring problems with psychological difficulties will enter a therapy situation with statements such as, "I have to be here"; "They make me come and talk to you"; "I have no choice". It is important for the clinician to create an atmosphere of choice and self-determination by focusing on choices the client has. The following reactions by a therapist when faced with statements such as those given above demonstrates this.

> *Client*: I have to be here.
>
> *Self-efficacy reaction by therapist*: So you have to be here. How did you make the decision to go along with that demand?

Or

> So you have to be here. How would you like to make use of the time we have?
>
> *Client*: They make me come and talk to you.
>
> *Self-efficacy reaction by therapist*: They make you come and talk to me. Have you decided what you want to talk about?
>
> *Client*: I have no choice.
>
> *Self-efficacy reaction by therapist*: You feel you don't have a choice . . . how did you come to that conclusion?

Techniques of MI

We differentiate between basic MI techniques (selective active listening and fine-tuned reflections) and advanced MI techniques (positive restructuring and provocative techniques).

Selective active listening

Selective active listening consists of three components: active listening, selection of motivational elements, and asking motivational questions.

Active listening

Active listening means that we are tuned in to what clients are telling us. We are focused on "getting" what they are trying to convey. We use non-verbal signals of eye-contact, nodding, and hmm-hmm-ing to show that we are interested. We use repetitions, reflections, and summaries to feed back to clients how we have understood their stories. In MI, the clinician tries to do this in a way that invites the client to expand on what they have said. Often, a reflection or summary is ended with a question such as, "Could you tell me a bit more about that?"

Here, we revisit a conversation from the second session with Ann, this time using it as an example of active listening. Comments are given in square brackets.

> *Therapist*: So you're feeling really worried and feeling anxious?
> [Empathic response, but would have been better if followed by "Could you tell me a bit more about that?"]
>
> *Client*: Yes.
>
> *Therapist*: That's a very good example because anxiety is a real signal that something's not right. Anxiety is a good feeling to have when we're in a really dangerous situation. When an unpleasant person with a big gun stands in front of you and threatens to shoot you, then it's very appropriate to feel anxious, isn't it?
> [Working with the client's short answer and going into some brief psychoeducation about anxiety.]
>
> *Client*: Yes.
>
> *Therapist*: But, in your situation, when certain tasks in the house aren't done, when certain things aren't as clean as other people might want them to be, to feel anxious about that is perhaps—
> [Attempt at summary.]
>
> *Client*: You see, I know you're going to say it's silly and it's about what people think about you, isn't it? It's about how people see you and you

just think it's silly because it's not a gun. Well, it's like a gun to me. [Client brings across what the real issue is: how people see you!]

Therapist: So that's very good, your saying that, excellent. So what you're saying is that an unclean house feels like someone is holding a gun to your head?
[Therapist gets only 50% of client's message, but . . .]

Client: No, not an unclean house, what people think about you.
[. . . the therapeutic relationship is strong enough for the client to have the courage to correct the therapist.]

Therapist: What people think about you, it feels like there's a gun held against your head. That's a very good example of how anxiety can really be a very unpleasant problem.

Selection of motivational elements

Active listening is not a "blind" activity. Not everything the client says is treated equally. Signs of the building blocks of motivation (knowledge, concern, self-appreciation, felt competence, and trust in the change process) are given more attention in the repetitions, reflections, and summaries of the therapist. This works as reinforcement of desirable behaviour (for most people, a therapist focusing on issues that they just talked about themselves is perceived as something positive) and what is reinforced is likely to occur more frequently. If this reinforcement is combined with an invitation to talk more about these issues, we have a very strong combination: motivational talk by the client is reinforced. This is followed by an invitation to expand on the topic. The result is *more* motivational talk. The consequence of this should not be underestimated. We know that the best way to convince ourselves is to hear ourselves talk. So, the more we get the client to talk motivational talk, the more we increase the client's belief in what he/she is saying.

Asking motivational questions

Motivational questions are questions focused on getting the client to talk about any of the five motivational building blocks. For example: "You mentioned your tiredness. Could you tell me a bit more about the problems this tiredness causes for you" (eliciting factual problem information), or "You mentioned your tiredness, how do you feel about being tired all the time?" (Eliciting concern.)

Padesky (1993) describes Socratic dialogue as following these steps:

1. Informational questions: getting the facts.
2. Empathic listening: bringing across to the client that the therapist is interested and can see the client's perspective.
3. Summaries: summarising the facts, including the client's emotional and cognitive reaction to the facts.
4. Analytic/synthesising questions.

The active listening component of motivational interviewing would follow similar lines, but the therapist would be very careful not to overwhelm the client with informational questions, since this can quickly become a very one-sided affair.

Fine-tuned reflections

Selective active listening is the foundation technique of motivational interviewing; without this base, all other interventions will fall flat. Fine-tuned reflections are a set of techniques that look and sound like reflections and, to all ends and purposes, they are presented to the client as reflections, but their intent and effect is often not the same as with a standard reflection.

Feeling reflection

A feeling reflection can be used when the therapist senses a strong feeling behind the spoken words of clients. The therapist can then reflect the feeling in a low-key manner, leaving it to clients to "accept" or "reject" the educated guess of the therapist. If the therapist gets it wrong, and the client rejects the feeling interpretation of the therapist, then it is vital to accept this rejection and not push the client into accepting that they were feeling angry or anxious. The impact of carefully presented feeling reflections is a deepening of the therapeutic rapport between therapist and client.

Conflict reflection

Conflict reflections are used when the therapist notices ambiguity in the client. Sceptical clients might be in two minds about certain issues:

"On the one hand, I really would like to get rid of this tiredness, but I certainly don't have a mental illness"; or "I don't want to end up like my friend Bob, he was killed in a car crash, but I really like getting completely wasted with my mates". It is a bit like an approach–approach or an avoidance–avoidance conflict. In MI, it is important to feed these internal conflicts back to the client but *finish with the side promoting change*, followed by an invitation to expand. What happens is that clients will expand on the element that promotes change, as this was the last element before the invitation to expand.

Overshooting and undershooting reflections

Overshooting and undershooting are used when clients seems to have rigid beliefs that go against motivation for change. The aim of these reflections is for the client to *disagree* with the therapist. What the therapist does is to feed back to the client in the style of a reflection, but many times exaggerating or minimising what the client has just told the therapist. The presentation style of the therapist needs to be very empathic, hesitant, trying to really understand the client. Some examples follow.

Example 1

> *Client* I am *sooo* depressed, it is all awful.
>
> *Therapist* If I understand you correctly, you are in the deepest pit of depression twenty-four hours per day; there is not one second when things are less black.
>
> *Client's response*: Well, it is not as bad as that, when I walk the dog . . .

Example 2

> *Client*: I can't help that I am in prison. I didn't make myself kill my parents. If they had just given me the money there would have been no problems.
>
> *Therapist*: If I understand you correctly, you are saying that you are completely powerless; you are a pawn in the game of life with no influence over your fate whatsoever.
>
> *Client's response*: I wouldn't say I was completely powerless . . .

These "shooting" reflections are followed up by "normal" reflective listening. The response of the client to the "shooting" is often in the direction of motivation. In the first example, the client adds that there are moments that are better than others, and in the second example, the client takes back some self-efficacy.

Overshooting and undershooting need to be presented with empathy, otherwise they soon sound sarcastic and critical.

Positive restructuring

This is the first of the advanced strategies. Positive restructuring is based on the premise that, apart from people with a psychopathic psychological disorder, humans are well meaning and have good intentions. People's behaviour might have a negative impact, but the intent is, in general, positive. Therapists enhance clients' self-esteem by focusing attention on their positive intentions. This is *not* praise; it goes beyond the words and deeds: it focuses on the intention.

For example:

- A client who has been attempting to change for many years has tried many therapists and now wants to give it another shot with this therapist: focusing on the intention, "You are a very persistent person."
- A client who arrives at the office in a desperate state has been told that her three children will be taken into care unless she demonstrates some radical change: focusing on the intention, "You want the best for your children."

It is often much easier to focus on negative intentions. In the first example, we could easily say that the client lacks will-power and is not able to tolerate discomfort. In the second example, we could have said that the mother has been neglecting her maternal duties because of her gambling addiction. However, would that have influenced motivation for change?

Provocative techniques

Provocative techniques should only be used when nothing else works. There are different kinds of provocations. There is the "Columbo technique", whereby the therapist displays clumsiness and relative incompetence. This can be used in situations where the therapist has a captive audience (the client *has* to meet with the therapist), and where the client feels very threatened by the supposed competence and superiority of the therapist. By becoming clumsy and slightly incompetent, therapists reduce their standing and, as a result, make clients more comfortable. Another provocative technique is the "devil's advocate" technique. This can be particularly well used in situations in which clients find it difficult to reach a decision: for instance, to begin therapy or not. The therapist then starts subtly to advocate for the side of lacking motivation/not wanting to change *but presents that in a slightly negative light*. For instance, a client who finds it very difficult to decide whether to embark on an anger management programme to curb his aggressive and self-destructive outbursts could be told: "Well, entering a therapy programme like this is not easy; many people don't have the will-power and strength of character to bring it to a successful conclusion, and it would be such a shame if you were disappointed in yourself. Why would you want to risk that?"

Reflections on engagement strategies

MI is not a panacea for all sceptical and unmotivated clients. It is a tool to assist clinicians to talk to sceptical clients without getting into unproductive arguments and, furthermore, it is a set of techniques aimed at gradually building motivation for change.

MI is proposed as an engagement strategy for sceptical clients. Many clients could fall into the sceptical category. The model we can use to assess the level of their scepticism is the stages of change model. This will provide a roadmap for the motivation enhancement work that needs to be done. Specific and detailed motivational interventions are described; however, it is important to emphasise that they are not a panacea for all challenging clients.

CHAPTER FOUR

Cognitive behaviour therapy from a new perspective: different strokes for different folks

Introduction

Classification or formulation

The psychological suffering of humans has been described in many formats. For the past fifty years, a very popular way of thinking about psychological problems has been the classification system published by the American Psychiatric Association (2000) in the *Diagnostic and Statistical Manual of Mental Disorders* (*DSM*). It provides a common language and standard criteria for the classification of psychological problems. It is used in the USA and, to varying degrees, around the world by clinicians, researchers, psychiatric drug regulation agencies, health insurance companies, pharmaceutical companies, and policy makers. There have been five revisions since it was first published in 1952, gradually including more mental disorders, although some have been removed and are no longer considered to be mental disorders—most notably, homosexuality. The manual evolved from a system for collecting census and statistics. It was significantly revised in 1980. The last major revision was the fourth edition (*DSM-IV*), published in 1994. The fifth edition (*DSM-V*) is currently in consultation, planning, and preparation, and is due for publication in May 2013.

The *DSM* system has attracted controversy and criticism as well as praise. Some critics argue that the *DSM* represents an unscientific system that enshrines the opinions of a few powerful psychiatrists. Glasser (2003) refers to the *DSM* as "phony diagnostic categories", arguing "it was developed to help psychiatrists—to help them make money".

The party

You are invited to a party and by chance you arrive early and have a good opportunity to observe all the guests as they arrive. You soon realise that this is a very interesting party with a bunch of rather special people. Could you decide which personality disorder would apply?

First you meet *Beatrice*. You notice that she has had a few drinks before the party. At first, she seems very shy and withdrawn. She does not talk to anybody, but, after you have seen her consuming a few more glasses of wine, she becomes more and more talkative. After a while, she is unsteady on her feet and needs the support of a wall or door. She tells everyone with enthusiasm that she is a much better driver with a few drinks inside. When someone comments that this sounds dangerous, she drifts to a different group of people at the party. Later in the evening, you notice Beatrice being the centre of attention of a small group, and she describes that she is always on top of the world, nothing can bring her down. The evening ends with Beatrice having fallen asleep on the floor just outside the toilets.

At exactly 8.30 p.m. the doorbell rings and there is *Keith*, dressed immaculately and pleasant and polite to everyone. You notice how Keith holds his drink in a very special way and that he seems to take sips at regular intervals. Keith also mingles well with the other guests. You notice, however, that he rarely has a real conversation; he talks at people for exactly six minutes and then moves to the next person. He frequently checks his watch and leaves at 10.15 p.m. exactly.

Lisa makes a very quiet entrance and remains quietly spoken during the rest of the evening. She only speaks when spoken to and never initiates any conversation. She makes a sad impression and all her comments sound very negative. After a while, you see her sitting by herself on one of the sofas, trying to hide her tears.

Daniel makes a quiet entrance and quietly stands at a certain spot, without moving too much. He does not initiate any conversation, but when spoken to answers questions, but does not volunteer anything or ask questions. People speak to him briefly before moving on, which does not seem to bother him. He is in the last group to leave, when several people have voiced that it is very late and that this is the end of the party.

Bob arrives at the party and is immediately full of stories about his recent visits to doctors and how worried he is that they have missed something. He is eager to explain in minute detail how he thinks his symptoms are the first signs of a rather serious disease called XYZ. He does not take kindly to people saying that if the doctors cannot find anything wrong with him then he should stop worrying. Towards the end of the evening, Bob is surrounded by a small group of people and they are all talking about illnesses and how the medical system is a conspiracy against them.

Jennifer has spent a long time debating with herself whether she should go to the party. She arrives late and hesitates for a while at the entrance of the room. She does not make eye contact with anyone, and when people speak to her she looks frightened and surprised. She spends most of her time at the party with her back to the group studying the pictures on the wall and the books in the bookcases. She leaves early.

You realise that all these people probably could be diagnosed with a psychological problem.

According to the official classification systems of mental health problems (the *DSM-IV* and the tenth edition of the *International Classification of Diseases and Related Health Problems* (*ICD-10*), published by the World Health Organisation, 2001), there are more than 300 clinically recognised mental disorders, each characterised by problem feelings and behaviours that can create a life of instability and misery.

Would we be able to diagnose our friends at the party using these guidelines? The answer would be a tentative yes, but whether we all would agree on who fits which mental disorder or psychological problem would be questionable.

Pinpointing which classification "fits" with an individual client's presentation is not an easy task, despite repeated improvements in both commonly used classification systems (Harvey, Watkins, Mansell, & Shafran, 2004).

In other words a heterogenic group of people is frequently captured under the umbrella of one disorder. No wonder that there are strong moves to focus more on a dimensional model of mental disorder as opposed to the current dichotomous model (Parker & Hadzi-Pavlovic, 2001; Verheul, 2005; Widiger, 1992).

The *DSM* and *ICD* classification systems are important for cognitive behaviour therapy because recent years have seen the development of "disorder specific treatment models". For depression, the two main interventions are "Beckian CBT" (Beck, 1963, 1976) and "behavioural activation" (Veale, 2008). Treatment of specific phobias is mainly based on *in vivo* exposure and response prevention (Choy, Fyer, & Lipsitz, 2007). For generalised anxiety disorder, there are three CBT models (Department of Health, 2008) that are suggested as evidence based: the "avoidance model of worry and GAD" is proposed by Borkovec (1994), the "intolerance of uncertainty model" by Dugas and Ladouceur (2000), and the "metacognitive model" by Wells (1999). Treatment models for obsessive–compulsive disorders have been suggested by Foa, Steketee and Groves (1979), and the focus is again on exposure and response prevention. For post traumatic stress disorder, various treatment models have been proposed, of which a few are: Ehlers and Clark's (2000) cognitive model of PTSD and Foa and Rothbaum's (1998) prolonged exposure therapy for PTSD. Social phobia treatment models have been postulated by Heimberg, Liebowitz, Hope, and Schneier (1995) and Clark and Wells (1995). Treatments for panic disorders have been presented by Barlow and Craske (1989) and Clark (1996). All these idiosyncratic interventions focus on offering CBT treatment for a specific disorder. The development of these treatment models brings many benefits, not least of which is the ability to conduct specific research into the effectiveness and efficacy of these treatments.

When all these different treatment models are compared, a number of commonalities can be noted.

- People pay attention to issues that make their problems worse (e.g., a depressed client pays attention to negativity and a socially anxious client to other people's disapproval).
- People remember things better that reinforce their problems, as opposed to things that would reduce their problems.
- People engage in distorted thinking that enhances negative feelings that the person would prefer to avoid.

- People engage behaviourally in a trial and error fashion to avoid experiencing negative feelings and, when successful, they repeat the process.

A different approach

For the purposes of this book, I would like to adopt a different approach. This will be based on (1) the processes that underlie many psychological problems, and (2) a unified treatment model for psychological problems (Barlow, Allen, & Choate, 2004).

Harvey, Watkins, Mansell, and Shafran (2004) list as important transdiagnostic processes responsible for human misery attentional processes, memory processes, reasoning processes, thought processes, and behavioural processes. They evaluate the traditional diagnostic approach in comparison to a transdiagnostic approach. In the former, the diagnosis is meticulously established based on sets of strict criteria (resulting in treatment options fitting with the diagnosis), while in the latter, the processes are analysed in detail. This detailed analysis makes the application of individualised treatment options to counter the unhelpful process possible. Harvey and colleages state that a transdiagnostic process is the preferred model. First of all, thinking in diagnostic categories leads easily to an "us and them" response, in which "us" equals the "good" people and "them" implies the "bad" or "mentally ill" people. We have, unfortunately, seen many examples of this during our years of clinical practice. Clinicians often clearly perceive people with a diagnosis of personality disorder as "them" (to be despised, mistreated, and judged) and not "us" (respectable, upstanding people). It also leads to easy stigmatisation. Harvey and colleages also make the case that a classification/diagnostic approach is an impossible task with, at the moment, 350+ disorders described in the *DSM* (no person is capable of having this amount of information in their working memory). They further argue that in a diagnostic approach, valuable personal and idiosyncratic information is in danger of getting lost. It also becomes very difficult to deal with comorbidity in a categorical model, as we see in the case presentation example that follows (see p. 141). From our perspective, we favour a transdiagnostic and problem-based approach, here not the diagnostic category, but the processes involved in problem presentation, with the identified problems being analysed in an idiosyncratic model to form the basis of formulation and treatment.

Transdiagnostic processes

Attentional processes

In many problem areas, we can observe that people give more attention to certain issues and less to others. The process is general; the content is problem specific (Harvey, Watkins, Mansell, & Shafran, 2004). Depressed people pay more attention to negative experiences, negative attributes of themselves, and negative interactions with others.

Memory processes

What people store in their memories, what they spontaneously remember, and what they can deliberately retrieve seems to be very much habitual, and again can be observed as a process in a variety of problem categories, but with content specificity. For a depressed person, moments of despair are remembered better than moments of happiness, and occurrences in which others do not treat him/her with kindness are stored away very well.

Reasoning processes

How people apply reason to their lives is also described as a transdiagnostic process. Applying unsound reasoning seems to be a transdiagnostic process, but the exact content of the unhelpful reasoning appears to be connected to the specific problem area of the person. A socially anxious person will believe that others are talking about her/him in a negative way and that this is terrible.

Thought processes

How we use our brains is also a transdiagnostic process. Some people have one thought in their minds and ruminate about that endlessly, others flit from thought to thought, while others again do both, depending on the content of the thoughts.

Our socially anxious person might ruminate constantly about the negative thoughts that he/she believes others are thinking about him/her.

Behavioural processes

A well established transdiagnostic phenomenon is that people use behaviour to eliminate negative feelings, and these behaviours might become habitual (through the process of negative reinforcement). This general process acquires problem-specific meaning; for instance, the practice of aiming for short-term relief with long-term negative consequences is seen in

- social anxiety: avoiding people reduces the anxiety in the short term, but makes it more difficult to meet people in the long run;
- depression: avoidance of all challenges (for example, staying in bed all day) excludes disappointments from the possible repertoire of experiences in the short term, but leads in the longer term to a deepening of the depression.

Example: the case of Peter

Peter is a thirty-five-year-old man who has spent the past seven years imprisoned by his social anxiety. He has lost his job and now only leaves the house on brief trips to do some shopping in the local supermarket (he goes to the shop at 3.00 a.m., to avoid meeting other people). Peter and his wife were divorced ten years ago, after a marriage that lasted four years. He describes himself as always having been shy, but says life was all right when he was married. It seemed that Peter could function within the protection of the marriage, where his partner took care of the social interactions, and Peter was, in general, accepted by friends and family as "the quiet one".

Diagnostic/assessment information

During assessment, Peter qualifies for a diagnosis of social anxiety disorder. In interactions with other people, he experiences high anxiety; he limits interactions with others to a minimum and when he does interact with others he uses many self-defeating behaviours (no eye contact, speaking very softly, etc.).

Transdiagnostic processes applied to Peter

Attentional processes. Peter describes how he is focused on other people's facial expressions (he does not look at people, he just briefly glances at them) and notices people not looking at him, people looking away, or facial expressions that he interprets as disapproving. He also notices his own bodily response clearly: swallowing, blushing, sweating, his way of speaking, etc.

Peter reports that his attention is drawn immediately to people that he thinks are disapproving of him.

Memory processes. Peter remembers painful and embarrassing moments with others much more clearly than positive interactions with others.

Reasoning processes. Peter engages in disqualifying the positive (positive interaction with others only happens because they take pity on him), catastrophising (other people thinking negatively about you *is* terrible), and mind-reading (Peter pretends to know what other people think: negative views about him).

Thought processes. When Peter starts to think about social interactions, it seems as if a tapeloop has started. He repeats the same scenario of thoughts and images over and over again.

Behavioural processes. Peter has over-learnt an avoidance strategy: avoid interpersonal contact as much as possible and, when meeting people, make the interaction as least interactive as possible: no eye-contact, speak little and only when spoken to, speak softly, no gestures—in other words, avoid anything that could be seen by others as negative.

A unified treatment protocol

The second pillar on which this book rests is Barlow's "unified treatment protocol" (Barlow, Allen, & Choate, 2004). A number of specific psychological treatments have gained empirical support in the treatment of emotional disorders, surpassing, in most instances, the efficacy of pharmacological treatments over the longer term (Barlow, Allen, & Choate, 2004). Despite this success, there are some problems: with a success rate of 50–80% for CBT, this leaves a significant number of people who achieve less than optimal response or do not respond to CBT (Barlow, Allen, & Choate, 2004). In addition, these CBT treatments are often complex and target individual disorders. This results in there being quite a number of these disorder-specific interventions (e.g., separate treatments for panic disorder, generalised anxiety disorder, major depressive disorder, etc.). These separate interventions make dissemination a challenge, since clinicians would need to obtain competence in all the different protocols, which would prove to be rather costly and time-intensive. It also assumes that different disorders can be treated in isolation; for example, Beatrice's drinking problem, her social anxiety, and her depression could be treated in sequence as separate and unconnected issues. Any therapist with some experience will be able to state convincingly that this is not possible.

Barlow, Allen, and Choate propose that the solution might lie in the development of a common treatment approach applicable to a range of emotional disorders: a treatment approach that applies the basic principles of CBT to the various disorders and designs an intervention package from first principles: cognitive psychology, reinforcement theory, and the transdiagnostic processes. Barlow and colleagues suggest a protocol that starts with a psycho-education phase. In this phase, the client learns about behaviours, thinking processes, and emotions, their functions, and how they become disordered. The ensuing treatment then focuses on (a) altering antecedent cognitive appraisals, (b) modifying emotion-driven behaviours, and (c) preventing emotional avoidance.

Altering antecedent cognitive appraisals

This aspect of the unified treatment approach focuses on changing the unhelpful thinking that often leads to emotional distress and/or unhelpful behaviours. The bottom line here is that if we alter the thinking that produces or promotes the negative affect, subsequently the negative affect will be significantly decreased or completely removed.

Some examples are shown in Table 4.1.

The following CBT interventions would fit:

- cognitive restructuring through working with thought records;
- cognitive restructuring through working with behavioural experiments;
- cognitive restructuring through Socratic dialogue about emotionally upsetting events;
- psycho-education about rational and irrational thinking.

Table 4.1. How antecedent cognitive appraisals can change negative affect thinking.

Negative affect	Problem behaviour	Antecedent cognitive appraisals	Changed cognitive appraisal
Depression	Avoidance, staying in bed all day.	It is pointless. I am useless. It will be too difficult.	A thing being difficult does not mean that it will be too difficult. Not feeling like doing doing things is my depression talking; in the past I felt better after doing things.
Anxiety	Avoiding people.	They will reject me and that is terrible.	It is unlikely that I will be rejected by X, but if it happens, that will be unpleasant and not terrible.

Modifying emotion-driven behaviours

Negative feelings often trigger an action tendency to remove or suppress the negative feeling. Anxiety results in a tendency to avoid the stimulus that triggers the anxiety; depression results in avoiding events that could result in more disappointments. The longer the problems have been in place, the more entrenched these emotion-driven behaviours (EDBs) are. In real life, we often see an avoidance of specific approach behaviours based on an emotional state (the client is depressed and, as a result, refrains from engaging in any challenging activity) in combination with a skills-deficit (the depressed person might lack the communication skills to express their wishes and wants in social situations, or they might have the skills but have learnt not to use them). You could say this is a double whammy, two for the price of one: the client, in general, avoids and, more specifically, would not have the skills or would not use the skills needed in the situations if they stopped avoiding.

Emotion-driven behaviours are, at first, reinforcing, since they reduce the impact of the negative feelings. In the mid- to long-term, they are highly maladaptive. For example, avoidance in response to fear of criticism produces further social isolation and prevents new positive experiences (e.g., learning that social situations are not often associated with criticism and embarrassment). "A century of tradition in emotion science suggests that one of the most powerful methods for modifying emotions is to change EDBs and thereby change feelings" (Barlow, Allen, & Choate, 2004).

EDBs are over-learnt and extremely powerful in the field of addictions. They are, in most cases, self-defeating; for example, the negative feeling is escaped from or reduced but will return with a vengeance in the mid- to long-term. Examples of EDBs are:

- escaping from situations in which the anxiety provoking stimulus is present (crossing the street when confronted with a dog for a dog-phobic person);
- redirecting a conversation towards submission when noticing (hypothesised) disapproval on the other person's face (when discussing a topic with a colleague for a person with social phobia);
- drinking alcohol to excess/eating chocolate to excess when feeling depressed;
- avoidance of assertive behaviour and engaging in submissive behaviour in order to avoid the guilt that would be the result of asserting one's personal rights;
- expressing nasty critical comments to partner when feeling depressed (the ensuing row will result in an escape from the feeling of depression for a brief period);
- a cognitive example of "emotion-driven behaviour" is, of course, worrying. This cognitive activity is fuelled by anxiety and the worrier attempts to reduce the anxiety through worrying.

EDBs are working according to an escape paradigm. The feelings are occurring, are registered by the person, and the person deploys methods to "escape" from the negative feelings. In itself, this is a rational process, were it not that the escape behaviour results in even more negative consequences in the mid- to long term. EDBs are, therefore, strongly linked with the next element of a unified treatment model, which is the prevention of negative feelings occurring (an avoidance paradigm). This is also not a deliberate and planned process. For instance, in the last example, it is highly unlikely that the depressed person deliberately plans this. It is more a question of over-learnt behaviours, whereby one thing almost automatically leads to the next. If we adopt a reinforcement theory perspective for a moment, this becomes very clear, and we can see the principle of negative reinforcement at work in these examples.

This is an example of the inner dialogue of a particular client, with the resulting "real" dialogue with her partner in quote marks, and comments from a learning theory perspective in square brackets.

> *Client*: I am feeling very depressed; why does he always have to ask how I feel? Doesn't he know it makes me more depressed?
> [Highlighting the negative emotional state and linking it with partner's behaviour.]
>
> "Why do you always have to ask how I feel, can't you just see how miserable I am? I can't believe you are such an idiot!" (I can feel my adrenaline flowing through my body.)
> [Angry/aggressive behaviour. The act of speaking these angry words gets some adrenaline flowing and reduces the depression slightly; mild negative reinforcement.]
>
> Partner defends.
>
> *Client*: (shouting now). "Are you stupid? Can't you see I just need an apology from you for being so insensitive?" (No wonder I am depressed, no one really understands me. I would expect more from a partner.)
> [Adrenaline is really flowing and depression abates.]

Human beings are learning organisms and, having been confronted frequently enough with the need to escape from a negative feeling, we will often find a way to avoid the feeling occurring in the first place.

The following CBT interventions would be suitable for teaching clients *not* to use EDBs:

- exposure and response prevention;
- skills training (e.g., acquiring and using new skills that are incompatible with the EDB);
- self-control training.

Preventing emotional avoidance

EDBs are deployed to reduce (escape) negative emotions or reduce the intensity once the emotion has occurred; emotional avoidance strategies are used to prevent the experience of the negative emotion in the first place. There are several forms of emotional avoidance. Avoidance can be in the form of specific overt behaviours like avoiding every form of exercise for the person with panic attack problems (each hint of physical arousal is seen as impending doom). Cognitive avoidance can occur when a person simply tries to prevent thinking about certain things (events from the past or certain thoughts/images that are seen as wrong). Sometimes, it takes the form of "superstitious" behaviour in the person concerned (hand-washing in OCD), or the person might need to carry with them certain items in order to ward off the negative feelings (the person cannot leave the house without their pills, talisman, favourite shirt, for instance).

The following CBT interventions would be suitable for teaching clients to prevent emotional avoidance:

- exposure and response prevention;
- skills training (e.g., acquiring and using new skills that are incompatible with the EDB);
- self-control training;
- mindfulness training.

CHAPTER FIVE

Making sense of the facts: formulation and treatment planning in cognitive behaviour therapy

Introduction

With what we have learnt in Chapter Four, we can now go back to thinking about formulation. A formulation is a pocket-sized theory that explains how the person acquired the problems and how they are maintained. The theories applied are, of course, learning theory and cognitive psychology. In this chapter, we will review formulation from three perspectives, using the BASIC-ID model (Lazarus, 1973) and the SORCC model (Goldfried & Sprafkin, 1976; Junge-Hoffmeister, 2006; Narciss, 2006; Rinck & Becker, 2006) in combination with the transdiagnostic processes.

The client: You never can work too much!

Jason is a thirty-eight-year-old senior accountant in a very successful accountants' firm. He is married, and the family consists of his wife Joan and three children aged six, nine, and eleven. Joan is a stay-at-home mum, so Jason is the only salaried worker in the family. Jason has been very successful in his life. His parents were kind and hardworking people, who created a positive and pleasant home atmosphere. He was successful at school and university. He has held three jobs and left each with a solid promotion. Jason complains of feeling tired all the time, he only has energy to do his work and is completely exhausted when he arrives home. Weekends are often spent on catching up on sleep. Jason mentions that things he enjoyed doing in the past do not give him pleasure any more: he has stopped going for long walks with the dog, stopped playing golf, no more theatre and cinema visits, and even playing with the children has become a chore. His wife and colleagues have given him feedback that he has become very irritable and can explode as a result of small mistakes others make, or because of simple misunderstandings. Jason says that he feels he is caught in a straightjacket and cannot get out. He knows something is not right, but does not know what or how to fix things. Looking back, he states that things have not been all right during the past four years, but it has now come to a head because he completely lost it with the children when one of them had to go back into the house to fetch a book needed for school. Jason spent fifteen minutes screaming and shouting at the children, telling them how ungrateful they are and how they never consider him. After that, he went to bed and called in sick at work. The next day he went back to work and would have left it at that if his wife had not told him that he really needed to seek some help.

On depression rating scales, he scores in the moderate to severe range. There are no relevant scores on anxiety questionnaires, and in one questionnaire focusing on beliefs and core beliefs there are elevated scores for unrelenting standards, self-sacrifice, entitlement, and self-worth based on achievement.

SORCC and BASIC-ID from a unified treatment model perspective

The SORCC model

The letters stand for stimulus, organism, response, and consequence. The main aim of this model is to understand the problems from a learning theory perspective. The S is the external stimulus that constitutes the trigger for a sequence leading to problem behaviours and/or problem feelings. The O indicates the internal response of the organism to the trigger. These are the internal operations of humans: feelings, physiological sensations, and thoughts. The R indicates the overt response of the person, and, finally, the C indicates the consequences (short, medium, and long term) of the overt response and the connection between response and consequence (is the consequence always present after the response or is it an intermittent ratio?).

The SORCC model is an empirical model: it is based on observations of what actually happens in the client's life. The therapist gains access to these observations through structured dialogue with the client and by teaching the client to become an "objective" observer of his/her own life.

Clients come for therapy because of problem feelings or problem behaviours. These are the starting point for the therapist. The client's problem response could be regular avoidance of social situations to such an extent that the client's work is now suffering. The therapist can refer to a recent situation when the client avoided being the focus of attention. Our client was scheduled to do a presentation to a group of suppliers to the company, but thirty minutes before the event he reported sick to his boss and a colleague had to take over. So the R (response) here is: "Telling my boss that I don't feel well, go home and stay home for three days." The situation (S) that triggers this is the work demand that the client does a presentation to thirty-plus people who are important to the company. The internal reactions of the client to this demand are: ruminating about how difficult suppliers can be in these presentations, how he will make mistakes during the presentation, and playing over and over again a disaster film in his mind about how badly the presentation could go. This results in a general physical agitation and arousal and a feeling of anxiety. These spike at moments when our client is actively reminded of the presentation (a colleague might say: "This is a good example to include in your presentation"). On the day itself, the client feels very anxious and firmly believes he will make a complete mess of the presentation. He goes home, claiming to be ill and (the consequence) his anxiety and agitation rapidly disappear. From a learning theory perspective, this is negative reinforcement.

The SORCC model is very flexible and allows the therapist to identify accurately exactly what is happening with the client, which is translated into the model.

The SORCC model applied to Jason

The SORCC model is behaviour specific; this means that the core of the model is behaviour of the client that is seen as problematic or that leads to problems. In Jason's situation, a number of behaviours seem to be relevant to his problem presentation: working many hours (at least around seventy, and sometimes more), critical and grumpy with family and colleagues, anger outbursts with family, avoidance of doing personally pleasurable and satisfying activities. If we focus on Jason's hard work, then we can construct the following SORCC model (Figure 5.1).

What can be seen clearly from this SORCC model is how the response leads to consequences that are perceived as positive by Jason. Either he receives something positive (praise, a full calendar, and a full desk), or something negative is taken away (the fatigue is replaced by feeling energised briefly when focusing on the work). In the mid- to long term, the response elicits the same situations, feelings, and sensations that triggered the response in the first place and thus becomes a vicious circle. Figure 5.2 depicts how this results in Jason becoming critical and grumpy with his family, which demonstrates operant learning at work: a combination of positive and negative reinforcement maintains the critical behaviour. In Figure 5.3, we can see how Jason's angry outbursts with his family are sandwiched between demanding thinking and the negative reinforcement following it.

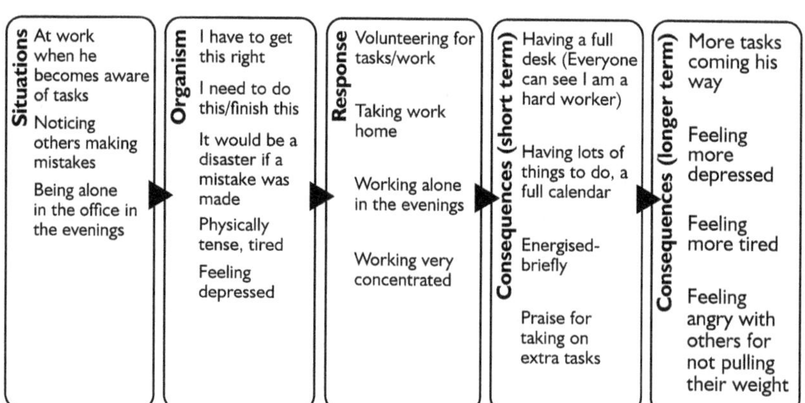

Figure 5.1. The SORCC model, based on Jason's hard work.

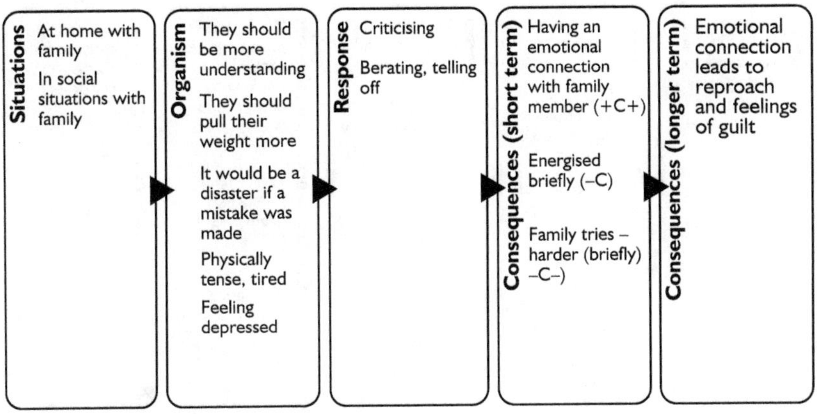

Figure 5.2. Jason becomes critical and grumpy with his family.

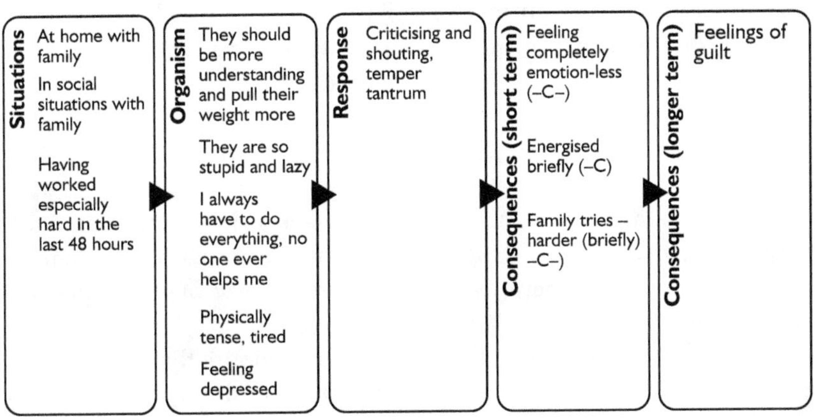

Figure 5.3. Jason has angry outbursts with his family.

Figure 5.4 shows how working and worrying offer both reinforcing consequences for the behaviours and keep Jason locked into not using the weekends for rest and recuperation.

Preliminary conclusions

It seem that Jason invests a lot of time in work (self-monitoring showed he spends an average of seventy hours at work and works another ten hours from home) and little time is invested in activities

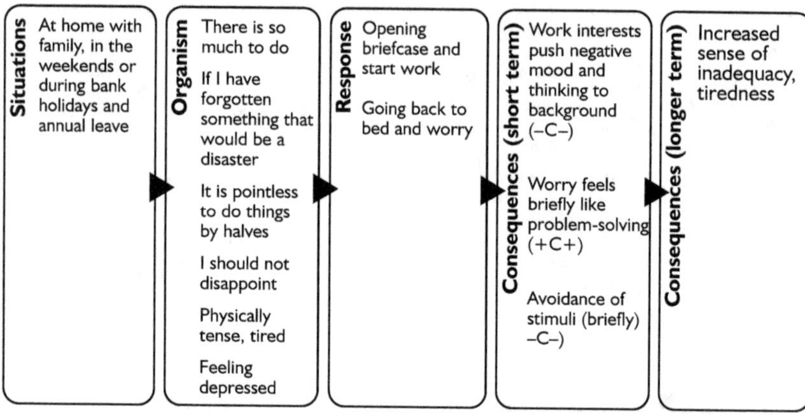

Figure 5.4. Avoidance of personally pleasurable and satisfying activities.

that previously he found rewarding (playing with the children, playing golf, dog walking, evenings in and out with his wife).

The BASIC-ID model

The letters stand for behaviour, affect, sensations, interpersonal, cognitions, imagery, and drugs and alcohol. This model is excellent in assisting client and therapist not to overlook any of the important domains in life.

Behaviour encompasses all the client's behaviours that are relevant to the issues at hand: for example, working, studying, playing with the children, hair-pulling, and checking face/body in the mirror.

Affect includes all relevant emotional experiences of the client: for example, depression, sadness, happiness, anger, guilt.

Sensations include all physical experiences, often outside voluntary control, that are relevant to the problems: for example, sleep, fatigue, craving, pain, blushing.

Interpersonal encompasses all interpersonal aspects of a person's life as far as they are relevant to the person's problems. This has two components: potential and actual. Someone working as part of a team of counter staff in a relaxed coffee shop will have more opportunity-*potentially*—for interpersonal interactions than someone working alone in the storage facility of a department store with one or two visitors per day. How that person then *actually* utilises the opportunities for interpersonal interaction is the second component. Examples are: smiling, joking, criticising, hugging, playing games.

Cognitive includes the content of the thinking, the relevant thinking processes, beliefs, and core beliefs that guide these. Examples are: various forms of thinking errors ("They will criticise me and that is terrible"), maladaptive core beliefs ("I am worthless"), rumination, attentional focus, and selective memory.

Imagery stands for all images that are relevant to the problems: for example, images of being the centre of attention, images of the self as being small, images of others as being all-powerful.

Drugs and alcohol encompasses any substance use that is relevant to the problems at hand: for example, coffee, alcohol, illegal drugs.

The BASIC-ID model is excellent in understanding links between various areas of a person's life; for example, what leads to what. Jason's BASIC-ID profile is shown in Figure 5.5.

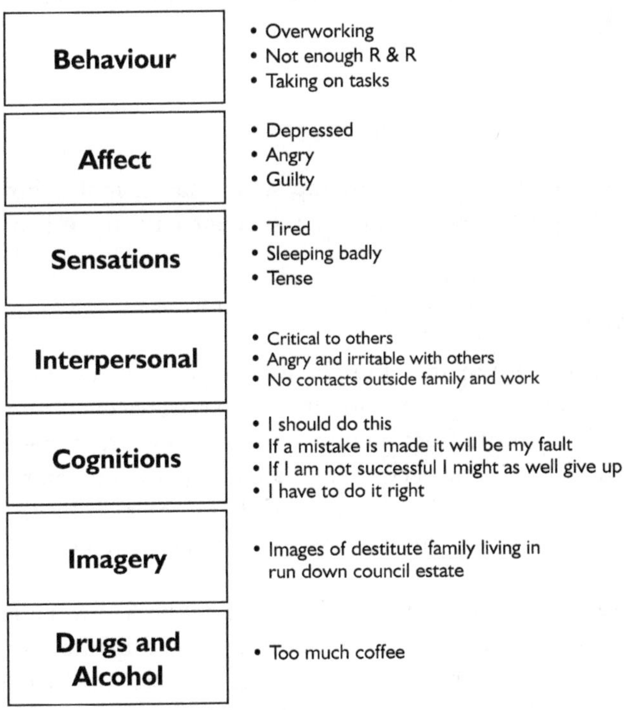

Figure 5.5. Jason's BASIC-ID profile.

By studying this BASIC-ID profile for a while and discussing it with the client, the connections will become clear:

- too much coffee connects with feeling tense and sleeping badly;
- the cognitions and the imagery must be real "pushers" for the hard work and the lack of rest and recreation (R & R);
- the hard work and the lack of R & R must result in tension and feeling tired;
- the depression fuels not investing in R & R;
- the critical and angry behaviour towards others results in feelings of guilt;
- guilt feelings result in feeling depressed and coping strategies that have been used in the past in dealing with guilt (working hard).

Jason was also asked to monitor interactions with family and colleagues on a friendly ↔ critical continuum. This showed that friendly interaction are virtually non-existent and that Jason hardly expresses positive and negative feelings to others in a productive, pro-social manner.

Transdiagnostic processes

A formulation is complete when the therapist also has insight in how the transdiagnostic processes operate for the client with these problems.

Memory processes

It is important to know whether the client gives certain memories preferential treatment. Some people find it easy to retrieve everything that went wrong in their life from memory, while others are prone to remembering when others criticised them. To what types of memories does the client give preferential treatment? It might also be that certain memories are being discriminated against in a negative manner (repressed).

In Jason's situation, he was often thinking of how he had received praise in the past for working very hard; also, he was thinking often about how humiliated and ashamed other people must have felt when they had made a mistake. These memories and images prompted him to work harder.

Reasoning processes

In cognitive behaviour therapy, thinking plays a pivotal role in influencing emotions and behaviour. People apply incorrect inferences and evaluations to their experiences and, consequently, experience strong negative feelings. To learn about a client's specific style of making incorrect inferences and which type of evaluations are used by the client is essential if the therapist wants to be able to assist the client in overcoming the problems.

For Jason, here are some of the reasoning processes that were identified.

- Mindreading: Jason assumed that people wanted him to work so hard; he also assumed that people were deliberately trying to sabotage him (hence his irritability and anger).
- Catastrophising: Jason made mountains out of molehills; when small things went wrong he was convinced it would all end in disaster;
- All-or-nothing thinking: from Jason's perspective one could perform a task to perfection or not at all; if he made a small mistake, or others made small mistakes, he was inclined to completely condemn himself and the other person ("you stupid imbecile!").

Thought processes

Reasoning is to do with the content of the cognitive domain, while thought processes refers to how the cognitive domain deals with its products. Rumination is one of the more well known thought processes. When ruminating, we repeat the same content many times over, sometimes in the same format, sometimes in a slightly different format.

Jason was a real ruminator; he could spend hours reviewing small mistakes he had made and chastising himself for that.

Behavioural processes

The name "operant conditioning" comes from the word "operate": to operate on one's environment results in changes in that environment. If we like the changes, we will repeat the operation, and if we do not like the changes we will select a different operation. In other words, our behaviour is the tool we can use to change our environment in such a way that it becomes better (less anxiety provoking, less chaotic, less unpleasant) for us. Many problem behaviours start as solutions for problems (the need to reduce or erase a negative feeling or the desire to gain access to (more) positive feelings). Problem behaviours are, in general, successful in producing the desired effect in the short term, but in the long term will produce a similar situation to the one that triggered the problem behaviour in the first place.

Jason's behavioural processes were based on a desire to avoid even the slimmest possibility that he would not achieve enough. The idea of under-achieving (which, for him, meant achieving less than top marks) was highly anxiety provoking. The way in which Jason avoided was overworking and under-investing in his own rest and recuperation.

Formulation

Formulations that draw on SORC-models and a BASIC-ID profile in combination with identifying relevant transdiagnostic processes can be very powerful in describing how a problem came to be and how it is still maintained. The road to a good formulation is via detailed topographical analyses, functional analyses (the SORCC model is a good format for these), a detailed historical analysis, self-monitoring by the client, problem-specific questionnaires, questionnaires focused on cognitive content, and processes.

Composing a formulation is much more then a tick-box exercise. Some of the problem-specific formulations available really invite clinicians to do just that. The danger is obvious: the end product reflects more of the author of the model than of the client in question. Formulations need to be individualised and linked to the idiosyncratic presentation of the client; that is why a good formulation contains one or more diagrams and a narrative that explains how the client developed the problem and what the current maintenance processes are.

I think it is good practice to put the formulation on paper and use this when discussing it with the client. It is also good practice to ensure the client has a copy of the formulation and treatment plan.

Treatment plan

A treatment plan identifies the goals of the treatment and details the chronological order of the CBT interventions that are going to be used to achieve these goals. The interventions can work in two ways: directly and indirectly. If we take the example of overworking and under-investing in R & R (Jason's problems), then it is clear that behavioural activation and contracting regarding activities are directly focused on goal attainment. Cognitive restructuring by way of thought records and behavioural experiments is focused on removing a roadblock to goal attainment. This intervention is focused on decreasing the positive valence of hard work and increasing the value of decent self-care. It is also focused on reducing the anxiety stemming from making mistakes.

A treatment plan is, therefore, firmly based on the formulation. A treatment plan without a decent formulation is a house without a foundation.

Here are some of the things that you should know before you start on a treatment plan.

- Is the client aware of the target behaviours of therapy?
- Does the client know how to execute the target behaviours?
- Does the client know when to execute the target behaviours?
- Does the client have effective strategies to overcome the negative feelings that might block execution of the target behaviours?
- Is the client prepared for a possible negative reaction of the environment?
- Does the client have strategies to reduce the possible negative feelings as a result of the target behaviour?

Example formulation and treatment plan for Jason

The formulation and the treatment plan for Jason was drawn up using the SORCC and BASIC-ID models in combination with the transdiagnostic processes identified, as described above. The problems identified and the goals set to deal with them are shown in Table 5.1.

Table 5.1. The problems identified and the goals set for Jason.

Problems	Goals
I work too hard and that makes me depressed.	Limit work to not more than fifty hours per week.
	Return to old hobbies: golf (once a week); dog walking (daily), playing with the children (five times a week), and social outings with wife (twice a week).
	Leave non-critical tasks unfinished (one per week).
I set my standards so high that I never achieve them; this makes me work too hard.	I need to set reasonable standards for tasks by deliberately planning for "average" results (at least once per week).
	When mistakes are made, I need to react with kindness and understanding (each opportunity).
	Plan mistakes (at least one per day).
I mainly communicate in a critical and angry manner with family and colleagues; this makes me feel guilty.	Express positive feelings to family (once per day).
	Express positive feelings to a colleague (at least once per day).
	Express negative feelings as suggestions for a change in behaviour by others to make me feel better (each opportunity).

Comments

For each problem, several goals are identified. The goals involve specific behaviours of the client (sometimes internal behaviour, as in the case of "I need to set reasonable standards for tasks by deliberately planning for 'average' results (at least once per week)" and "When mistakes are made I need to react with kindness and understanding (each opportunity)". It is also clear that "feeling better" or "feeling less depressed" are not featured in the list of goals. This highlights an important distinction between treatment goals and the overarching aim of therapy. It is clear that for Jason the overarching aim of therapy is to feel better and to feel less depressed. These treatment goals are identified because, in achieving these goals, the client will start to feel better. How do we know that? We know it because we have composed a good formulation that demonstrates that when these goals are achieved, the maintenance forces of the current problems are interrupted. Setting goals can only be done specifically towards the end of the assessment process, when the formulation is almost complete. Client and therapist need to know how the client functions in order for them to set goals that are really meaningful and will definitely interrupt the problem-promoting maintenance processes.

Treatment plan

The treatment plan drawn up for Jason is depicted in Table 5.2 on the next page.

In consultation with the client, a sequence of interventions was decided upon, as indicated by the numbers in the interventions column.

Comments

A real advantage of making time to explain the formulation to the client is that the client will become the therapist's co-therapist. The client can, therefore, discuss with the therapist what they think is the best therapeutic chronology. This, of course, does not mean that the therapist becomes a quiet bystander. On the contrary, the therapist provides the client with ideas and information to base his or her decisions on. In Jason's case, he felt that he needed to address his overworking and exhaustion before he could muster the energy to address anything else.

Table 5.2. Jason's treatment plan.

Goals	Interventions	Domains
Limit work to not more than fifty hours per week.	Behavioural activation, contracting (1).	Modifying emotion-driven behaviours.
Return to old hobbies: golf (once a week), dog walking (daily), playing with the children (five times a week), and social outings with wife (twice a week).	Behavioural activation, cognitive restructuring (thought records and behavioural experiments) (1).	Altering antecedent cognitive appraisals, and modifying emotion-driven behaviours.
Leave non-critical tasks unfinished (one per week).	Cognitive restructuring (thought records and behavioural experiments) (2).	Altering antecedent cognitive appraisals.
I need to set reasonable standards for tasks by deliberately planning for "average" results (at least once per week).	Cognitive restructuring (thought records and behavioural experiments) (2).	Altering antecedent cognitive appraisals.
When mistakes are made I need to react with kindness and understanding (each opportunity).	Compassion skills training, communication skills training (3).	Altering antecedent cognitive appraisals, and modifying emotion-driven behaviours.
Plan mistakes (at least one per day).	Cognitive restructuring (thought records and behavioural experiments) (3).	Preventing avoidance of negative feelings, altering antecedent cognitive appraisals, and modifying emotion-driven behaviours.
Express positive feelings to family (once per day).	Skills training (3).	Modifying emotion-driven behaviours.
Express positive feelings to a colleague (at least once per day).	Skills training (4).	Modifying emotion-driven behaviours.
Express negative feelings as suggestions for a change in behaviour by others to make me feel better (each opportunity).	Skills training (4).	Modifying emotion-driven behaviours.

CHAPTER SIX

Cognitive behaviour therapy strategies focused on altering antecedent cognitive appraisals

Introduction

Strategies focused on altering antecedent cognitive appraisals can also be called interventions focused on the cognitive domain. If we take the building blocks of our formulation, then we can see that these interventions try to bring about change in the O (organism) element, or, from a BASIC-ID perspective, in the C (cognitive) and I (imagery) domains. From a transdiagnostic perspective, the change would focus on reasoning processes.

The aim of all interventions is to bring about an improvement in the extent to which the client is plagued by unhealthy negative feelings and/or engages in maladaptive behaviours. Although the interventions reviewed in this chapter have as a primary focus bringing about a change in thinking, this change is not a goal in and of itself. In CBT, we want to change thinking only if there is a subsequent change in emotional experience and/or behaviour. Cognitive behaviour therapists are not the thought police; for example, the aim is not to eradicate irrational thinking. The aim is for people to feel better and to behave better. Thinking is merely the helpful intermediary that brings about this change. A change in thinking without a subsequent change in emotion and/or behaviour is meaningless. If a client with a dog phobia learns to think of most dogs as harmless, tail-wagging, furry, slobbering mutts who have no harmful intent towards her, but this same client continues, at all costs, to avoid dogs and situations that might result in an encounter with a dog, then therapy has been no more than an academic exercise.

In this chapter, I will review three methods of changing thinking: Socratic dialogue, daily thought records, and behavioural experiments.

Socratic dialogue

There are several other names for this CBT technique: Socratic questioning and guided discovery. Personally, I like the term Socratic dialogue, because it emphasises the client–therapist link. Socratic dialogue can be used in three ways. First, it is used to assist the client to explore with the therapist what exactly is happening at crucial moments and how the client's mind works. A mistake I often see made by novice CBT practitioners is to start using Socratic dialogue and then turn it rapidly into an evidential hearing in which the client's irrational thinking is laid bare by the therapist. This is not the aim of Socratic dialogue; in this instance, the aim is to explore, to learn about the client's way of doing and thinking. The second use of Socratic dialogue is when the therapist wants the client to reflect on their thinking and meaning-giving process and method. Implicit in this is the aim to assist the client in drawing new and more rational conclusions. Here, the aim is indeed to "change the client's mind", not by convincing the client, but by guiding the client's process of self-discovery. This is where Padesky's term "guided discovery" originates. Four steps are identified in Socratic dialogue (Padesky, 1993): asking informational questions, active listening, summarising, and synthesising and analytical questions. A third application of Socratic dialogue is to communicate with clients during the implementation of change-directed interventions.

Step one: asking informational questions

Padesky (1993) defines this step as asking the client questions that:

- the client has the knowledge to answer;
- draw the client's attention to information that is relevant to the issue being discussed, but that might be outside the client's current focus;
- the client can, in the end, apply the new information to either re-evaluate a previous conclusion or construct a new idea.

Asking informational question in Socratic dialogue is never a quest for information; instead, it is an exploration of the client's experiential inner world. What is actually happening, from the client's perspective, and how does the client evaluate these experiences? So, the facts are important, but also the client's response to these facts: feelings, cognitions, and, if relevant, physiological reactions.

Step two: active listening

A common mistake of inexperienced CBT therapists is to fire off a salvo of questions to the client and follow up each answer with another question. Needless to say, this is wrong, and will lead to clients feeling interrogated. It is important to acknowledge the client's answers with repetitions, reflections, and paraphrases.

Here is an example of the first two steps of Socratic questioning. This is how the client—Gemma—introduces herself.

> "I am thirty-six and I am married with two children. The oldest, David, he is six now, and he has ADHD, so he's quite a difficult character at times and I feel quite worried about his behaviour and how I'm looking after him. I am also worried that my younger daughter is showing signs of having ADHD as well, so I'm worried about that. I feel like just a lot of the time—and I'm in my second year now of a Nursing Degree, which involves quite a lot of placements in hospital settings, working with patients, and I feel very anxious throughout the placements whether I'm doing the right thing, if I'm putting my training to good use and making the most of the opportunity. I also worry about assignments, deadlines, coursework. Another thing that I feel worried about is I'm not earning any more and, although my husband earns a very good wage and he's supporting, I feel that I'm not contributing financially to the family, which does worry me. I just find it very difficult day-to-day to stop feeling anxious. I've lost contact with some of my friends from my previous jobs since I've started this degree and I find it very difficult to make new

friends on the course; everyone's a lot younger than me and, yes, I just worry about how I'm coming across to them. I find it very difficult being in social situations around other students and, yes, at home as well I think I'm quite snappy and irritable with my husband and with my kids, and it's mainly just because I feel really worried and anxious all the time, so it's sort of spreading into my home life as well as I'm finding it very difficult to concentrate."

The following excerpt is from the first session and occurs just after the setting of the agenda. As before, the explanatory comments are in square brackets.

Therapist: So you started off by saying, "I've come here to talk about how I'm feeling" and why you're feeling like this and what I can do to improve it. Can you tell me a bit more about that?
[A brief summary and an open question to allow client to expand in any direction she desires.]

Client: Well, I think I have always been a bit of a worrier.

Therapist: A worrier?
[Repetition with a question mark to allow client to expand.]

Client: Yes, even from quite a young age. My mum always used to describe me as being quite anxious as a child, quite emotional.
[And we get a lot more information.]

Therapist: So, anxious, emotional as a child?
[Repetition with a question mark to allow client to expand.]

Client: Yes, and I think that I've always managed to cope, and I've just sort of accepted that I am one of those people who is just a bit highly strung.

Therapist: "I am one of those people who is highly strung." Is the way you would describe yourself?
[Repetition, followed by a question to confirm that therapist heard it right.]

Client: Yes, but now it just feels like I don't feel highly strung any more, I just feel on the edge and very nervous and anxious and worried in general, but then there are a couple of things I get more anxious and worried about. It's just getting to the point now where I don't really know how to manage it any more and I just want to go back to how I was where I felt that, yes, I was anxious, but I also could cope with it.

Therapist: So you are saying that now you don't know how to manage it any more. Can you tell me a bit more about that?
[Paraphrase followed by an open question.]

Client: Well, I guess I used, yes, to worry and feel nervous and anxious, but it wouldn't ever stop me from doing things.

Therapist: So, you would worry and things would make you nervous, but it wouldn't stop you from doing the things that you wanted to do.
[Paraphrase.]

Client: Yes, because I always used to put it down to being that kind of person who's, yes, just highly strung, but now it is getting to the point where I feel that it gets in the way of day-to-day life.

Therapist: It gets in the way of day-to-day life, so what kinds of things does it get in the way of?
[Paraphrase, followed by informational question.]

Client: I think it affects my studies because I get so worried and anxious about getting things right that I often don't start things because I'm so nervous about messing it up or not doing the best that I can, so I tend to have these periods of, yes, just working myself up over it.
[Now we are getting information about the self-defeating impact of the worrying. Client worries about grades, but the worrying results in not studying, therefore making bad grades more likely.]

Therapist: So you're worried about getting things right and, as a result of that, you don't start studying because you're so worried about getting things right.
[Paraphrase, should have been followed by an open question!]

Client: Yes.
[The client merely confirms what the therapist said, so the therapist needs to ask another question.]

Therapist: When you say "getting things right", can you tell me a bit more about that? You're studying, so how does that fit in with getting things right?
[Information question aimed at increasing therapist's understanding of the situation.]

Client: I think that, because I've started my degree later on in life, I need to make it worthwhile, all the changes and disruptions it's caused, so I'm always aiming to get really high grades to make sure that my assignments are as good as they possibly can be. I'm always aiming for, like, first-class feedback and high scores, and we do placements as well because it's a nursing degree, and I always worry that my performance on the placements isn't good enough.

Step 3: Summarising

In this third step, the therapist summarises a larger part of an interview. The therapist can combine various parts of the session in a summary and follow this up with more informational questions.

An example of this occurs in the interview with Gemma.

The first excerpt follows immediately from the one given above.

Therapist: So, if I get it right, you were saying that you'd be worrying about lots of things from a very young age as a child, and your mum may have called you anxious and emotional, highly strung, and that's been OK, but lately you've noticed that it gets in the way of getting things done, and what you're saying is that you're really quite worried about doing things right, whether at studying or whether that's in your placements. The way you say that, would it be true to say then that you've had lots of experience with getting bad grades and getting bad evaluations, and have you done lots of placements where people have said, "We think that was really a very bad job you did with us"?
[This is a summary and an inference from the therapist that will allow the client to confirm or disconfirm whether her worries are reality based.]

Client: Not really.

Therapist: Not really, so you worry, but it's not something that's happened frequently?
[Paraphrase.]

Client: No, it's not really based on constantly getting feedback that says that I need to do better or it's not good enough.

Therapist: So it's not based on that kind of feedback with language like, "Come on! You have to give it a bit more energy because look at your grades"?
[Paraphrase.]

Client: No.

Therapist: Your worries are not based on your experience of getting bad grades or bad evaluations. Could you tell me a bit about your grades and evaluations?
[Paraphrase and an informational question.]

Client: In general they are very good. All my grades are either distinctions or merits and the feedback from my internships is very good. One of my supervisors called me a bit of a perfectionist.

There are no rules for summaries regarding the order in which the therapist put the elements and the frequency of summaries. Sometimes, a summary produces a simple "yes" or "no" from the client, and then it is prudent to try again with a summary that is slightly differently phrased.

Another summary to elicit more information about client's internal processing is this one, formatted as previously described.

Therapist: So, it is this kind of worrying that makes you anxious and makes you feel on edge. Are there any other things in your life that make you anxious?
[Brief paraphrase and open question.]

Client: At the moment, yes. It's not that we're struggling financially because my husband has a good job and he earns enough money to provide so that I don't need to work full-time, and I get a bursary from the NHS, so there is money coming in, but it's only like £6,000 a year. Before, I used to have a reasonably well-paid job myself and I worry now that, because I'm not bringing in as much money and because we do have quite a fifty-fifty relationship, it feels unequal and that maybe my husband thinks that I should be working instead of studying.

Therapist: So you have the worry about getting low grades and not being up to standard in your placements, and you said that that is what you worry about, but you also said it has no connection with reality as you haven't received critical reports from your placements and you haven't received critical feedback from your lecturers. The worry about your husband being unhappy about you not contributing 50% of the household finances, is this also one of those worries where your husband hasn't said anything about the money, but you worry about it?
[Summary linking two experiences and question to get client to evaluate the worry.]

Client: Well, he has never said: "You need to go out to work. It's not fair that I earn all the money". But I still worry that he is thinking that.

Step four: asking synthesising or analytical questions

These types of questions combine various points of information and ask the client to evaluate them. The evaluation of the various sources of information is aimed at bringing about a change in client's thinking. In the case of Gemma, the therapist had established that Gemma is a habitual worrier and that the worrying has negative emotional consequences. Despite this, Gemma formulates that: "But I need to worry. If I am not worrying I don't feel prepared. Worrying also motivates me to work hard and to achieve. I think I just have to pay the price of this anxiety in order to have any real achievements." Gemma and the therapist have also established that she simply does not study at all if her worries and anxiety get bad. She has also reported that her money worries are starting to irritate her husband, who has repeatedly stated that their money situation is fine and she can take as long as she needs to complete her degree. The synthesising question is often preceded by a summary. In this case, the therapist said, "If I get it right, you think that worrying serves a productive purpose: it prepares and it motivates. You have also told me that as a result of your worries and anxieties, your study time has decreased by at least 70%. You also mentioned that your worries about money have resulted in some irritations between you and your husband. How does all this information fit with your belief that worrying is productive?"

By asking questions like this, the client is invited to look at her experiences from a new perspective. Not a perspective imposed on the client by the therapist, but a perspective the client already had, but was not linking with other elements of her life.

Daily thought records

Many clients with psychological problems will put not being able to deal with strong negative feelings high on their list of problems that need resolving. Based on the premise that negative affect is strongly influenced by thinking, an essential intervention is the daily thought record (DTR). The CBT model assumes that irrational thoughts influence negative affect and that this negative affect can be instrumental in promoting maladaptive behaviours or blocking pro-social behaviours.

With the DTR, the client learns to change

- the unhelpful and irrational thinking into more helpful and rational thinking;

- the maladaptive self-defeating behaviour that supports this irrational thinking into more adaptive behaviour that supports the new helpful and rational thinking.

Working with the DTR assumes that three things are already in place:

- the client has been introduced to the CBT model of psychological problems and wants to give working in that model a chance;
- the therapist has explained the formulation to the client (explaining how the problems became established and how they are maintained);
- the client and the therapist have identified problems and goals to work on, and reduction of negative affect was one of the goals.

The DTR is introduced to the client as a skill that client can learn to reduce the impact of negative feelings and enable the client better to engage in desirable behaviours (Davidson, 2007). There are many variations of DTRs available in the literature. I particularly like the one presented here, which has been developed over the years. The good thing about it is that it can be explicitly taught to clients in three steps. In step 1, the client learns to describe the situations as they occur at the moment. In step 2, the client analyses the current situation, and in step 3, the client focuses on change.

Learning to carry out DTRs is only the start of the process. The more important task is to be able to access the rational thoughts the next time that the client is exposed to a similar situation.

DTRs' instructions

Step 1: That is how things are now!

- What is the situation?
  Here, the client is invited to record the situation he/she was in when the negative feelings were very strong. The client describes when, where, with whom, what they were doing, and any other relevant circumstances.
- How did you feel in that situation and how strong were the feelings on a scale of 0–100?

The client writes down the negative feelings experienced. It is very important to teach the client to write down feelings and not sensations, or words describing heightened arousal. Clients are also invited to record the strength of their feelings. So, *not* upset, uptight, stressed, *but* anxious, depressed, guilty.

- What do you do that really does not work to get over the problem? Here, the client writes down the behaviour he or she engages in as a result of the negative feelings (self-defeating behaviour). This is sometimes difficult, especially when the client does not seem to engage in any behaviour and abstains from pro-social behaviour.
- What are your thoughts in that situation, especially thoughts that promote the feelings under the second bullet point above?
  This is the real one! This is what it is all about. Here, the therapist needs to get the client to disclose their thinking. Often, crafty Socratic dialogue is necessary, as well as continually checking whether the thoughts match the emotions.
- How much do you believe these thoughts to be true: give each of the thoughts a rating from 0 (= not true at all) to 100 (= completely true).
- Each of the thoughts needs to be checked out with respect to how much the client believes the thought to be true in the specific situation. (As a flexibility of mind check, the therapist could ask the client how much they believe the thought while sitting in the consulting room of the therapist; if there is a discrepancy, this can be worked with.)

Step 2: your self-analysis of how things are

- Do you want to feel like this?
  This question is a motivation check. Sometimes clients are "attached" to their negative feelings and don't really feel motivated to give them up.
- How helpful is it to behave like this?
  Here, the therapist checks with the client what the pragmatic value is of the behaviour triggered by the emotions and thoughts.
- Now analyse your thoughts:
  Is this thought a fact or is it your opinion?

Does this thought help you feel the way you want to feel and behave the way you want to behave?
Is this thought an example of (1) demanding, (2) catastrophising, (3) low frustration tolerance, (4) self/other downing, or any of the other thinking errors (or you use another list of thinking errors).

Step 3: this is how I want things to be

Well, the situation is the same! Beware that the client does not put changes in the situation so that it becomes easier for her/him to deal with the situation.

- How would you like to feel in these situations?
  This is a very important question. Most clients want to go from a strong negative feeling (very depressed) to a strong positive feeling (very happy). The therapist needs to introduce a reality check here and explain that CBT is not a positive thinking movement. When you feel depressed and you have been feeling like this for many years, to expect that you will feel very happy in similar circumstances is several bridges too far. Here, we teach clients that to say that it smells like roses when "the shit hits the fan" is highly irrational. When the shit hits the fan, it stinks and that is unpleasant, but it is not terrible, it is not a catastrophe.
- How would you like to behave in these situations?
  Here, we ask the client how they would like to behave in the given situation. This might often be a bit of challenge, as the client might have reacted to these situations in this style for a very long time. As a result of that, they might not be able to imagine that they could react differently. The therapist needs to be guided by the formulation, but also common sense plays an important role. It is also the moment for the therapist to be open to the possibility that the client might need to acquire certain skills before they can embark on pro-social and adaptive behaviour.
- Are there alternative factual and helpful thoughts that "promote" how you would like to behave and would like to feel, but which go against the original negative automatic thoughts?
  For each of the unhelpful thoughts, the client and therapist need to compose a rational alternative. These rational alternatives need to

 - evaluate the badness of the actual situation;
 - be based on preferences;
 - focus on high frustration tolerance;
 - promote self/other acceptance as fallible human beings;
 - be believable by the client.
- How much do you believe these new thoughts 0–100.
  The client rates each of the new thoughts on the 0–100 scale.
- Go back to Step 2 and the original negative automatic thoughts. Check to what extent you still believe these and rate on a scale of 0–100.

Some further comments on getting the thoughts "right" and disputing irrational thinking

Here, the thought is written down. A word of warning about thoughts. Often clients disclose their thoughts to therapists in a sanitised way. The thought might have been: "Those bastards can drop dead, I hate them and will fucking destroy them", but the client might say to the therapist, "It is not very nice that they did that." It is very important to get the client's real thoughts included in the thought record. Another thought pitfall is when clients write down very moderate thoughts but, given their feelings, they should have had much stronger thoughts. Socratic dialogue to get the real thoughts is the name of the game.

Is this thought a fact or is it your opinion?

Here, client and therapist check whether the thought was based on facts; is it a factually true statement?

Does this thought help you feel the way you want to feel and behave the way you want to behave?

This focuses on the pragmatic value of the thought. Is the thought helpful in achieving our personal goals, in feeling better, or getting along better with people?

Which thinking errors do you recognise in this thought?

Here, client and therapist try to "label" the thought with a thinking error.

An example of a DTR

Step 1: That is how things are now!

What is the situation?
I (Claire) arrive at work in the morning and say "Good morning everybody" and Gavin, my boss, does not respond. He was in the office with four other people and no one responded.

How did you feel in that situation and how strong were the feelings on a scale of 0–100?
Extremely depressed.

What do you do that really does not work to get over the problem?
I went to my office, locked the door, and when no one came to check on me, I left work again after fifteen minutes. I called in sick from home and did not answer any of the phone calls from colleagues.

What are your thoughts in that situation, especially thoughts that promote the feelings identified above (please number these thoughts):

1. They are ignoring me again.
2. He is planning to get me fired; it is so unfair.
3. No one can be trusted; he is going to stab me in the back.
4. I can't stand being here any more.
5. They should not treat me so badly.

How much do you believe these thoughts to be true? Give each of the thoughts a rating from 0 (= not true at all) to 100 (= completely true).

They are ignoring me again.	100
He is planning to get me fired; it is so unfair.	90
No one can be trusted; he is going to stab me in the back.	90
I can't stand being here any more.	90
They should not treat me so badly.	90

Step 2: Your self-analysis of how things are

I (Claire) arrive at work in the morning and say "Good morning everybody" and Gavin, my boss, does not respond. He was in the office with four other people and no one responded.

Do you want to feel like this?
No, I don't want to feel like this!

How helpful is it to behave like this?
Not really helpful, walking away from the job and calling in sick for a week is not going to do my career prospects any good!

Now analyse your thoughts:

- Is this thought a fact or is it your opinion?
- Does this thought help you feel the way you want to feel and behave the way you want to behave?
- Is this thought an example of
  1. Demanding
  2. Catastrophising
  3. Low frustration tolerance
  4. Self/other downing
  5. Any of the other thinking errors . . .?

Thinking about your thinking

1. *They are ignoring me again.*

Is this thought a fact or is it your opinion?
Well, people were on the phone and busy; they probably did not notice me (as I did not exactly speak loudly when I said good morning). This is a belief, not a fact.

Does this thought help you feel the way you want to feel and behave the way you want to behave?
Not helpful, it made me very depressed.

Which thinking errors do you recognise in this thought?
Overgeneralising.

2. *He is planning to get me fired; it is so unfair.*
Is this thought a fact or is it your opinion?
I have no evidence that Gavin is planning to fire me. My last performance review was OK. This is an opinion.

Does this thought help you feel the way you want to feel and behave the way you want to behave?
Not helpful, makes me feel afraid and when I get afraid I get angry at the people who I think make me afraid!

Which thinking errors do you recognise in this thought?
Mind reading.

3. *No one can be trusted; he is going to stab me in the back.*

Is this thought a fact or is it your opinion?
Many people at work have been rather reliable and helpful. There have been people in the past who treated me badly, but I have no real evidence that any of my colleagues or Gavin is planning to do so! Opinion!

Does this thought help you feel the way you want to feel and behave the way you want to behave?
No, makes me depressed and filled with self-pity.
Overgeneralising, fortune-telling.

4. *I can't stand being here any more.*

Is this thought a fact or is it your opinion?
This is really an exaggeration. I found it unpleasant, but it was not intolerable.

Does this thought help you feel the way you want to feel and behave the way you want to behave?
Thoughts like this make me avoid important things.

Which thinking errors do you recognise in this thought?
An example of low frustration tolerance.

5. *They should not treat me so badly.*

Is this thought a fact or is it your opinion?
There is no law in the universe that dictates how people should or should not treat me. Opinion.

Does this thought help you feel the way you want to feel and behave the way you want to behave?
Depression and poor-me-ism!

Which thinking errors do you recognise in this thought?
Demanding thinking.

Step 3: This is how I want things to be

I (Claire) arrive at work in the morning and say 'Good morning everybody' and Gavin, my boss, does not respond. He was in the office with four other people and no one responded.

How would you like to feel in these situations?
Well, fact is I said "good morning" and people did not respond (because of my depression I did not notice the circumstances—people were on the phone or busy). So I would like to feel disappointed.

How would you like to behave in these situations?
I would want to stay at work and look closer at the situation. If I had done this in the situation we discussed I would have seen that people were rather busy and simply did not notice me coming in and saying "good morning". I could have repeated my good morning a lot louder!

Alternative factual and helpful thoughts that "promote" how you would like to behave and would like to feel? Put belief percentages in brackets after each new thought.

- *They are ignoring me again.* That they are not responding does not mean they are ignoring me. They are busy and probably did not hear me. (70)
- *He is planning to get me fired, it is so unfair.* My performance reviews were positive, there is no evidence that anyone wants me fired. (80)
- *No one can be trusted; he is going to stab me in the back.* No evidence that anyone is planning to stab me in the back, people have been kind and friendly. (80)
- *I can't stand being here any more.* Because of my irrational thinking, I feel uncomfortable, but that is not unbearable. (65)
- *They should not treat me so badly.* Apart from in my mind, there is no evidence of bad treatment. (70)

Go back to your original negative automatic thoughts, how much do you believe these thoughts now? Rate on a scale from 0–100.

- *They are ignoring me again.* (20)
- *He is planning to get me fired; it is so unfair.* (15)
- *No one can be trusted; he is going to stab me in the back.* (30)
- *I can't stand being here any more.* (30)
- *They should not treat me so badly.* (20)

Working with daily thought records (DTRs) should never become a form-filling exercise! DTRs work only when they are solidly based on good Socratic dialogue. When the therapist and client are too focused on the correct completion of the form, then CBT turns into a tick-box exercise. It is, therefore, important to ensure that the therapist really "gets" what the client finds upsetting in a given situation. Only when we understand how the client makes sense of a situation can we assist the client in interpreting the same situation in a more helpful way.

DTRs are also not one-off exercises. The aim is not to assist the client to think differently in this particular situation, but, rather, to introduce the client to a new way of dealing with upsetting moments: a more rational way. When the client's work with a DTR is properly supervised, most clients will learn to use this tool in three to five sessions. Some are much quicker and some are a lot slower.

The behaviour in DTRs

The question "How would you like to behave if the situation were to arise again?" can be met by clients with disbelief. They might say things such as, "Of course, I could ask for a day off, but the reaction of my boss would be terrible!", or "I would like to speak up for myself and disagree with them, but I would not know how to!" The therapist has uncovered a new roadblock to change in the client. Informed by the client's reaction to the idea of "new" behaviour, the therapist can suggest interventions to overcome this roadblock.

If the client's reaction is one of fear of predicted negative consequences, then a behavioural experiment is an option, while if the objections are based on not knowing how, then skills training is indicated. Sometimes, the predicted consequences are mildly negative, but, as a result of the client's lack of problem-solving skills, they become very negative. For instance, for Joanne, asking for a day off work so she could prepare for her house move became a big problem. She planned to move house in the busiest period of the accountancy firm she worked for, and her boss had said no to a previous request. Joanne interpreted this as a complete definitive veto on having time off to prepare for her house move. She could not resolve this problem, so we taught her the problem-solving process. This resulted in her wanting to ask for the help of an older colleague (how to do this required some skills training) and, accompanied by this colleague, she approached the boss again and explained her predicament (how to do this also needed some skills training). This resulted in the employer suggesting a specific day that she could take off, and also saying that if colleagues wanted to help her, they could leave work early on that day.

The DTR is really one of the centrepieces of working with clients with psychological problems since all cognitive, emotional, and behavioural problems will come to the fore in carefully done DTRs.

An example of an almost complete session focused on working with a thought record.

The client is forty-four years old and single. She (Louise) has been depressed all her adult life. When she is in a relationship, she feels good and can actually activate herself, but the minute that the relationship collapses, she feels that she has hit rock-bottom and is extremely handicapped. She struggles to get to work and certainly does not want to go out, and that is how she is feeling at the moment, very withdrawn. The excerpt starts after the agenda setting.

Therapist: So, we come to our session today and it's going to be quite active. What we agreed last time was that I would start showing you how to use this thinking record. It's a straightforward form that will help you to see the links between how you feel and think and how you end up behaving; it really helps to make sense of how it all comes together. Then, once we've done that, we'll be looking to change some of these thoughts that have got you into a depressed spin.

Client: I know that the thoughts just get me down and then they just go round and round and round, and that's the problem.

Therapist: So, these thoughts that go round and round in your head really bring you down. The beauty of actually writing things down is that you can start to address them. Without this, everyone gets caught up in thoughts of a worrying nature and of a really doom-like nature, and it's very hard to escape them, so what we know is that if we write them down, it actually helps us step back a bit from them, so that's what I'd like to do with you today. I asked you last week if you would think about something that happened that we could focus on today.

[Gentle introduction to the DTR and informing client about advantages of writing things down.]

Client: Yes, well, it actually happened at the weekend and it's quite a good example. I was asked out to this party and it just started again; I just couldn't go, I just couldn't face going, and I didn't go, I didn't actually go to the party. I just felt so bad, so bad.

Therapist: That sounds like a really good example.
[Reinforcing therapy supporting behaviour.]

Client: Is that a good example because this is what happens to me all the time?

Therapist: Yes.

Client: When I'm like this, I can't go out.

Therapist: So this negative feeling, what do you call that?
[So we have some information about the trigger (asked to go to a party) and we have information about self-defeating behaviour (not going), so the logical next step is affect!]

Client: I feel horrible.

Therapist: That kind of tells me about the strength of it in a way, but, if we think about it in emotional terms, is it anxiety?
[Without "correcting" the client, the therapist gets the client to state the relevant affect.]

Client: No, no. Low, very depressed, very miserable.

Therapist: Miserable and depressed, all right. Can you measure that in terms of numbers something out of ten, or would words work better for you?

Client: I'd say ten.

Therapist: Ten, the worst?

Client: Yes.

Therapist: I'm going to record that here. In this column where we record emotion, we want to know how bad you felt at the worst possible moment, so you reckon it's a ten for depression and miserable?

Client: I took to my bed.

Therapist: That actually moves us into the next column, and the heading is "Unhelpful behaviour". What it means is: did you do anything that didn't really help?

Client: Well, I didn't phone to say I wasn't going. I was just thinking about going and thinking about going, but I just couldn't face it, so I took to my bed.

Therapist: And, ordinarily, you're quite a sociable person, aren't you, so, if you want to be out socialising and you like to take up the opportunity to party, then going to bed, do you think that is very helpful, given that you're more than upset?

Client: I'm a failure.

Therapist: So you think that was unhelpful behaviour?

Client: Yes.

Therapist: Anything else? Did you do anything else that didn't really help your mood in the moment?

Client: Well, I kept thinking about what I was doing. I kept thinking I couldn't go and I kept thinking about not being able to go and I felt, "Here we go again. It's all happening again".

Therapist: So, in the first column we've got a heading, "Trigger", and very briefly we just need to write down a few words to capture what it was about and, if I paraphrase you, it would be being invited to a party.

Client: Yes, I had a call. What really sort of brought it to a head was a call, asking if I was going. A friend called to say, "Are you going?"

Therapist: OK, so "being asked if I was going"?

Client: Yes, to the party.

Therapist: What triggered the depression then, because that sounds like a fairly normal thing for a friend to do?

Client: Well, I think the friend knows I don't always go, so it was because I don't always go and she knows that, when I'm not feeling good, I don't go, so she was phoning to just see whether I was actually going because she, I think, guessed I might not go.

Therapist: And the act of telling her, "No, I'm not", how did that trigger the depression?

Client: Because it forced me to acknowledge how I felt then.

Therapist: So that would be interesting. Perhaps I can start trying to pick up on these thoughts. We call them "negative automatic thoughts" because they're like in a blink or in a heartbeat, and we're not often conscious of thinking them and that's why they're quite subtle and sometimes hard to pick up. Just putting yourself back in that Saturday evening moment, can you capture any of those thoughts for me?

Client: "I can't face it, I can't be with people, I can't talk to people".

Therapist: What is this, "I can't be with people, I can't talk to them"? It sounds very similar, but what's it based on?
[Gentle exploration of the client's thinking.]

Client: Well, I've got nothing to say, I'm not interesting. There might be someone new there, but I'm not going to be cheerful, boring to be with.

Therapist: Is that another way of saying, "I'm not interesting".

Client: I'm not interesting; I'm certainly not going to meet anyone because I feel so unattractive at the moment. No one's going to want to talk to me; no one's going to want to be with me. I just may as well stay at home and go to bed.

Therapist: That would be like your solution?

Client: Yes.

Therapist: "I just may as well stay at home and go to bed". That is not in itself a negative thought. I suspect there's a little bit more to it. It's like there's something behind, "I can't face it, I can't be with people", or is it just, "I've got nothing to say"?

Client: Well, you said, "I'm not interesting", and I think that's something, that I'm not a very interesting person. I think it's about—I feel unattractive and uninteresting. I think that probably would be—

Therapist: That's the nub of it?

Client: Yes, unattractive, uninteresting and, therefore, I'm dull and people will be bored and then I'll probably feel rejected.

Therapist: Do you think people would actually reject you, that they'd walk away after a minute or so?

Client: Because I'm boring. They don't want to be with me.

Therapist: "People would be bored and reject me"?
[Now we are getting to strong negative automatic thoughts.]

Client: Yes.

Therapist: So, this notion of not being able to face it, is it because then you'd be brought face-to-face, as it were, with the horrible truth about yourself?

Client: It's that, but also I don't have the energy to make the effort. It's the thinking. I just imagine that's what I'm going to think and then I just feel, "I can't be bothered. I just haven't got the energy even to get ready, even to try and make myself look reasonable. I just haven't got the energy".

Therapist: So, "I can't face it, I can't be with people, I'm not interesting, I'm unattractive, no one wants to talk to me, people will be bored and reject me, and I haven't got the energy". This is it in a nutshell?

Client: That sounds pretty much like me, pretty much.

Therapist: Again, it's a useful practice to measure how much you would have believed the thoughts at the time, so how strongly out of ten would you have believed, and I will run through them, "I can't face it"? [Further introducing the client to the DTR-model.]

Client: I suppose there's a little bit of me that knows that it's a bit silly, but on Saturday I felt 98–99 per cent. Today maybe, looking back, I would say 90.

Therapist: So, not as much. But that is still a lot.

Client: Weekends are hard. Weekends are bad.

Therapist: So, from the point of view of doing this for other issues, you want to measure your thoughts, how intensely you believed them at the time in the sort of heat of the moment, as it were.

Client: Won't that make me feel worse?

Therapist: Well, no. If you were doing the thought record there and then, like, if you had already had this skill on Saturday night and you decided to do a thought record on it, it would simply be accurately measuring how strongly you were telling yourself these thoughts, and that's important for us to know. We need to know how to challenge them, so partly we need to know how much you believed them at the time.

Client: So it's me taking the responsibility, me telling myself that I'm thinking this?

Therapist: Well, it's always *you* thinking your thoughts. It's just that most of the time we don't track our thinking, we don't pay much attention to the way we think, so this is rather an unusual activity for most of us. We're very aware of how we behave and we're usually very switched on to how we feel, emotionally and physically, but we don't really pay much attention to what we're saying to ourselves internally, what our thoughts are, so, when people feel very depressed, it's quite important to be able to recognise exactly what you're telling yourself and often what you will find is that there are patterns.

Client: Well, as you've said, they're automatic. For me, they're feeling automatic.

Therapist: Yes, they are automatic.

Client: I think it's just that they're there. I don't feel in control; they just come.

Therapist: One of the ways that you can break this automatic cycle is to actually be a little bit like a detached scientist and just observe them, so you record what you see, you record what you experience. In this case, when you're looking at your thoughts, yes, we want to know what you're saying to yourself and, yes, we want to know how much do you really feel at the time, so it's part and parcel of the business of being able to observe and record and then take another look at it. In the first instance, before we can even begin to think about changing anything, we need to know exactly what we're dealing with, so, one, the thought and, two, the intensity of it, how much it's got a grip on you.
[Kindly explaining the process.]

Client: It felt, just going through it, very real again, just thinking it through then.

Therapist: "I can't be with people", out of 100?

Client: Now or then?

Therapist: Then.

Client: Then, I'd say 90.

Therapist: "I'm not interesting"?

Client: 95.

Therapist: "I'm unattractive"?

Client: That's a biggie. I feel that's 100.

Therapist: "No one wants to talk to me"?

Client: 95.

Therapist: "People will be bored and reject me"?

Client: That's a biggie too. That's a 98–99.

Therapist: "I haven't got the energy". I'm actually wondering, and you kind of touched on it earlier, "I can't face it and I haven't got the energy", should we link those two together?

Client: Yes.

Therapist: OK, so previously you said 90-something.

Client: Because the energy's more of a feeling, I suppose. Is it more of a feeling?

[Now the therapist focuses on each thought and gets strength of belief ratings for all of them.]

Therapist: It's physical?

Client: It's just a physical feeling, just lethargy.

Therapist: So that would be 90-something?

Client: Yes.

Therapist: So it would make sense, wouldn't it, that, if anyone were experiencing these thoughts and believing them this strongly, they'd end up feeling really depressed and miserable, and how could they feel anything but?
[Re-affirming the CBT model of negative feelings.]

Client: That's me.

Therapist: But, you know, it would be anyone. If you sincerely believed these this strongly in the face of having a party invitation and, if you truly believed this, then you would be depressed and miserable, wouldn't you? There'd just be no other emotion.

Client: And no one would want to be with me.

Therapist: Well, if it was true, but here's the interesting thing about doing this cognitive work: one of the reasons we want people to look at the way they think is because thoughts are not necessarily facts. It sounds weird when you first hear it because most people just take their thoughts at face value and they think, "Well, if I thought it, then it must be true".
[Further explanation of the CBT/DTR model.]

Client: I can see a bit, that it's not as bad as that today, it's not as bad as it was then, but they're still there. That's still my thinking.

Therapist: That would be fair enough for them to be there because, you know what, you haven't done anything about them, and that's the thing with depression. If you don't learn to work with your thoughts, and there's a few key ways in which we teach people to work with their thoughts when they're depressed, if you don't develop these strategies, then they remain very powerful and they do interfere with mood, even though there are pleasant, good, sociable things that are happening, but the thoughts are very dominating and powerful. Therefore, in order to be able to work with your thoughts, we need, first of all, to see what we're working with, and it would apply to anyone. If you truly believe these thoughts, then you will end up being depressed.

Now, the next column is called "Disputing", and there are two steps here. The first is that we want to identify thinking errors. Now, do you remember during our assessment stage I gave you a couple of thinking error sheets, you know, descriptions of the sorts of distortions that people, all of us, readily get into?

Client: Yes.

Therapist: What we know about distortions is that they're always there when we're feeling particularly bad, when we're angry, when we're hurt, when we're feeling ashamed or guilty, and certainly when we're depressed. One of the first ways that we can step away from our thoughts and just see that there's a bit of a distortion going on there, and perhaps it's not the fact we thought it was, is to be able to identify these thinking errors that go with each thought.

The second task in the "disputing" column is that we want to ask three questions of each thought, and the three questions are, first: is it helpful? In other words, "Does thinking this thought, that I'm boring, does that help me feel more confident or happier?", and clearly not. In fact, what you'll notice is that none of the thoughts that are negative automatic thoughts ever makes us feel better, so they're always unhelpful. The second question is: "Is it logical?" which is another way of saying, "Does that make sense? Does that really stack up?" This one about "I'm unattractive", that you feel it, does that logically mean that it must be so? Beauty, as they say, is in the eye of the beholder, so you could look at each of these, and we will, and check them out for how logical they really seem, but, as I say, most of the time we don't examine our thinking, so we don't get round to any kind of analysis, which is what this is. Then, the last question, and it's the most interesting question of all, is: "Is it true?" Now, in order for a thought to qualify for being true, it has to be factual or reality-based, so the opposite of fact would be opinion, so something's either a fact or it's opinion, but what happens in normal conversation is that we normally run the two together. If we were friends and I said to you, "Have you met the new neighbour?" and you said no and I said, "Well, he's really lovely. He works at the university, he's got teenage kids himself actually and he's got the best sense of humour and, goodness, he's just quite a guy", can you see that I've run together a number of facts, but I've also put in a lot of opinions?

[Quite a lengthy explanation. This could have been split up in several shorter ones or the therapist could have asked the client to summarise and give feedback more frequently.]

Client: Well, your thoughts, your opinion.

Therapist: Exactly, they're my thoughts and, if you trust me and like me, you'll give my opinion the same kind of credibility as the factual bits.

Client: Yes, I can see that.

Therapist: And that's what we do in our own minds; we run together thoughts and opinions very easily and we just assume that whatever we think is truthful, that it's real, it's factual.

Client: So I'm affecting how I'm thinking?

Therapist: Yes. The other way of looking at determining if a thought or an idea is true or not is reality versus idealism. Now, this is a slightly trickier one to understand, but I think I can best explain it to you if I give you an example. I was working once many years ago with a man who was angry and he was angry because his daughter had done something he didn't like (she'd lied to him), and his thought was, "She shouldn't have done it", and I said, "Well, is that true?" He said, "Of course it's true". I said, "Well, tell me why it's true". He said, "Well, first of all, we're a very religious family and we go to the synagogue every day. We're big on the Ten Commandments, honour thy father and mother and do not lie". I said, "Well, you, you know, you've given me all the reasons for why it would be ideal, but the reality is that teenage children do lie and that you don't like it doesn't make it less real". It's like, if we've got a planned picnic and we notice it's raining, we don't say, "Hey, that shouldn't happen"; we just accept it is and then we move on to Plan B. One way of determining whether a thought's truthful or not is sometimes we can use this: is it reality-based or idealism?

Client: So I'm making demands? Am I making demands?

Therapist: Good question, if you look back at your own thinking, what do you think?

Client: Well, I'm thinking that I'm demanding, "I must be attractive".

Therapist: Yes, that's a good point because sometimes demands are hidden. You know, if we know someone really well, we don't always speak grammatically correct sentences, and it's the same with our thoughts. We think half the thought, so, "I'm unattractive", now that could be an example of a hidden demand, and, "I should look better than

I do" or, let me just point out, actually it could be an example of "catastrophising": "I'm unattractive and that's terrible".

Client: I think it's both.

Therapist: It could be.

Client: I'm thinking with this one too with your saying that I think I'm demanding, "I should be interesting, I've got to be interesting, but I'm not".

Therapist: So, we've got a couple of more subtle demands here, because that's the thing—

Client: But I'm doing that catastrophising too; I can see them both.

Therapist: So here's what we need to do: we need to identify the thinking errors and we also need to quickly ask, "All the thoughts that I've got here, are they now no longer helpful? Are they logical and are they true?" That then gives us a chance to step back and be looking at the thoughts in an intellectual sort of way, and then we're in a position to move on to the next step, which is to see if we can change some of the thoughts. OK? Is that making sense so far?

Client: Yes.

Therapist: So, "I can't face it, I haven't got the energy", what do you think that would be an example of? What kind of thinking error would that be?

Client: Black.

Therapist: It's very negative, isn't it?

Client: Yes.

Therapist: So we simply label it and we put against that "very negative". The second one, "I can't be with people"?

Client: I was going to say, yes, it's like, "I can't be with people because I'm not interesting or attractive enough".

Therapist: So three thoughts actually turn into one.
[This is a good example of the therapist making the DTR more manageable. The reduction of the number of thoughts, if done well, is really helpful.]

Client: Yes, correct.

Therapist: So it's easy, it isn't it? "I'm not interesting and I'm not attractive", what would you call that? Do you want a moment to think or should I help you?

Client: Well, other than being negative?

Therapist: There are two other words that fit more accurately, and I will run them by you and see what you think. It's either very critical or very judgemental.

Client: Isn't it both?

Therapist: I think both words work, but choose whichever word you think.

Client: "Critical", I think, has got more—

Therapist: Yes, you recognise that it's very self-critical. "No one wants to talk to me", is that linked into—

Client: Because I'm not interesting.

Therapist: OK.

Client: No one wants to be with me because I'm not interesting.

Therapist: Should we scrub this out? Is it, "No one wants to talk to me because people will be bored"?

Client: They're bored because I'm not interesting enough.

Therapist: OK, so bored is a consequence of not interesting? OK, that's a separate one.

Client: They'll be bored.

Therapist: "They'll be bored and they will want to reject me". "No one wants to talk to me", shall we treat that as a separate one, a separate thought?

Client: I think that's because I'm not interesting too.

[This kind of discussion with the client about her thoughts increases both therapist and client's insight into her inner world.]

Therapist: In itself, there's a separate error here. Now, if you look at the tense of it, is it past, present or future?

Client: Present. No, I'm predicting, I'm predicting.

Therapist: So, very simply, we call it "a negative prediction"?

Client: Yes, I'm predicting that they won't want to talk to me.

Therapist: Likewise, "People will be bored and will reject me"?

Client: It's the same, isn't it?

Therapist: Exactly the same. Now, we might think of it as negative or we might think of it as catastrophic, but it's just a matter of degree: how hard does it hit you?

Client: Or jumping to conclusions.

Therapist: Exactly. The jump to conclusions is the same. In fact, if you look at Burns' list, he calls it "jumping to conclusions" and, if you look at the other list, and I've forgotten who authored it, but I think it's from REBT, it's the same thing, it's just different words. "Jumping to conclusions" is another way of saying "making a prediction". So is it really negative, and I'm asking you about degree here? Is it a negative prediction or is it a catastrophic prediction? How bad would it be if you're right?

Client: I think when I feel that low, it's not so much, I don't catastrophise, I just feel horrible.

Therapist: OK, let's leave it as a negative prediction then.

Client: I feel it's just negative, very negative rather than . . .

Therapist: OK, let's do the second part of disputing, which is asking: are other thoughts logical? If we take number one, which is, "I can't be with people because I'm not interesting and I'm unattractive", is there any logic to that?

Client: It feels like it at the time.

Therapist: That's interesting, because that highlights another error, which is what we call "emotional reasoning": because it feels like it, it is.

Client: I know.

Therapist: A bit like the agoraphobic in the supermarket: because it feels scary, then there's something truly to be scared of. You and I know that's not the case, but they feel scared, there's no doubting that. So, this not being logical, we would say, "This isn't logical because actually it's based on an emotional reasoning".

Client: And I know that because I know, when I feel better, I know I can face it, I know I can be with people.

Therapist: So this is not logical then?

Client: At the time, it feels it, but—

Therapist: Yes, at the time, but, now that you're a couple of days away from the weekend and you're looking at it in a slightly more detached way, the logic doesn't hold up, does it? And is it true? Is this a fact or is this your opinion?

Client: It's my opinion.

[This is a very important part; here the therapist "forces" the client to hold on to the reality: that it feels like something does not make it real.]

Therapist: No other predictions that no one would want to talk to you and people would be bored and reject you?

Client: People try, I know people try, so—

Therapist: To engage with you?

Client: Yes.

Therapist: OK, so there's no logic there.

Client: I know that I run away from it. I know people do try.

Therapist: So I guess that's not logical or true?

Client: Yes.

Therapist: OK, well done. We can see then that these thoughts aren't as valid as you first thought and there is distortion in them and none of them is true, none of them is helpful, so now we want to come up with the next column, which is, "Creating more rational thoughts, rational alternatives". Now, it's quite important that we don't get muddled up with being positive, because positive is really great for salespeople, but it's not good for depression, so we want something that's rational, pragmatic and, above all, believable, so we want to come up with alternatives for the main thoughts that we've identified here. Now, is there one in particular, because we don't have to work with them in the order they are here, so is there one in particular that you want to go with first?

Client: I know that I can't be with people.

Therapist: "Because I'm uninteresting and I'm unattractive"?

Client: I think, logically I know I can be with people, but I still feel that I'm not interesting and unattractive.

Therapist: OK, let's work with that then.

Client: Because I do go to work.

Therapist: And what happens at work?

Client: I get on with my work and I'm with people, so I know that I can be with people, but it's the party that's a problem.

Therapist: The social circle, the socialising?

Client: Yes.

Therapist: Well, what would be a more helpful thing to say because, clearly, repeating this message drives your mood down and gets you into quite a miserable spin? What would be something more realistic to say? Any thoughts off the top of your head?
[Moving the client on to formulating a more rational alternative.]

Client: I can be with people, but I don't feel good about myself.

Therapist: Now, here's the thing: "I can be with people" on its own just sounds positive, so on its own we can't write that down. Also, it's the opposite of "I can't be with people", so you don't actually want to write down anything that's the dead opposite of your negative automatic thought because it'll just end up that it is, it isn't, it is, it isn't and, the next time you're in a similar situation, you could simply not believe it because it won't be strong enough. So, if you want to start here or include this belief that "I can be with people", we need to back it up and we need to put some context round it. Now, something that's useful to begin with sometimes is putting in context this bunch of thoughts and feeling like this and to be able to say to yourself, "These negative automatic thoughts are a part of my illness/depression" as opposed to, if you like, the thinking of symptoms of depression as opposed to facts about you.
[Very educational and important to do when doing a first DTR.]

Client: OK, so I can say, "Because I'm depressed, I'm feeling unattractive and uninteresting"?

Therapist: And what are you going to say about that?

Client: When I feel better . . ..

Therapist: No, no.

Client: No?

Therapist: Sorry, I want you to stick with it, feeling unattractive, and what was the other word?

Client: Uninteresting.

Therapist: What comment would you make about that?

Client: That it's not helpful.

Therapist: Definitely that. One thought that occurs to me is that this is often best described as a habit; just it's a thinking habit.

Client: Very much so.

Therapist: So would it be helpful and give some context to it to say, "This is just a thinking habit that goes with depression"?

Client: Yes.

Therapist: Because, although I know you know this, it actually helps to state the obvious because, when you're depressed and on your own, you can't work this out. This is just a, what, unhelpful, negative thinking habit?

Client: A pattern.

Therapist: That's better.

Client: An unhelpful pattern that I get stuck in, which is true.

Therapist: You recognise that?

Client: It's very true, yes.

Therapist: So our alternative to "I can't face it, I can't be with people, I'm uninteresting, I'm unattractive", our alternative to it is, "I can be with people and it's because I'm depressed that I'm feeling unattractive and uninteresting, and this is just an unhelpful pattern I get stuck in".

Client: Yes.

Therapist: That would seem like a reasonable alternative?

Client: Yes.

Therapist: How much would you believe it?

Client: I believe that, I believe that, but the problem is I get stuck, but I do believe that.

Therapist: Sometimes it's helpful to do two ratings here. One is, what I'd call, an "intellectual" or a "head rating", and the other is a "gut rating", so the head rating, the intellectual rating's always higher, so it sounds like you believe it quite easily and that would be your head rating of 90-something or 90?

Client: Yes.

Therapist: OK, so that would be your intellectual rating, 90. What, do you think, would your gut rating be?

Client: Less, a bit less.

Therapist: Usually, it is less. As much as you know it's true intellectually, it just somehow doesn't sit well, as easily and as comfortably.

Client: Fifty per cent.

Therapist: OK. This is all we've got time for this afternoon, but do you have a sense of flow?

Client: Yes.

Therapist: That we started with the problem, and the problem was how awful you felt, feeling depressed and miserable, we identified the situation and it was your friend ringing and asking if you were going because she knew you often didn't. Then, we looked at what you did that didn't help, that you went to bed. Then, we managed to pick all the thoughts that you were having, which clearly fuelled this miserable state, and then we started looking intellectually at what's wrong with these thoughts, what are the distortions, and we asked these questions: is it helpful and is it real; is it truthful and is it logical? Then, we began to pull together an alternative way of thinking about still the same content, but just getting it in a different context and something that's more helpful to you.

Client: Yes, and I can see that. I can really see that's what happens.

Therapist: Any questions about that?

Client: No, no.

Therapist: And it flows?

Client: It does, and that certainly makes more sense. Thank you.

It is not straightforward! Don't expect this process of cognitive restructuring to be smooth sailing. Many thought records and many repetitions of challenging and disputing the same thoughts and beliefs might be necessary. It is worthwhile to iterate that the aim of doing thought records is, of course, to bring relief in current problem situations of the client. However, more importantly, the aim is for the client to learn to use thought records in future difficult situations.

Sometimes disputing seems not to work! The therapist and client review the client's negative automatic thoughts and both agree that they are not helpful and not based on facts, and subsequently the client surprises the therapist by stating that they still believe it is true and the negative emotions have not shifted at all.

More often than not, when this is the case, it is not a question of the disputing does not work, but that the work of disputing has not been done. This is one of the moments when haste is always bad. Quietly reviewing clients' thinking against true, logical, and helpful parameters cannot be hastened, especially if we want to educate clients so that they can do this process by themselves in the future.

Accessing the new rational thoughts

Learning to recognise irrational thinking and replace it with more rational thinking during therapy sessions is only the first step. In the actual situation that triggered the strong negative feelings and/or maladaptive behaviours, it will be much more difficult to apply this new skill. This is the moment when the DTR work is tested. We use the following methods to prepare the client for this.

Repetition

When we have identified the new rational thoughts and the client believes them to be true for more than 50% of the time, then we can ask the client to put these new rational thoughts on small cue cards and carry these cards with them at all times. Then we would ask the client to read the new rational thoughts before any ordinary activity they do with a high frequency. Before having a cup of tea/coffee; before getting in the car, before going into a meeting, before starting to answer the next e-mail. This is based on the Premack principle (Premack, 1959). High frequency behaviours act as reinforcements for low frequency behaviours. And, as we all know, reinforced behaviours are more likely to occur.

The client can give this repetition a bit more spice and also involve other parts of the brain, not just the rational—frontal cortex—thinking part of the brain, by practising saying the rational thoughts out loud with various emotional intonations with accompanying facial expressions. This ensures that the new rational thoughts also create links with emotional parts of the brain and emotional states. It will be helpful to practise this in the sessions and it might be necessary for the therapist to model the various expressions.

Externalising of dialogue

The internal debate between "irrational" and "rational" thinking is externalised here. The best way to start this process is again to put the rational thoughts on a cue card and then client and therapist conduct a role-play. This can be done in two ways. The client can play both roles, rational and irrational thoughts, or the therapist plays the role of the client's irrational thinking while the client holds the fort for the rational perspective. The therapist needs to keep a careful eye on the client's reactions and stop the role-play if the client starts to waver, for example, the rational thoughts crumble. When this happens, stop the role-play and go back to the drawing board: find more, better rational alternatives. A good starting point for these exercises is for the client to start by describing what actually happened.

Preparation is crucial here. The client and therapist need to have established a library of rational counters for the client to use and they need to be visible to the client. When the client plays both roles, it is best that the client uses different chairs for each perspective, so we have a rational and an irrational chair.

Here is the "externalising of dialogue" Claire did with her therapist.

> *Claire*: I arrived at work, as per usual, around 8.30 a.m. and walked into the open plan office and said "Good morning". Sally and Peter were standing at the coffee machine and said "Good morning, Claire!" The others (Jack, Allan, Moira, and Gavin) did not respond to my good morning.
>
> *Therapist*: But that is just horrible, they deliberately ignored you, the bastards!
>
> *Claire*: Well, you could be over-generalising there; it is true they did not greet me, but they were all on the phone and Gavin was also being talked to by his PA.
>
> *Therapist*: But still, when someone says good morning and colleagues and the boss don't respond, that must be a sign that they are planning something behind your back. You are probably going to get fired. How can you accept being treated so unjustly!
>
> *Claire*: Mind-reading and fortune-telling, that is what you are doing. I don't have any evidence to support the idea that I will get fired or that people are planning something behind my back. Everyone has been friendly and my performance reviews with Gavin have been OK to very good.
>
> *Therapist*: But people stab you in the back when you least expect it.
> [The therapist really tries all the "dirty" debating tricks to unsettle the client's rational resolve (because that is what client's own mind will do).

Yesterday-ing

The song "Yesterday", made famous by the Beatles, is a song that is suited for this process *par excellence*! Here, therapist and client, or the client alone, change the text of the new-found rational thoughts into a song. The original text is replaced by a text describing how to go from the irrational thoughts to the rational thoughts. If the song is chosen wisely, for example, a song that the client really likes and can remember easily, then doing this will be of invaluable assistance in helping the client recall the rational thoughts at crucial emotional moments.

The client can actually sing the song, in private, in public, or record it and bring it to the session. The aim is to anchor the new rational thoughts in the client's brain so they can be reproduced when needed.

Negative automatic thoughts and beliefs

There are no clinical trials supporting the idea that for certain psychological problems it is imperative that interventions are focused on changing beliefs or core beliefs. Maladaptive schemas, or core beliefs, might be influential in causing and maintaining problems, but this should be demonstrated through the assessment and therapeutic work. In other words, when we work with thought records to help the clients bring about change in their lives and we notice that certain negative automatic thoughts are frequently returning, or we find that there is a commonality in all the cognitions we elicit in the situations we review, then we can hypothesise that there is an underlying belief or core belief at work. This belief might need to be addressed directly when working with thought records produces insufficient change, despite covering the skills deficit issue.

First, the underlying belief needs to be identified. This can be done by using the thought record and adopting the "downward arrow technique". When using this technique, the therapist acts like a very curious bystander who really wants to know how the client's brain operates, by constantly asking for the meaning if a certain event were to happen.

- If they were to reject you, what would that mean for you?
- If she were to say no, what would that mean to you?
- Why is making a mistake so bad?
- What is so bad about being disapproved of?

Doing this persistently will lead to the client's beliefs, core beliefs, and/or rules for living. Once this has been "found", or established as being instrumental in the client's problems, the following steps need to be taken to help the client work towards a different, more adaptive belief, core belief, or rule for living:

- historical perspective;
- pragmatic perspective;
- rational perspective;
- behaviour supporting the rational perspective.

Belief change and a historical perspective

The aim of this step is to assist the client in understanding how he/she learnt these beliefs or rules for living. Questions to ask are: how did you learn . . .; how did you come to believe . . .; who taught you . . . As homework, the client can be asked to put in a timeline how this belief has influenced their life. Get the client to answer questions such as: Which good and which less good things have happened to you as a result of adopting this belief/rule for living?

The aim is for the client and the therapist to understand that these beliefs do not drop out of the sky, but that there is a reason for developing these beliefs: either life's experiences, or modelling from parents.

This step is complete when the client can complete the following sentence (or one similar): "No wonder I developed the belief that XXX, because YYY happened to me, and believing XXX seemed to be a logical option, given my life's experiences after that and my current circumstances, ZZZ seems to be more realistic belief".

Pragmatic perspective

Here, client and therapist check out how useful adhering to the belief/rule is *now*. This can be done in the session by checking the advantages and disadvantages of the current belief/rule for living. The aim here is to help the client to come to the conclusion that although this belief might feel familiar, it is not a belief that is advantageous to keep adhering to. The end-point is when the client sees more disadvantages in adhering to the belief than advantages.

Rational perspective

Here, client and therapist try to formulate an alternative to the original maladaptive belief or rule for living. Adaptive beliefs need to be based on reality, helpful for goal achievement to the client, and believable to the client, just like alternative thoughts in the DTR. Similar strategies as we discussed for confirming rational thoughts in the client's mind can be used for beliefs: repetition, externalising of dialogues, and "yesterday-ing"

Behavioural experiments

How to conduct behavioural experiments has been very well described (Bennett-Levy, 2006). Behavioural experiments are aimed at testing the client's hypothesised outcome of engaging in certain behaviours:

- "If I speak up for myself I will be mercilessly criticised."
- "If I say no, they will all reject me."
- "If I apologise, they will humiliate me."

A behavioural experiment is warranted when a client is confronted with beliefs that they *have* to behave in a certain way or else . . . Sometimes, the "or else" is so toxic for the client that this needs to be addressed in a gradual manner. The gradual approach could mean that the therapist demonstrates the behaviour and the client and therapist evaluate if the predictions come true. At other times, it might be that the client can do the experiments, but the situations are staged in increasing difficulty.

Socratic dialogue and having completed one or more DTRs often precede behavioural experiments. The core of a behavioural experiment is that the client will engage in behaviours that they previously had not engaged in, and this non-engagement was based on specific predictions of what would happen if one were to engage in these behaviours. So, specific prediction of what could happen and what each course of action means for the beliefs is essential.

The client and therapist prepare carefully what behaviour the client will engage in, and work at making the client's prediction as specific as possible (e.g., what exactly will people do to humiliate you?). The client then executes the experiment and the results are followed by an evaluation between client and therapist. The focus in this evaluation is whether the hypothesised outcome happened. There are a few "specials" to which the therapist might need to pay attention.

- Beware of skills deficits in executing the behaviours. It might be prudent to role-play situations before asking the client to test things outside the therapy session. It would not be the first time that what a client considers to be an assertive request is, in fact, a very submissive way of begging.
- Beware of catastrophic misinterpretations by the client. The client might interpret a polite refusal as a massive rejection. The therapist can prevent this from happening by investigating in detail the predictions of the client.
- Beware of "yes, but . . ." from the client. Here, the client does not really go along with your reasoning and you might need to review his/her "but" with a DTR.

Examples of behavioural experiments

Claire: *"I will be rejected."*
Based on the discussions with the therapist and reviewing several DTRs, it seemed that Claire avoids any friendly contact with co-workers because she believes that she will be rejected by them because they all know that she will be fired soon, and, therefore, that there is no point in investing in collegial relationships. The experiment involved joining a group of co-workers at least twice a day for a week and engaging in small talk (this was practised in the session). During this practice, therapist and client discovered two things: Claire was not good at small talk and she misinterpreted other people responses. For instance, when a colleague said, "OK, time to get back to work", at the end of a coffee-break, she would interpret that as a personal rejection and not as the normal finishing line of a conversation. Some training and psycho-education was required before embarking on the experiment. "Being rejected" was also very clearly defined as: "Not responding at all to Claire's verbal prompts, no eye contact, and walking away mid-sentence". In the reviewing of the behavioural experiments, the responses of the colleagues were a mixed bag: some colleagues were not very good with eye contact, but were quite chatty,

others were not chatty but made eye contact, while no one walked away in mid-sentence. Doing the behavioural experiment significantly reduced Claire's belief in the idea that she was being rejected as a precursor of a redundancy.

Louise: *"I will be rejected."*
Louise also fears rejection, because she believes she is boring and uninteresting. She predicts that people will walk away from her at a party; no one will speak to her and she will spend the whole evening on her own. When reviewing her experiences at parties and social gatherings, it became clear that Louise has a habit of "waiting to be spoken to" and, when spoken to, "waiting for the other person to walk away from her"; that is, she does not initiate any conversation and when people speak to her, her answers are monosyllabic, as she expects that whatever she says will be regarded as boring. She has created her own self-fulfilling prophecy. As in the case of Claire, the experiment for Louise was to engage in unusual behaviour: first of all, go to a party and, instead of "waiting", she would actively approach people with questions such as: "Hello, how are you, how do you know X (the organiser of the party)", and other conversation openers. This was role-played with the therapist before she did the experiment (the agreement was to attend four social functions and observe people's reactions to her new behaviour). She soon found that people would also ask her questions and were genuinely interested in what she did.

Behavioural experiments should not be thrown at clients when the therapist finds the going difficult, as they require careful preparation.

It is sometimes postulated that that it is necessary to aim for schema change or core belief change in order for CBT to be effective. I have, however, found no clinical trials supporting this statement.

CHAPTER SEVEN

Cognitive behaviour therapy methods for modifying emotion-driven behaviours

Emotion driven behaviours

What are emotion-driven behaviours (EDBs)? EDBs are behaviours that result in the short term removal or reduction of unwanted negative feelings. It concerns behaviours that are "triggered" by negative feelings and are instrumental in suppressing, reducing, or removing these feelings (even if it only works for a short time).

Behaviours deployed to eliminate, avoid, or reduce negative affect are subsequently negatively reinforced if they produce the desired result, however fleetingly. The negative reinforcement keeps these behaviours going, notwithstanding the client's knowledge that these behaviours are self-defeating; that is, they produce only temporary results and sometimes lead to negative consequences.

This seems like an easy to follow idea: the client experiences negative feelings and subsequently does something that is not helpful, so let's change the unhelpful behaviours to more helpful behaviours. Sometimes, it is that simple, but at other times it is far more complicated.

Some examples

Ann being grumpy and snappy with her children and her husband

This is an example of a complicated EDB. What Ann reports is feeling and acting grumpy, snappy, and irritable with her husband. On the surface, this looks like (and is) an uncomplicated EDB: she experiences irritation and instead of using effective communication skills, she starts to accuse, shout, and gets herself into a real state of anger. However, her irritation is the result of other EDBs. She feels guilty (as a result of her high standards) and, as a result of that, *overworks*, with no time for herself. The guilt feelings also *stop her from making reasonable requests* of the children and her husband for help. The overworking results in an ongoing heightened state of arousal (making anger more likely), and the lack of expressing her needs results in her needs hardly ever being met (because others do not know what her needs are). So, what we have is a chain that starts with a normal trigger (the normal range of activities to do in a household with two children). Ann's high and unrelenting standards lead to feelings of guilt, which lead to EDBs (1) overworking and (2) not making reasonable requests. These EDBs result in feeling hyper-stressed and disgruntled which results in another EDB (3), angry outbursts to husband and children.

Drinking helps me relax

John tells us that he does not have a drinking problem; he just has the odd drink to help him unwind. After having monitored his alcohol intake, John is shocked to find out that he drinks around eighty standard alcohol units per week. This is four times the recommended limit. John says he cannot understand it, because he is not an unhappy person; he does not feel overly stressed. So what is going on here? When we analyse some of John's drinking moments in detail, the following picture emerges. The following scenario occurs regularly when John has had a good day at work and he feels pleased with this. This positive feeling unravels quickly and some worrying thoughts pop into his mind ("what if X should happen"), these worrying thoughts make him anxious and the anxiety makes him do two things: he stays in the bar/pub because he does not want to take his anxiety home with him, and he drinks more. Of course, consuming alcohol has only a very brief anxiety-reducing effect and the whole exercise needs to be repeated several times. When John has had a bad day, the first step, feeling pleased is skipped. Here we have three EDBs: (1) feeling pleased leads to worrying and thinking in worst-case scenarios; (2) anxiety leads to a reduction in communication or avoidance of communication with his partner; and (3) drinking more alcohol.

The following interventions are helpful in assisting clients to break away from the tyranny of EDBs.

- Increasing awareness of EDB activation: self-monitoring of behaviours in their internal (emotions and cognitions) and external contexts.
- Exposure and response prevention: learning to tolerate the presence of the emotion, while *not* engaging in the behaviour.
- Skills training (e.g., acquiring and using new skills that are incompatible with the EDB): communication skills and problem-solving skills.
- Self-management training: bringing the behaviour back under personal control.

Increasing awareness of EDB

Knowledge precedes any successful attempt at change. Clients need to develop an understanding of how specific feelings trigger certain maladaptive behaviours. The fact that it is the client who experiences this, and has been experiencing this for a while, does not mean that he or she is fully aware of the connection.

Increasing client awareness of EDBs follows, essentially in two steps. Step one is "in-session" reviews of problematic moments, and step two is the careful monitoring by the client of problem moments and their internal (emotions and cognitions) and external contexts. When interviewing clients, the focus of the interview is often a client's complaint or primary symptom ("I feel anxious", or "I am depressed", or "I never speak up for myself"). By discussing a specific occurrence of this ("It would be really helpful to focus on a moment last week when you felt very anxious/very depressed", or, in the case of not speaking up, "When during the last week would you have wanted to speak up for yourself, but didn't?") the therapist really focuses the mind of the client. The therapist needs to think SORCC and BASIC-ID while doing this.

Figure 7.1 might be helpful in this respect.

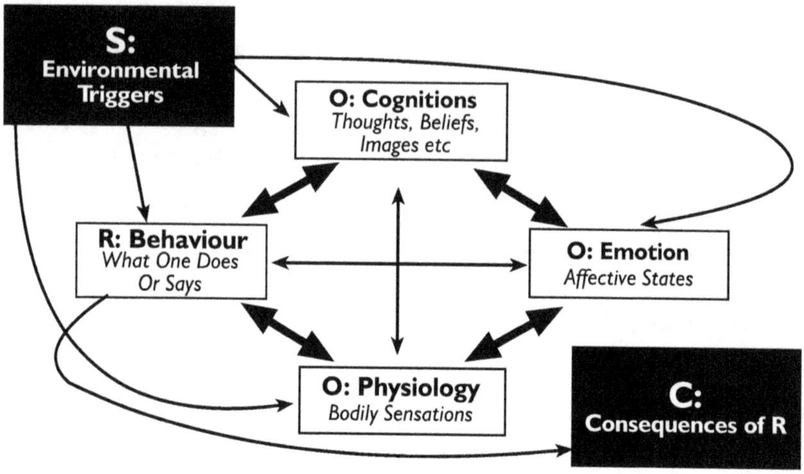

Figure 7.1. The sequence of events in emotion-driven behaviour.

The client will present as *the* problem issue either the emotion or the behaviour. The first step is to learn more about the behaviour (I am feeling anxious. → What do you do when feeling anxious?) or the emotion (I never go out any more. → When you want to go out and don't, which feeling stops you?). The next step is to explore the impact the behaviour has on the client with respect to the negative feelings that were being experienced (and any other desired or undesired effects). For instance, not going out might result in a reduction of anxiety, to be followed by an increase in irritation and anger with one's self for having given up again. Both client and therapist will gradually develop the insight that the behaviours create reinforcement (negative reinforcement, mostly in the form of a brief reduction of the negative emotion) that keeps this problem behaviour going. It is also important to explore how the client responds internally to the external trigger/situation that starts the process. There are three ways here in which antecedent cognitive appraisal can play a pivotal role: (1) the meaning the client gives to the situation, (2) the meaning the client gives to experiencing this specific emotion, and (3) positive connotations are connected to the EDB and negative connotations are connected with most other behaviours.

Sometimes, clients report that experiencing a specific emotion "means" that they "have to" walk away, stay in bed, explode, that there is real danger ("I feel anxious, therefore something dangerous must be happening"). The meaning-giving process is almost a behavioural instruction, telling the client what to do, and in doing so blocks pro-social and adaptive behaviours.

The meaning-giving process regarding the possible and potential behaviours in the given situation is also important as guidance for the client. For a client who is angry, the only behaviour that is positively evaluated might be strong aggressive behaviour towards the person he/she perceives as being the cause of the anger. All other behaviours might be negatively evaluated ("If you don't show them who is boss, they will think you are weak"). It might, therefore, be necessary to combine EDB-focused interventions and cognitive interventions focused on changing antecedent cognitive appraisal.

In exploring situations in which the client experienced strong negative feelings, or behaved in a way they did not want to behave, or did not behave in a way they really would like to behave, the focus needs to be on uncovering maintenance cycle issues: how does reinforcement play a role here, and which skills need to be learnt to break the maintenance cycle? Detailed questioning about what happened, what the client experienced, how the client decided to engage in certain behaviours, and what was the result of these behaviours is key. The parameters of this questioning are guided by the BASIC-ID: which behaviours, which affect, which sensations, which interpersonal events, which cognitions, which images, and which drug and alcohol use were the trigger or the consequence of the sequence.

Let's review an example (Figure 7.2).

The client is depressed and suffers from sleeping problems. Each day he works until he is so exhausted that he keeps making mistakes, but up until that point he cannot stop for fear that he has not done enough or has not done it well enough. The client is terrified of making mistakes and of being seen as not working hard enough. Therefore, he needs to learn to tolerate making mistakes and learn the cognitive and communication skills that will enable him to deal with criticism from others.

Exposure and response prevention: learning to tolerate the presence of the emotion, while not engaging in the behaviour

Exposure and response prevention is the best strategy to use for strong negative feelings resulting in persistent avoidance of the

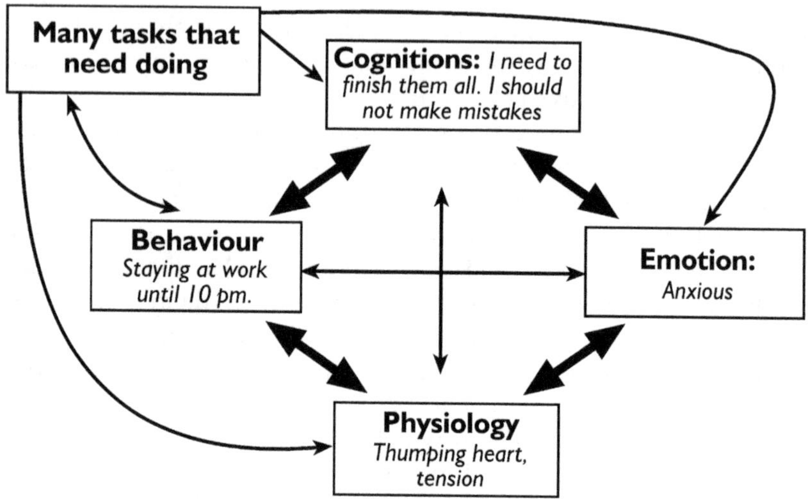

Figure 7.2. An example of EDB: overworking as a result of perfectionism.

stimulus that triggers such a feeling. It simply means that the client stays in the presence of the stimulus until the negative feeling is reduced to a level that it no longer interferes with daily functioning. Experiencing a strong negative feeling, staying with the stimulus causing this feeling, *and* not doing the things one usually does to reduce the feeling sounds very counter-intuitive. It is, therefore, not surprising that many clients need a careful explanation of the reasons for such an intervention.

Here is an explanation that I often use. The specific example is of a client with panic attack problems.

"We have investigated what happens when you feel anxious. Your anxiety is triggered by bodily sensations that are, in fact, normal (heart rate, sweating, lump in throat) for people becoming anxious. You know now that they are not signs of impending doom, but when you are out and about and these things happen, the anxiety still hits you like a gale-force wind. You react to this by doing things that reduce the anxiety briefly (sitting down, stopping any physical exercise, holding on to things). In CBT, we call these behaviours safety behaviours, and they can be quite annoying and cause interference with leading a fulfilling life. What you do, by behaving in this way, is confirm to your brain that something really dangerous is happening, so that your brain does not learn that these physical sensations are, in fact, completely innocent signs of anxiety. So, what do we do when someone's life is ruined by a fear of dogs? Well, they need to learn to play with a dog! We need to experience the anxiety, triggered by the things we fear, and allow ourselves to be anxious while not making any attempts to reduce the anxiety. What will happen is that gradually the anxiety will disappear. Mostly, we do this in a gradual manner, starting with triggers that cause lower levels of anxiety and gradually moving to situations that trigger high levels of anxiety. So, in order to overcome your anxiety problem, you have to learn to experience anxiety and not react to it in your usual way."

Before the actual exposure can start, the client and therapist need to explore the full extent of the client's safety behaviours. Discussions with the client and self-monitoring of problem situations will be helpful here. Both client and therapist also need to decide on how to execute the exposure.

Flooding or gradual exposure

Flooding means the client is exposed to a trigger that elicits high levels of the negative emotion and remains exposed to the trigger until the anxiety is vastly reduced (at least to a level of not more then 50% of the original level). An example is a client who is afraid of public transport embarks on a journey on the London Underground and does not leave the train until their anxiety has gone down to a pre-set level. In gradual exposure, client and therapist make a list of triggers ranging from high negative emotion eliciting to barely manageable levels of negative affect. An example of a hierarchy for a client with panic problems is given in Table 7.1.

Therapist guided exposure or client alone

The best results in exposure can be achieved by doing the exposure sessions under the supervision of the therapist. The therapist can spot the subtle way in which the client introduces old and new safety behaviours and can help the client to reduce these. The therapist is probably also more aware of the process of anxiety reduction and can assist the client in sticking with the task until the anxiety has been reduced to not more then half the original value. In my experience, the investment in therapy time to have the exposure conducted under the supervision of the therapist is really worth it.

Table 7.1. Hierarchy of levels of anxiety and concomitant symptoms.

Level of anxiety	Symptoms (activity client could do to trigger these symptoms)
40	Noticing heart rate and breathing (shopping in supermarket with a full trolley).
50	Heart pounding in chest, breathing fast (walking at a brisk pace).
60	Heart pounding in chest, breathing fast, getting flushed (walking upstairs fast).
70	Heart pounding loudly in chest, breathing very fast, getting flushed and sweaty (gentle run on the treadmill in the gym).
80	All of the above, but getting short of breath (a more forceful run on the treadmill).
90	All of the above and really having trouble catching your breath (working hard on the cross-trainer in the gym).

"Escape" should be allowed

In my original training, I was told that it was essential that clients needed to remain exposed to the trigger and not escape from the situation. If this were to happen, it could push the client's progress back weeks, if not months. The question that was never answered was: "How do you keep a very anxious person in the presence of the anxiety provoking trigger, if they want to leave?" Using force and handcuffs was illegal even then . . . The best approach is to have an agreement with the client that "escape" is permissible, as long as the session is completed with a successful exposure. This might mean that if the client is working at an anxiety level of 80 and this gets too much, so they escape from this trigger, that they go back into a situation at level 60 or 70 and remain in that situation until the anxiety has been reduced to not more then half the original level.

Frequency of sessions

Spacing out sessions in the normal weekly or fortnightly manner might not be the optimal use of therapy time. Massed practice in the form of longer and more frequent sessions is a more efficient and effective method of planning exposure sessions. If the time between sessions is too long, then the client might engage in avoidance behaviour to such an extent that this annuls all the progress made with the exposure and in the next session the therapist and client have to start from the beginning (lowest level of negative emotion) again.

Therapist's style and conduct

It is of vital importance to be as kind and gentle with clients as possible, while at the same time keeping the client on task. A gentle reflection of client's comments during the exposure tasks is essential, as is not becoming "hyped up" by the client's emotional state. The more emotion the therapist adds to the mix, the more difficult it will be for the client to remain task focused.

The task of the therapist is to assist the client to continue with the exposure and to motivate the client to abstain from anxiety reducing responses that are normally used. The therapist could focus the client's attention on the fear-inducing stimuli ("Now your hands have touched the floor and you think they are really dirty"), while at other times the focus will be on the client's emotional processing ("How much anxiety does that cause you?", "OK, stay with that, feel this level of anxiety, and notice what happens. How is the anxiety level now?"). Impatience on the part of the therapist, irritation, and anger are, of course, natural, but should not be expressed or shown. The client is doing the best they can and if the therapist gets worried ("No change yet and my next client is in fifteen minutes") that is a problem for the therapist; the client should not be confronted with that. The lesson is to plan your exposure sessions generously and with breaks between sessions.

If clients find it difficult to move up the anxiety hierarchy, it might be helpful to ask them to stay with the current level and make small modifications. For instance, a client, who could not progress in an exposure to dirt from being close to the dirty floor to touching the floor with the whole hand was asked to bring one finger closer to the floor and check if she could touch the floor with one finger; subsequently, finger by finger, the client increased her floor touching. Successive approximation with tiny steps is sometimes the name of the game here.

Skills training (i.e., acquiring and using new skills that are incompatible with the EDB): communication skills and problem-solving skills

The emotion-driven behaviours are always focused (perhaps not deliberately or intentionally) on achieving a specific effect: the reduction of a negative feeling. The negative feeling is often connected with client's appraisal that they lack the skills or the ability to deal with a specific situation. This will become clear through careful analysis of a problem situation (topographical and functional analyses). In other words, clients use EDBs to get out of life what they want and it does not produce the intended results. There are two groups of skills that are very important in getting out of life what we want: problem-solving skills and communication skills.

The following skills are very important and frequently appear to be missing in people with psychological problems:

- communication skills such as active listening, expressing positive feelings, expressing negative feelings, and making positive requests;
- problem-solving skills.

In dialectical behaviour therapy (Linehan, Schmidt, Dimeff, Craft, Kanter, & Comtois, 1999), skills training is one of the pillars of the treatment programme. I cannot stress enough the importance of this as part of a CBT treatment for people with psychological problems. I mean *real* training, whereby client and therapist practise the skills in various role-played situations. Especially for clients with more enduring problems, whose ways of handling life are entrenched and rigid, it is extremely important to include practice in the treatment.

I have included these skills under the umbrella of changing EDBs, since the problem behaviours the client engages in, instead of using communication or problem-solving skills, are incompatible with these. The negative feeling (for example, anxiety) results in the client keeping quiet and not expressing a negative feeling and a request for a change in the other person's behaviour.

Lacking communication skills

Communication is our tool to interact with the world and the other people in it. Communication is what we use when we want other people to know that they have done something that we really liked or when they are doing something we do not like. We also use communication to "understand" other people. Psychological problems are often connected to not possessing the skills and/or not actually using the skill. A person might know how to be assertive and express negative feelings, but might not do so for fear of rejection.

I suggest a uniform strategy of teaching these skills. In step one, the client and the therapist discuss the skill and design a checklist for this skill (the checklists are based on the bullet-point lists that follow). The next step is that the therapist demonstrates the skill to the client in the form of a carefully scripted role-play. It is important for the client to recognise the various elements of the skill. In step three, the client is invited to practise the skill in the session in a role-play. It is important to get the client to practise until the client demonstrates a basic competence with these skills before moving to step four, which is to practise the skill in real life with people that the client feels he/she can practise with easily. Step five is in session practice of the skill in difficult situations; again this practice is to be done until a good level of competence is achieved, and step six is to practise in real life in difficult situations.

With expressing positive and negative feelings, some in-between step is needed, whereby I ask clients to observe others expressing positive and negative feelings and to be alert for when others "deserve" an expression of positive or negative feelings by the client. Both exercises sensitise the client to the work and will make the practice more successful.

Active listening

Listening is an important skill; it allows us to understand people and it signals to others that we are interested in them. For many clients, this is an essential skill to learn: hearing what really is being said instead of jumping to conclusions.

Many clients try to convince the therapist that they are indeed excellent listeners and do not need to learn this skill. A brief active listening role-play is often very helpful in establishing the need to learn this skill. The exercise I do is to ask the client to listen to me talking about my weekend experience and then we reverse roles, after which we discuss the differences.

These are the elements of this communication skill.

Non-verbal:

- make eye contact;
- adopt an attentive facial expression;
- use a kind tone of voice;
- use plenty of "Ah-ha's".

Verbal:

- repeating certain key words works wonders;
- paraphrasing what the other person has told you (content) and how they told you (emotion);
- use plenty of summaries, simply summarising what the other person has told you;
- ask questions, so you can understand better.

Too often when we are pretending to listen to another person, we are just preparing our own counter-argument. Listening is really trying to understand where the other person is coming from.

Expressing positive feelings

Expressing positive feelings is the tool we have to let other people know when they behaved in a way that we appreciated. It is *the* tool to tell others that they were behaving in a way we want them to behave. By being appreciative and nice about it, they will be inclined to do it more often (yes, the basic principle of positive reinforcement!). The expression of positive feelings also creates a nice atmosphere in the moment.

When we introduce this skill, many clients try to convince us it is not necessary, because "People know that we appreciate them", and there is no need to say it. In other words, many clients expect other people to read their minds!

These are the elements of this communication skill.

Non-verbal:

- make eye contact;
- adopt an attentive facial expression;
- use a kind tone of voice;
- Use plenty of "Ah-ha's".

Verbal:

- look at the person, and speak in a friendly way;
- you may smile, shake hands, or make some other warm gesture if that seems right for the situation;
- tell the person exactly what things they did that pleased you;
- tell the person exactly how it made you feel when they did that; "I was pleased ...", "I was happy...", "I enjoyed ...", "I was delighted...", "I was excited ...", "I liked..." .

Expressing positive feelings is also, in and of itself, an antidepressant strategy. By practising the expression of positive feelings in language and behaviour, there will be a positive impact on mood very soon.

Expressing negative feelings

Many people think that the only way to express negative feelings is to start screaming and shouting; that is not the case. Expressing negative feelings is extremely important, because we let other people know what they have done that caused us to be irritated, hurt, angry, sad, or disappointed. This skill can be very well combined with making positive requests.

Non-verbal:

- make eye contact;
- adopt an attentive facial expression;
- use a kind tone of voice;
- Use plenty of "Ah-ha's".

Verbal:

- look at the person and speak in a firm manner;
- say exactly what has triggered your unpleasant feelings;
- say exactly what they did that triggered you to feel what you feel;
- say exactly what you are feeling;
- use the tone of voice, facial expressions, and gestures that convey these feelings;
- suggest ways that they might help you get rid of these feelings: for example, make a positive request or arrange a problem-solving discussion.

Expressing negative feelings is often even more difficult to "sell" to clients. Many people expect other people to "know" what they have done wrong, without ever having told them so ("Everyone would know that that is not right!"), and they are surprised that the world does not consist of experts in mind-reading. Other objections to expressing negative feelings are that "It should not be necessary!", "It will hurt people's feelings", or "If I do this, people will reject me". This, of course, means that before the therapist can embark on the skills training, some work on the cognitive appraisals of the client is needed.

Making positive requests

Making a positive request is, essentially, asking another person to change their behaviour.

Non-verbal:

- make eye contact;
- adopt an attentive facial expression;
- use a kind tone of voice;
- use plenty of "Ah-ha's".

Verbal:

- look at the person and speak in a warm tone;
- tell them exactly what you would like them to do;
- tell them how you expect to feel when they have done that;
- use phrases such as: "I would like you to . . .", "I would be pleased if you would . . .", "I would be grateful if you . . ."

Problem-solving skills

Many people lead unhappy and unfulfilled lives because they allow problems to fester and ruin everything for them. Most problems can be resolved, but will not simply go away through the passage of time.

Let's take as an example, Catherine. She tells us she is depressed and she displays all the tell-tale symptoms of serious depression. Upon further analysis, it seems that Catherine avoids dealing with a range of small problems (paying bills, for instance) by completely avoiding the issue. She knows her bills at the moment exceed her expendable income, so she has been stuffing unpaid bills in a big box. Now debt collection agencies are knocking on her door. When organisations she is indebted to have approached her to discuss a solution to her debt problem, she has become angry and told them to mind their own business. This situation has been going on for two years and now has got on top of Catherine emotionally, hence the depression.

It is clear that Catherine did not use appropriate problem-solving strategies to resolve the issue of increasing debt. She also did not use appropriate communication skills when assistance was offered. Catherine's treatment for depression would need to include teaching her problem-solving skills and communication skills, otherwise there would be no lasting change.

Problems need to be confronted and resolved. I suggest a four-step approach to problem solving (D'Zurilla & Nezu, 2007):

- Define the problem and the goal.

  "Here is where you think about what is the problem really and what would be a reasonable solution to the problem. For example, my problem is that I stepped into a big pile of dog-poop and I don't want to smell of poop and make the whole floor in the office dirty. A solution would be if I could clean my shoe."
- Brainstorm solutions and, when you have at least four, select the best one.

  "Brainstorming means just listing all possible solutions, without disregarding any of them. Sometimes they just flow, and at other times, you will have to think hard. When you have at least four, you make a selection of the best. In the dog-poop example, we could come up with: (1) go back home and change shoes; (2) throw shoes away and buy a new pair; (3) go to the nearest supermarket and get a plastic bag and put it over the soiled foot, go to work, and wash off in the toilet; (4) clean the shoe as best you can on the street (find some grass, some water, some paper) and go to work as normal. Selecting the best solution is always based on the solution that best reflects your goals. In the dog-poop situation your goals might be not to miss work, and not to spend money on new shoes unnecessarily."
- Selection: in the dog-poop situation, immediate cleaning of my shoes as best as I can clearly has most advantages: compared to the other solutions, it saves time and money.

- Implementation: in order to implement the solution, I need to find a way to clean my shoes, perhaps on the curb of the pavement or by finding some grass to wipe my shoes clean.

Clients are often surprised at the fact that they can follow a step-by-step process in resolving problems. Their previous strategies had been based on avoidance and/or impulsive action.

Self-management training: bringing the behaviour back under personal control

This can be about two types of self-management: reducing unwanted behaviours (for example, drinking alcohol, eating cream cakes, and watching television) and increasing behaviours we appreciate (going to the gym, being kind to others, and studying for a CBT course). The second type of self-management is when the client needs to bring their lifestyle in general into more balance by increasing activities or reorganising the "shoulds" (things we *have* to do, such as going to work) and wants (things we really like to do, such as soaking in the bath).

Self-management and values

A feature borrowed from acceptance and commitment therapy (Hayes, Strosahl, & Wilson, 1999) is to identify the individual's valued directions and what they want their life to stand for. Values (valued directions) are not goals—they are more like a compass and must be lived out by committed action. Thus, getting married is a goal, but being a good partner is a value: you never reach your destination, since there is always something more you can do. If a valued direction in life is to be a good parent, then the first goal for a depressed patient might be to spend a specified time each day playing with, reading to, or talking with their child. Hayes and colleagues (1999) identify five areas that can be identified as topics for values.

- Relationships.
- Education/career.
- Recreation/interests.
- Mind/body/spirituality.
- Daily responsibilities.

The step that can be taken after having identified which values are important for the client is to identify activities (that the client can start doing or that can be increased in frequency) that would be indicative of this value. Here are a few examples.

- Value: being a loving parent.
- Activity: tell my child I love him/her every day.
- Activity: make a special breakfast for my child on Saturday.
- Activity: pick up my child from school promptly each day.

- Value: being an attentive and caring friend.
- Activity: call my friend once a week.
- Activity: text my friend.
- Activity: ask my friend about his/her week.

- Value: caring for the needs of your spouse.
- Activity: make special plans with spouse.
- Activity: tell spouse I love him/her every day.
- Activity: buy my partner a surprise gift.

In my practice, I tend to have a discussion about values with a client first, before we embark on a programme of behavioural activation or on a self-management programme focused on some behavioural excess (e.g., drinking alcohol). By establishing values and linking it with activities, we establish something really positive for the client: in a way, we set out a plan to design a life worth living.

Intermezzo: what does the client want from life?

Good question, what do we want from life? Not easy to answer and, to make it easier, I have designed the following exercise that will help your client to make a start in finding out about this.

Ask the client to imagine he or she has lived to the ripe old age of eighty-five and it is his/her birthday. Today, family and friends will be visiting. They will congratulate the client and there will be speeches. You have one question for the client: "What would you want other people to say about you in these speeches? When they talk about you in these speeches, what would you like them to say about you?"

Ask your client to write one such speech. Other people included things such as: *hard working, loyal, kind, generous, funny, serious, a good friend, very giving* in their speeches.

In the subsequent session, you then list the character traits the client has listed as desirable and make an inventory of which behaviours would demonstrate that someone possesses this trait. These behaviours can then become a guideline for planning activities.

Lifestyle imbalance

Many clients with psychological problems have developed unhealthy and unbalanced lifestyles. This can lead to depression, chronic boredom, and burn-out. Helping clients to adapt a more balanced lifestyle that, as a result, will reduce certain negative feelings is often a first port.

I teach clients behavioural activation in several steps, after we have had a few good discussions on values, and have identified behaviours and activities supporting these values.

Step I: Self-monitoring

This is what I tell the client about this: "Self-monitoring simply means observing your pattern of activities. It involves keeping a detailed record of what you do, hour by hour. You can do this in a notebook or diary, or I will give you a special record sheet. Rate your pleasure and satisfaction for each activity on a scale of 0 to 10.

"Your record will show you in black and white how you are spending your time, and will make you aware of how much satisfaction and pleasure you get from what you do. You will have a factual record to help you find out more about what is getting in your way, and to form a basis for changing how you spend your time."

I ask clients to keep a record of their activities for at least a week, using the Activity Schedule (see below). Sometimes, it might be worthwhile to pre-print activities based on values on these activity sheets and ask the client to monitor the frequency and duration of these valued activities (needless to say, many clients with anxiety and depression problems will return showing a very low frequency of these valued activities).

Step 2: Planning ahead

This is what I say to the client about this step: "Now that you can see how you are spending your time, the next step is to plan each day in advance, making sure that you include activities that are based on your personal values and which will give you a sense of pleasure and satisfaction.

"Planning ahead means that you are taking control of your life. The plan will prevent you from sinking into a swamp of minor decisions ('What shall I do next?'), and will help you to keep going even when you feel bad. Once the day's activities are laid out in writing, they will seem less overwhelming. You will have broken the day down into a series of manageable chunks, rather than an endless string of time, which you must somehow fill.

"Every evening, or first thing in the morning, set aside time to plan the day ahead. Find out which time suits you best to do this, remembering that you are likely to be able to plan most realistically and constructively when you are feeling relatively well and clear-headed. If you find it difficult to remember to make time to plan ahead, give yourself reminder cues. Put up signs around the house, for example, or ask someone to remind you that 7.30 is your time for planning tomorrow. As far as possible, try to ensure that your planning time is not interrupted, and that there are no other pressing demands to distract you. Turn off the television, and take the phone off the hook.

"Aim for a balance between pleasure and satisfaction in your day and remember to include activities based on the person you want to be! If you fill your time with duties and chores and allow no time for enjoyment or relaxation, you might find yourself feeling tired, resentful, and depressed at the end of the day. On the other hand, if you completely ignore things you have to do, you could find your pleasure soured by a sense that nothing has been achieved, and your list of necessary tasks will mount up. You might find it helpful to aim for the pattern of activities you found most rewarding in the past. There is a fair chance that, once you get going, you will find this pattern works for you again.

"Encourage yourself by starting the day with an activity which will give you a sense of satisfaction or pleasure, and which you have a good chance of completing successfully. This is particularly important if you have trouble getting going in the morning. And plan to reward yourself with a pleasurable or relaxing activity when you tackle something difficult. You might, for example, set aside time to have a cup of coffee and listen to your favourite radio programme when you have spent an hour doing housework. Avoid bed. Beds are for sleeping in, not for retreating to during the day. If you need rest or relaxation, plan to achieve it in some other way.

"At the end of each day, review what you have done. Take the time to sit down and examine how you spent your day, how much pleasure and mastery you got from what you did, and how far you managed to carry out the activities you had planned. This will help you to see clearly how you are spending your time, what room there is for improvement, and what changes you might like to make in the pattern of your day.

"If you have managed overall to stick to your plan, and have found what you did reasonably satisfying, this gives you something positive to build on. If, on the other hand you did not stick to your plan, or you got little satisfaction from what you did, this will give you valuable information about the kind of things that are preventing you from making the most of your time."

The structure of an activity schedule is shown the box below.

Activity schedule: Write down for each hour your main activity and rate your satisfaction and pleasure for each hour: × 10 = very little and +10 = very high

Hour	Monday	Tuesday	Wednesday	Thursday	Friday	Saturday	Sunday

I also instruct the client to go back to the eighty-fifth birthday speech and the behaviours we identified from there. I would ask clients to include at least one new activity that is evidence of one of the traits they value in their repertoire each week.

Self-management and self-control methods to counter EDBs

This method to develop different responses to experiencing negative feelings is particularly suited to when the problem behaviour has become habitual and feels as if it is outside the client's control: taking drugs, drinking alcohol, gambling, and over-eating.

Self-management methods use a combination of positive reinforcement strategies to assist clients in regaining control over these out of control behaviours. The process stretches out over a number of weeks and follows six steps.

Finding the facts

Here, the client and therapist find out the extent of the problem. In the case of drinking too much alcohol, the client will start keeping a record and detail how much they are drinking. Good practice is to get an overview of day, time, and amount of the problem behaviour.

Deciding on targets

When the client comes back to the session with the results of one or more weeks of observation, a decision needs to be taken regarding the client's goal for the future. This might sound a bit strange, since the client often wants to give up the problem behaviour completely: the client wants to stop drinking, using drugs, or indulging in sweet desserts. In this step, the client is asked to state his ultimate goal. With respect to—for instance—his drinking, what would he want to achieve by the end of treatment? This goal is separated into three components: maximum amount per week, maximum amount per day, and number of "free" days per week. Based on the discrepancy between how things are now (for example, a consumption of 143 standard alcohol units per week) and the goals (not more than fifteen units per week, not more than three on any given day, and two alcohol-free days), client and therapist set out a time frame for achieving the goals.

Rewards

People who have tried to change unwelcome habits (such as drinking or smoking) often start to use very strong and critical language when they are faced with temptation or when they have been unable to resist temptation. This will act as a punishment for their efforts and, instead of motivating, it will discourage. Here, we want to turn this around and work explicitly with rewards. We ask the clients to think of a reward they would be able to give themselves if they achieved their therapy goal.

Reduction through successive approximation, rules, and rewarding effort

After an end goal has been set and the time-frame has been decided upon, it is now time for the first change interventions to be implemented. There are three strategies working together here.

Cheese slicer

Each week, the client is invited to formulate goals regarding the frequency of problem behaviour he/she could engage in during the next week. This should be a reduction compared to the previous week, and the success or lack of it of the previous week's attempt is used as a guideline. So, for each week, the client decides on a weekly and daily maximum and the number of days without the problem behaviour. In the beginning, I strongly recommend using the "cheese-slicer method", as it is vitally important that the client builds up success experiences. The cheese-slicer method works by slicing off a little bit of the problem behaviour each week. The changes have to be small enough for the client to be confident that the change is possible.

Rules

Many of our behaviours are rule governed. Most of us have as a rule that we do not drink alcohol while at work at 11 a.m. on a Monday. Many of these rules are implicitly obeyed and when we or someone else breaks such a "normal" rule, we feel slightly awkward. When drinking, drug taking, or eating become problematic, it means that these behaviours are no longer governed by appropriate rules. Now it is time to start introducing new rules. Rules can be time-limiters (not before 10 a.m., not after 9 p.m., not on every even hour), they can be location rules (only in room X, or not in room X), or they can be behavioural rules (drinking alcoholic consumptions from the appropriate glass, making a glass last X sips, making a glass last X minutes, waiting X minutes between sips, when eating chew each mouthful for X minutes). It pays to have a brainstorm about these rules before starting to apply them, so that the therapist and the client can select from a list of rules.

Rewards

The client is also invited to select a small reward for the weekly achievement; this could be something in the order of giving oneself a real pat on the back, buying a nice cup of coffee, an ice-cream, or a newspaper.

Each week, the client and therapist review last week's progress and set goals for the forthcoming week, including rewards and introduction of rules.

Identifying and working with high risk situations

Once the client has developed some competence in "cheese slicing", the frequency of the problem behaviour downwards, and applying new rules (each week a new rule is added to the existing rules), a new strategy is introduced: identifying high risk situations. These are situations during which the client found it difficult to stick to the rules or identified goals. These situations are dealt with by analysing them with the help of a daily thought record, and appropriate cognitive restructuring or behavioural planning is implemented.

CHAPTER EIGHT

Cognitive behaviour therapy techniques focused on preventing emotional avoidance

Preventing emotional avoidance

As I stated in Chapter Four, habitual avoidance of negative feelings often leads to trouble. This is what I wrote there: Emotion-driven behaviours are deployed to reduce (escape) negative emotions or reduce the intensity once the emotion has occurred; emotional avoidance strategies are used to prevent the experience of the negative emotion in the first place. There are several forms of emotional avoidance. Avoidance can be in the form of specific overt behaviours like avoiding every form of exercise for the person with panic attack problems (each hint of physical arousal is seen as impending doom). Cognitive avoidance can occur when a person simply tries to prevent thinking about certain things (events from the past or certain thoughts/images that are seen as wrong). Sometimes, it takes the form of "superstitious" behaviour and the person concerned (hand washing in OCD) or the person might need to carry with them certain items in order to ward off the negative feelings (the person cannot leave the house without their pills, talisman, favourite shirt).

The emotional avoidance can become an over-learnt coping method in dealing with negative feelings. The client's response to the slightest hint of the negative feeling is the activation of the avoidance. This occurs frequently for people with chronic and long-standing problems.

Example: anxious and angry

Paula really did not want to feel anxious. The feeling of anxiety and all its cognitive and physical derivatives have become very aversive to her. She is hyper-vigilant to any sign of impending anxiety. Especially interactions with other people trigger feelings of anxiety. Her over-learnt response is one of irritability and anger. Paula is now forty-three years old and this pattern of "overshadowing" her anxiety with irritability and anger has been with her for most of her life. Her psychiatrist has given her a diagnosis of borderline personality disorder and has referred her for anger management, since her angry reactions to others have, at times, culminated in violence. For Paula, the negative feeling of anger is much less aversive then anxiety. From a learning theory perspective, therefore, one could postulate that this sequence (mild signs of anxiety → irritability → anger) is a negative reinforcement paradigm as something very unpleasant (anxiety) is taken away and replaced by something less unpleasant (anger). From a treatment perspective, it is indeed important for Paula to learn to control her anger and violence, but a precondition for lasting change in this would be for her to learn to tolerate feelings of anxiety. Part of the treatment needs to be assisting Paula in recognising and accepting feelings of anxiety and, subsequently, addressing them through cognitive restructuring. For many clients however the fear of the fear is the most toxic element.

Example: feeling "it" means that I am on the road to complete disaster

Ruth has learnt to find irritation and anger in any context very aversive. Her childhood was filled with many angry and aggressive models and, from a young age, she swore never to become like them. She associates disapproval, irritation, and even a healthy discussion among peers as signs of impending aggressive and violent behaviour. She has also learnt to associate her own feelings of discomfort, irritation, and disapproval as impending signs that she is about to commit acts of violence herself. As a result of this, she has become hyper-vigilant to even the smallest hint of these feelings and she engages in fierce attempts to deny or suppress them. She uses distraction (when she notices a hint of the dreaded feelings, she focuses on something else), positive self-talk (I am not angry, I am not angry, I can cope), and demands regarding her feelings (I should not feel this, stop it!) to try to suppress her feelings. This, of course, only works short term in suppressing the feelings, while her physiological arousal levels increase. The end result is frequent outbursts by Ruth, which confirm to her that she is a violent person and should suppress these feelings.

The following CBT interventions would be suitable to teach clients to prevent emotional avoidance:

- psycho-education about emotional processing;
- emotional sensitisation;
- exposure and response prevention;
- acquiring and using new skills that are incompatible with the emotional suppression;
- mindfulness.

Psycho-education about emotional processing

Experiencing feelings and understanding the purpose of negative feelings are two very different things. It is important to teach clients that negative feelings are part of an information processing system. Experiencing a negative feeling is an indication that something is not right. What it is that is not right can only be established through introspection. The something ("it") that is not right can be how people behave towards us (another person is rude to us), the circumstances we find ourselves in (a noisy and smelly work environment), how we behave ourselves (we have been slouched on the couch drinking coffee all day), or how we think about what is happening to us). Working out which something is instrumental in the creation of the negative feeling is an important step in learning to deal with negative feelings without suppressing them. Learning the point of negative feelings has a permission-giving impact on most people; it is no longer seen as "bad" when negative feelings come up.

Emotional sensitisation

Here, the client is invited to become a feelings detective. The client is asked to keep a record of feelings experienced, describe the circumstances, and what they assumed was the something that was signalled to them as not being right. The box below gives an example of a form we might give to the client.

Date and time	Circumstances	Feeling and strength	"It"	My reaction to the feeling

The aim of this exercise is to help the client to explore feelings, and learn to describe the different feelings and their varying strengths. Unfortunately, despite lengthy explanations, many clients perceive the aim of the exercise to be to have no feelings, and regularly clients proudly return their homework forms completely blank: "No negative feelings that means I am on the way to getting better, doesn't it?" It is important that clients become more sensitive to their emotional state. When people are aware of this, they can do something about improving it.

Discussions about the homework need to be conducted sensitively, to allow the client to explore their negative feelings, understand the "it" that brought them about, and what their habitual reactions are.

The role of the therapist is that of a very kind, but also very nosy, interviewer, who is simultaneously educating the client about negative feelings.

Exposure and response prevention

The diary the client has kept, with the aim of becoming more sensitised to the negative feelings, also provides information as to which internal and external "its" are instrumental in promoting certain negative feelings and which facilitate specific suppression strategies. This will provide sufficient information to create a hierarchy that can be used in a graded exposure format that is described in Chapter Seven.

Acquiring and using new skills that are incompatible with the emotional suppression

There are three sets of skills that people do not use as a result of negative feelings: communication, problem solving, and life planning.

Some examples follow.

- "If I spoke up in the meeting, I would feel *soooo* embarrassed" (expressing negative/positive feelings).
- "I feel so anxious about all the tasks that I have to do that I completely freeze and do nothing!" (problem solving).
- "I am feeling so bored and depressed that the only thing I can think of doing is to watch dreadful daytime television" (problem solving).

What is clear in all these examples is that the client experiences a negative feeling and, instead of dealing with the source of the feeling, selects avoidance as a strategy. The negative feelings either are (partially) caused by specific skills that the client lacks or the feelings suppress the application of skills that are already in client's repertoire. In each case, however, using the appropriate skills implies that the client has to accept the feeling and deal with it. The feeling needs to be communicated to others; it needs to be accepted as a fact to prompt problem solving, or both. Acquiring these skills or learning to use them again is an essential component in learning to accept and process negative feelings.

In the previous chapter, I explained how to teach communication and problem-solving skills.

Mindfulness

Mindfulness has enjoyed a tremendous surge in popularity in the past decade, in both the popular press and in the psychotherapy literature (Davis & Hayes, 2011). Mindfulness seems to have evolved from a largely unknown Buddhist concept to a mainstream psychotherapy construct. Davis and Hayes (2011) list the supposed benefits as self-control, objectivity, affect tolerance, enhanced flexibility, equanimity, improved concentration and mental clarity, emotional intelligence, and the ability to relate to others and one's self with kindness, acceptance, and compassion. The benefit "affect tolerance" is the important one for the purpose of this chapter.

There are various definitions for the term "mindfulness". Davis and Hayes list the following: a psychological state of awareness, a practice that promotes this awareness, a mode of processing information, and a character trait. An elegant description is "moment-by-moment awareness", or "a state of psychological freedom that occurs when attention remains quiet and limber, without attachment to any particular point of view", or the preferred description: mindfulness is defined as a moment-to-moment awareness of one's experience without judgement. In this sense, mindfulness is viewed as a state and not a trait, and, while it might be promoted by certain practices or activities (e.g., meditation), it is not equivalent to, or synonymous with, them (Davis & Hayes, 2011).

Mindfulness practice as part of cognitive behaviour therapy (mindfulness-based cognitive therapy (MBCT)) now has an evidence base in the prevention of relapse for people suffering from depression (Kuyken et al., 2010).

The aim here is not to provide a detailed introduction to mindfulness, merely to identify it as one of the effective strategies to assist clients to accept and process negative feelings. From a learning-theory perspective, mindfulness can perhaps best be understood as being "cognitive exposure and relapse prevention". There are specific and detailed training programmes that teach people mindfulness skills, but it is rather complex to integrate these fully in routine CBT practice. A more appealing strategy might be to include specific mindfulness exercises in routine CBT practice. The aim is to provide clients with the experience that potentially upsetting emotions and thoughts do not have to be dealt with. People suffering from anxiety or depression treat their negative feelings and associated thinking as if a phone is ringing that *has to be answered*. Mindfulness exercises and learning more about mindfulness will provide the experience that sometimes it is permissible to let the phone ring and not answer it.

CHAPTER NINE

Measuring competence in cognitive behaviour therapy

Introduction

More and more importance is rightfully given to reflective practice, clinical supervision, and monitoring the quality of psychotherapy. The tool that is mostly used for this purpose (at least, in the UK) is the cognitive therapy rating scale, revised (CTS-r) (Blackburn et al., 2001). There are some disadvantages to this tool (for example, it is very cognitive focused, very rigid in what *has* to occur in all sessions), which prompted me to start working on a more adaptive and inclusive instrument that is introduced here.

There are several measures for CBT competence available. I have tried to set up a CBT competence feedback tool that focuses on the learning process of CBT practitioners and takes into consideration requirements for "live" supervision. I do not claim that this is the definitive feedback tool for CBT competencies, or that it is the best one ever to be invented, but I hope that it will enable CBT practitioners to evaluate their performance and assist them in reflecting upon their self-identified room for improvement. I also hope that supervisors will be able to provide clear feedback to their students by using this structure.

The cognitive behaviour therapy model

The CBT model that I advocate is a structured model that can be applied with idiosyncratic flexibility. The structure I suggest is one whereby the beginning of CBT is always the establishment of *problems* and *goals*. Following on from this, the therapist will focus the assessment process on the identified problems and goals and will design a case conceptualisation or formulation. This formulation is shared with the client and problems and goals are reviewed and fine-tuned as a result of this. Based on this fine-tuning and the formulation, an intervention plan is decided upon with the client. The intervention plan is, essentially, a plan regarding a series of re-learning exercises during the course of therapy. The therapeutic interventions need to offer the client learning experiences so that she/he can go from problems to goals.

With this competence feedback structure, I aim to offer clinicians, supervisors, and supervisees an opportunity to review the level of competence in clinical practice. The competence feedback form is designed to be used in a variety of settings (live supervision, verbatim transcripts, and reviewing recordings of therapy sessions) and can be used for complete sessions or for shorter parts of sessions.

The CBT skills are divided into eight categories: assessment; interviewing; structuring; change directed interventions; overcoming resistance; evaluation; self-reflection; intervention planning.

I have chosen three possibilities for marking:

1. Insufficient evidence of competence in this specific element.
2. Sufficient evidence of competence, but with mistakes made and room for improvement in performance.
3. Sufficient evidence of competence, with some room for improvement.

Rating CBT competence is not the exact science we really want it to be. For each skill, there are several scoring points leading to a final score. The competence feedback structure requires the rater to make subjective judgements about the performance of the clinician, based on the guidelines in this volume.

The important question is when to give a specific rating of "1", "2", or "3". I would suggest that the piece of work deserves:

- A "3" (sufficient evidence of competence with some room for improvement) when the performance of the clinician with respect to this skill/aspect is correct at least 75% of the time.
- A "2" (sufficient evidence of competence, but with mistakes made and room for improvement of the performance) when the performance of the clinician with respect to this skill/aspect is correct at least 50% of the time.
- A "1" (insufficient evidence of competence, with mistakes made and lots of room for improvement in performance) when the performance of the clinician with respect to this skill/aspect is correct less than 50% of the time.

The first column in the feedback form indicates whether the skill was needed in this session or this part of a session. If the skill was needed, then subsequent columns are completed. In the second column, feedback is given as to whether the skill was applied at the correct moment, while the third column refers to the correct application of the skill. For example, agenda setting, if done at the beginning of the session, would receive a "3" for the correct moment element. If it is done after a fifteen-minute introduction and exchange of pleasantries, then it would only warrant a "2" for executing the skill at the correct moment. The next column concerns the correct execution of the skill. Expertly and elegantly conducted agenda setting might get a score of "3" here, but the end score might still only be a "2.5" if the supervisee did it at the wrong, or less than optimal, moment. The last column deals with exceptional circumstances: client posing challenges for the therapist, either by their therapeutic scepticism or their emotional presentation. Here, the supervisee can demonstrate the abilty to "hold her/his own" in stormy weather. The total score can still be one of competence, even if the supervisee makes some mistakes.

The feedback form can be used in routine clinical supervision. To each supervision session, the supervisee could bring a recording or transcript of a session with a client. Supervisee and supervisor listen to a pre-selected (by supervisee) clip of the session and work together on completing the form for this clip. In doing so, the supervisee learns to apply the competence checklist. In the feedback form itself, there is room for self-feedback. Both the supervisor's and the student's form have, in the last column, the following question: What needed changing to move to next level of competence? This gives supervisees a second chance at demonstrating their knowledge, and the self-reflection counts towards the end mark of the work.

Assessment

A pass for the assessment component is defined as: competent use of existing assessment tools and monitoring forms, as well as designing idiosyncratic ones for specific situations, combined with the ability to translate historical and assessment data in a cognitive behavioural framework (for example, BASIC-ID or SORC) leading to a case formulation.

Application of assessment tools

Competence is defined as using assessment tools in line with the defined and hypothesised problems. For a client entering therapy with a complaint of depression, the therapist should use tools to measure frequency, intensity, and duration of the depressive symptoms. If the therapist hypothesises a link between the depressed mood and the client's use of alcohol or overworking, then a measurement of the frequency, intensity, and duration of these issues would be warranted. Mistakes made here would be not using any assessment tools at all (would be scored as "1"), or using measurement tools only for part of the complaints (a score of "2"), or using measurement tools for issues not connected with the complaints (e.g., client is asked to complete a questionnaire on obsessive–compulsive problems and there is no hint of these problems present; this would be scored as a "1"). This includes the choice of assessment tools, the introduction of the assessment tools, and the provision of feedback to the client of their scores on the assessment tools.

Typical examples of competence:

- using specific assessment tools for anxiety, depression, OCD, etc., when appropriate;
- explaining the results of these to the client.

Typical examples of lacking competence:

- using specific assessment tools for anxiety, depression, OCD, etc., when no indication of such a problem is present or can reasonably be hypothesised;
- no assessment tools are used at all;
- using an overwhelming number of tools;
- not explaining results to the client.

Application of monitoring methods

Competence is defined as offering the client clear and specific methods to monitor symptom severity, frequency, and/or intensity. This includes the choice of monitoring tools, the introduction of the monitoring tools, and the provision of feedback to the client of their scores on the monitoring tools. Again, the use of monitoring should follow logically from the problems and goals definition; if not, the supervisee would need to have a hypothesis about the need for monitoring this specific symptom. No symptom monitoring at all, when needed, would be marked as "1".

Typical examples of competence:

- specific and detailed monitoring of behaviour, feelings, sensations, and/or cognitions is introduced;
- monitoring system is tried out in the session;
- monitoring instructions are specific and precise;
- monitoring task is do-able for client.

Typical examples of lacking competence:

- monitoring of behaviour, feelings, sensations, and/or cognitions bears no connection to identified symptoms, problems, and goals;
- results are not reviewed in the session;
- monitoring is not tried out in the session;
- monitoring instructions are vague;
- monitoring is too complex;
- monitoring suggested to client is overwhelming.

Conducting a historical analysis

Competence here is defined as the ability to interview the client about the history of his/her complaints and problems, and about the learning of assumptions and beliefs. This incorporates explaining to the client the need for a historical perspective, asking questions focused on the history of the symptoms and presenting the information back to the client from a CBT perspective.

Typical examples of competence:

- "When you first became aware of X being a problem, what was happening in your life?"
- Reviewing in detail the circumstances prevailing at the time the problem started.
- Reviewing the development over the weeks/months/years of the problems, linking with life events.

Typical examples of lacking competence:

- "So it started in childhood . . ." and leaving it at that.
- Accepting vague and non-specific statements of the client.
- Eliciting elaborate stories from the client that do not seem to be to the point or linked with the problems and goals.

Conducting a topographical analysis

A topographical, or SORC, analysis is the most rudimentary analysis of a problem. Competence is defined as the ability to focus with the client on one occurrence of the problem and create a detailed picture of what exactly happened, before, during, and after the problem occurrence. The competent supervisee demonstrates how to use the SORCC as a chronological timeline and the BASIC-ID as elements that need to be checked and reviewed. This incorporates giving feedback to the client about the hypothesised connections. An element of a competent topographical analysis is that the therapist can highlight safety behaviours and/or safety cues of the client.

Typical examples of competence:

- "If we could talk about a recent specific example of how the problem was bothering you, would that be helpful?"
- Focusing the client's mind and keeping it focused on a specific problem moment.
- Reviewing the problem incident following the SORCC model in a structured, but flexible, manner.

- Asking questions about the "content" of the S, the O, the R, and the C, while using the BASIC-ID paradigm.
- Asking a series of detailed questions to ascertain the exact connections between components of the O: feelings, thoughts, and sensations.

Typical examples of lacking competence:

- Allowing client to talk about how it usually goes; deviating from the specific moment.
- Not getting a clear and precise picture of the problem events.
- Vague questioning.
- Not trying to conduct a topographical analysis at all.

Interviewing for a functional analysis

Competence here is defined as being able to ask the questions that will increase knowledge regarding the functionality of problem behaviour. The supervisee needs to demonstrate having an understanding or hypothesis about the functionality based on one or more topographical analyses and focus questions on elaborating on this. This incorporates explaining a functional analysis to a client.

Typical examples of competence:

- Summarising previously completed topographical analysis and comparing a recent problem event with this.
- Asking specific questions, aimed at identifying triggers and reinforcements, asking: "What in that situation made you do . . .; was the result positive or negative for you?"
- Reviewing the problem incidents following the SORCC model in a structured, but flexible, manner.
- Asking questions about the "content" of the S, the O, the R, and the C, while using the BASIC-ID paradigm.
- Asking a series of detailed questions to ascertain the exact connections between components of the O: feelings, thoughts, and sensations.
- Explaining the maintenance cycle of the problem behaviour using learning theory.

Typical examples of lacking competence:

- Not aiming to create a functional analysis at all.
- Following a line a of questioning that indicates a lack of understanding regarding functionality of behaviour (e.g., not asking for consequences).
- Missing opportunities to identify reinforcers (vague questioning about consequences).
- Not summarising previous topographical analyses as a starting point.

Presenting a CBT formulation to the client

Collaboration is a key ingredient in CBT. Collaboration requires that both client and therapist know the journey and the means of transport. Sharing the formulation will ensure that client and therapist work from the same plan. The clarity of the presentation of the formulation is reviewed here, but also the adaptation of the explanation to the client's way of communicating, the answering of questions of the client, and the linking of the formulation to interventions. Competence is defined as the ability to present a clear CBT formulation to the client, in the client's language, that incorporates—using SORCC and BASIC-ID—how the client "got" the problem and why the problem still is a problem. Furthermore, it incorporates the ability to answer questions and link the formulation to interventions.

Typical examples of competence:

- Presenting a clear explanation of the emergence and maintenance of the problems to the client, using CBT theory to explain, in language understandable by the client.
- Using examples of the client's problem situations to clarify the formulation.
- The formulation includes suggestions for interventions.
- The explanation of interventions is clearly linked with core elements of the formulation
- The therapist carefully observes the client's reaction and builds in pauses in the explanation so the client can ask questions.

Typical examples of lacking competence:

- Clumsy explanation of formulation.
- Using inappropriate (technical, too complicated) language with the client.
- Incomplete formulation (e.g., no suggested interventions, no maintenance cycle, etc.).
- Therapist leaves insufficient room for client to ask questions.
- Therapist talks without summarising.

Identifying specific and concrete therapy problems

CBT is a problem-focused approach. The complaints of the client need to be translated into "problems the client wants to work on in therapy". Problem definitions need to be relevant, specific, and measurable. The best problem definitions include behavioural and emotional components: "I feel so depressed that I stay in bed all day", or "When I am with groups of people, I feel so anxious that I dare not speak." Taking the complaints of the client ("I am depressed") or a diagnosis ("I have social phobia") as a problem definition will be scored as "1". This includes presenting the problem list back to the client and revisiting the problem list after the presentation of the formulation. It also includes prioritising the problems.

Typical examples of competence:

- Problems identified are specific and measurable.
- Problems definitions include a behavioural component in combination with other BASIC-ID elements.

Typical examples of lacking competence:

- Problems are vague and unspecific.
- No problems are identified.
- Problems only contain one BASIC-ID element.

Setting specific, measurable, achievable, realistic and transferrable goals

For each problem, there needs to be at least one goal. Competence is defined here as having at least one smart goal for each problem. This includes presenting the goals list back to the client and revisiting the goals list after the presentation of the formulation. It also includes prioritising the goals.

Typical examples of competence:

- Goals are identified as specific, measurable, achievable, realistic, and transferrable (SMART).
- Goals are linked with problems.
- Goals are defined including a behavioural component in combination with other elements of the BASIC-ID.

Typical examples of lacking competence:

- Goals are *not* SMART.
- Goals are not reviewed with the client.
- Goals are not linked with problems.
- Goals are not prioritised with the client.

Application of report writing

This is reviewed by the written introduction the supervisee provides with the transcripts. Competence is defined as the ability to present a case using a CBT structure: basic data regarding client, identified problems and goals, assessment information, formulation, intervention plan, and intervention progress.

Typical examples of competence:

- Report includes necessary information: basic client details, topographical analysis, functional analysis, historical analysis, formulation, and intervention plan.
- Focused and specific use of language.
- Statements and hypotheses are presented with evidence to support it.

Typical examples of lacking competence:

- Rambling presentation.
- Chaotic.
- Presentation of opinions without evidence to back them up (e.g., "This clearly intelligent young man" without an IQ test to support it).

- Includes superfluous information.
- Incomplete presentation (e.g., some of the essentials, such as problems and goals, are missing).

Interviewing

CBT is a talking therapy. The way a cognitive behaviour therapist talks with clients is of the utmost importance. The same spoken words can trigger either comfort or emotional distress in the client. Interviewing skills will often be marked in combination with other skills.

Competence is defined as the ability to adapt interviewing and talking style to CBT therapeutic need of the moment.

Application of reflective listening

Competence is defined as the ability to use repetition, paraphrasing, and summarising in conversations with clients. To do this will have an impact on the client that will improve the therapeutic relationship. Reflective listening is a technique that is probably most underused in CBT.

Typical examples of competence:

- Repetition of key words of client.
- Reflecting and paraphrasing client's words.
- Summarising larger parts of a session.
- Doing the above in a kind, empathic tone of voice.
- Doing the above with reasonably high frequency (sufficient to keep the flow of the information going and to express to the client that the therapist is listening, but not so much that the flow of the conversation gets unnecessarily disturbed). Very elegant is to precede each question with a summary of the answer to the previous one.

Typical examples of lacking competence:

- No repetitions, reflections, paraphrasing, and summarising.
- Too low frequency of the above.
- Tone of voice when doing the above is too harsh.

Application of effective summarising of session content

I have highlighted the summarising of session content as a specific skill. Competence is defined as the ability to summarise concisely larger parts of a session in a way that highlights the important elements of the discussion. During a session, there should be several summaries, but the end of the session should definitely contain a summary of the items discussed and homework agreed during the session.

Typical examples of competence:

- Summaries include the important elements of the conversation.
- The issues the therapist would like to continue to talk about are mentioned last.
- Summaries are followed by an open question, inviting client to agree/disagree or to talk more about an element of the summary.

Typical examples of lacking competence:

- No or insufficient summaries.
- Incomplete summaries.
- Summaries not followed by a question.
- Summaries include interpretations and insights of the therapist.

Application of concrete and specific questioning

During the assessment, and later on when reviewing homework and checking for negative automatic thoughts, it is often necessary for the therapist to be persistent in concrete and specific questioning, oscillating between open and closed questions. Competence is defined as the ability to be persistent in concrete and specific questioning, oscillating between open and closed questions when needed.

Typical examples of competence:

- Questions guided by the BASIC-ID.
- Questions guided by what, where, when, and (with) whom.
- A flexible mix of open and closed questions.
- Using follow-up questions to get to the finer detail of issues.
- Frequent use of "Can you tell me a bit more about that?" or an equivalent.

Typical examples of lacking competence:

- Asking no questions but presenting assumptions.
- Asking only closed questions.
- Not asking follow-up questions when answers of client lack clarity.

Application of motivational interviewing

When confronted with sceptical or unmotivated clients, the therapist needs to use motivational interviewing. Competence is defined as the ability to recognise when to use motivational interviewing and the ability to use reflective listening, fine-tuning reflections, positive restructuring, and provocative strategies focused on increasing client's commitment for change. Continuing with standard CBT when signs of demotivation or scepticism are present would be marked as a "1" here. (For instance: Client: "I don't know why I am here, there is nothing wrong with me." Therapist: "One of the first things we do in CBT is to make a problem list. Which problems would you like to work on in therapy?").

Typical examples of competence:

- Frequent use of reflective listening.
- Adapt therapeutic tasks and actions to the stages of change the client seems to be in (precontemplation, contemplation, determination, action, or relapse).
- Use fine-tuning reflections, positive restructuring, provocative strategies when encountering motivational roadblocks.

Typical examples of lacking competence:

- Sticking rigidly to the proposed structure (agenda setting, etc.) of CBT, regardless of client's presentation.
- Asking questions without reflections.
- Attempting to convince the client by persuasion.

Application of Socratic dialogue

Socratic dialogue incorporates several skills: asking informational questions, reflective listening, summarising, and asking synthesising questions. There are two moments when Socratic dialogue can be used: during an assessment phase, when the therapist needs/wants to explore the client's thinking behind problem presentations, and during cognitive restructuring, when the therapist assists the client to adapt different ways of thinking about previously distressing issues. Competence is defined as the ability to patiently use asking informational questions, reflective listening, summarising, and asking synthesising questions to explore client's inner world. An often-made mistake is to omit the synthesising questions or to *only* ask informational and synthesising questions, and the supervisee will be marked down for these omissions.

Typical examples of competence:

- Asking open informational question in an empathic manner.
- Providing summaries to client.
- Asking questions that combine two or more elements of what client has been saying and will elevate client's understanding about themselves to a higher level.
- Frequent reflective listening.
- Frequent focus on the meaning giving process by the client.
- Questions such as: "What do you make of that"; "How do you make sense of this?"

Typical examples of lacking competence:

- Doing all the aspects of Socratic dialogue, but in the wrong order (e.g., asking synthesising questions without having done the groundwork with informational questions and summaries).
- Asking closed questions.
- Jumping to conclusions.

Giving feedback to clients

Competence is defined as the ability to recognise when feedback to the client is needed and to present the feedback in clear, specific, and understandable language to the client and in an empathic manner. Feedback needs to be given to the client whenever assessment results have been collected, when a formulation is completed and needs presenting, or when the client behaves in a counter-therapeutic manner.

Typical examples of competence:

- Asking the client whether they are interested in learning the results of the assessment.
- Presenting the results in a clear, concise, and personalised manner.
- Bringing up client's counter-therapeutic behaviours in an assertive, respectful, and empathic manner ("There are a few things that I would like to talk about. It concerns some things you do that seem to be not beneficial for therapy. Would it be OK for me to mention them so we can discuss and problem solve?").
- Giving clear and precise feedback to client regarding counter-therapeutic behaviour and suggest alternatives. ("I have noticed you have a habit of talking about your concerns in a non-stop manner without looking at me. To me that feels as if you are talking at me and not with me. As a result, it is very difficult for me to ask you questions and for you to see when I want to ask a question. I really would appreciate if you could look at me and keep an eye out for signals that I want to ask you something.")

Typical examples of lacking competence:

- Not giving client feedback when counter-therapeutic behaviours are noticed.
- Giving the feedback in a blaming way.
- Giving feedback in an emotional manner and not giving any alternatives.

Eliciting feedback from client(s)

Collaboration is the name of the game in CBT. It is paramount to elicit feedback from the client about: problems and goals, therapeutic interventions, and style of the therapist regularly, preferably at the end of each session. Competence is defined as asking for feedback in a specific and concrete form that enables the client to pinpoint problem issues. It includes responding in a non-defensive and empathic manner to critical feedback.

Typical examples of competence:

- Asking for feedback on sessions in a routine manner at the end of a session ("What were the good and less good things of this session"; "What were the helpful and less helpful elements of this session""; "Did I do anything that was not helpful?").

- Asking client to explain back to therapist their understanding of something therapist has explained.
- Using reflective listening to get the client to explain less good elements of sessions in detail.

Typical examples of lacking competence:

- Asking only closed "understanding" questions ("Is this clear?"; "Do you understand this?").
- Becoming defensive when the client criticises the therapist ("You misunderstood me"; "You got it wrong", etc.).
- Not asking for feedback at all.

Maintenance of a respectful attitude

Competence is defined by the absence of a number of therapist behaviours: being rude to clients, habitually talking over clients, calling the client names, etc.

Typical examples of competence:

- Therapist maintains a steady tone of voice.
- Therapist maintains reflective listening and gentle enquiry as a basic style.

Typical examples of lacking competence:

- Therapist puts the client down.
- Therapist calls the client names.

Structuring sessions

Competence is defined as the ability to impose and maintain the structure of CBT on clients in an empathic manner and to demonstrate good time management. This is perhaps the least understood element of CBT. Those who criticise CBT often take this element to mean a rigid and inflexible structure, whereby hard-nosed clinicians ignore a client's distress and demand in a strict sergeant-major voice:

"Agenda!" Nothing is further from the truth. The structuring of sessions needs to occur in a gentle and natural manner; when needed, the therapist can deviate from the structure and reflective listening continues to be the name of the game.

Application of agenda setting

Each CBT session starts with the setting of an agenda. The agenda is, essentially, a list of items the client and the therapist want to get through by the end of the session. Both client and therapist can contribute to the agenda. Competence in agenda setting is starting each session with the agenda (and not half-way through the session), asking the client for their contributions in an empathic and open manner, listing the agenda before starting (writing it down) and sharing this with client, and prioritising the agenda points in collaboration with the client.

Typical examples of competence:

- Statements such as: "What would you like to put on the agenda today?"; "Which things would you like to discuss today?"; "I have a few points for today's agenda but perhaps we can start by listing what you want to talk about?"
- Asking the client: "Is there anything else you would like to put on the agenda?"; "Where would you like to start today?"
- Therapist writes the agenda on a whiteboard, flipchart, or piece of paper and shares it with the client
- Therapist summarises the agenda.

Typical examples of lacking competence:

- "Let me set the agenda for today, let's start."
- "OK, what I would like to talk about today is XYZ, is that OK? So let's start with . . ."
- Doing the agenda setting half-way through the session.

Application of adhering to an agenda

Competence here is defined as the therapist following the agenda that has been set; the therapist completes each agenda point with a brief summary and checks with the client whether moving on is all right; the therapist brings the client back to the agenda when client deviates and checks with client when the therapist feels the need to deviate.

Typical examples of competence:

- Having the agenda visible for client and therapist during the session.
- Summarising the agenda before starting.
- Summarising the discussion of one agenda point before moving on.
- Making structuring comments such as: "Let's go back to the agenda"; "This seems to fit very well with point X on the agenda; shall we continue to discuss this now?"; "This sounds as if it is really important for you; would you like to add it to the agenda today?"

Typical examples of lacking competence:

- Making no attempts to structure the session.
- Making no reference to the agenda.
- Allowing the client to deviate without bringing him/her back to the agenda.
- Absence of structuring summaries.

Pacing in sessions

Competence here is defined as the ability of the therapist to "keep a steady pace" in the session. The pace of the session is always matched to the client's need. For a very distressed client, it will be necessary to slow the pace down to assist that client objectively to take stock of what is being said. Competence in "pacing" is recognising when to speed up and get the agenda done and when to allow for focusing on one issue that might lead to not getting everything done. An example of incorrect pacing is: sticking with one point of the agenda because the therapist is very interested in the issue.

Typical examples of competence:

- The therapist ensures that all points of the agenda receive suitable attention.

- The therapist ensures a steady working pace during sessions and resists pressure from the client to speed things up, and the temptation to focus on one element and not see the big picture.
- Frequent reflections and summaries are effective pacing methods.

Typical examples of lacking competence:

- Continuously asking questions, without interspersing them with reflections.
- Responding to client's pressure and haste.

Time management in sessions

Pacing and time management are connected, but slightly different. Pacing describes the interpersonal style and techniques the therapist uses to keep the session going, while time management is perhaps more about the listing of things on the agenda (fifteen points for an agenda is setting oneself up to fail . . .), keeping an eye on time and ensuring that about ten minutes before time, the session moves into its last phase (homework and feedback). So, competence in time management is starting and finishing on time, giving the client appropriate signals regarding the progress of time during a session, and putting a reasonable agenda together.

Typical examples of competence:

- The therapist ensures that sessions end in a timely fashion; for example, homework and session evaluation are done in an orderly manner.
- The therapist reminds the client of the progression of time in relation to the agenda: "We have spent quite a bit of time on this thought record. We now have twenty minutes left and still two big issues on the list and the usual homework and evaluation. Which of these two would you like to make a start with today?"

Typical examples of lacking competence:

- The therapist is short of time at the end of session and homework and evaluation are sacrificed.
- The therapist says things such as: "Let's just do this quickly . . ."

Reviewing and setting homework

Homework can serve two purposes: increasing knowledge (assessment) and change (interventions). Competence in setting homework incorporates clearly defining the task and its purpose, practising the task in the session, inviting the client to take note of the homework, checking the understanding and ability of the client regarding the homework, and, finally, ensuring the homework is linked with necessary assessment tasks and/or therapeutic change tasks.

Typical example of competence:

- The therapist puts review of homework on the agenda.
- At the beginning of a session, the therapist summarises homework and asks the client to give an update.
- The therapist links the homework results with problems, goals, and formulation.
- At the completion of a session, the therapist summarises homework and asks the client to say how he/she has understood the homework tasks.
- At the completion of a session, the therapist organises a written record of the agreed upon homework.
- The homework is SMART (specific, meaningful, achievable, realistic, and towards problems and goals).
- Homework difficulties are explored and problems solved.

Typical example of lacking competence:

- Homework set is not reviewed.
- No homework is set when relevant homework could have been set.
- Homework results are not linked with learning experiences regarding formulation, problems, and goals.
- Homework results are quickly dismissed by the client.
- Homework difficulties are not explored, but are dealt with by telling the client just to try harder.

Change focused interventions

Competence is defined as the ability to use a variety of CBT interventions to assist clients in working towards their goals. This is the crux of CBT. The main problems of novice therapists are that they start too soon with change-directed interventions. From our perspective, competent CBT follows the process of collaborative empiricism: problems and goals, assessment based on these problems and goals, formulating a case conceptualisation, sharing this with the client, revisiting problems and goals, working out an intervention plan with the client, and implementing the intervention plan. Incompetent change interventions might be well-executed thought records before the case conceptualisation is shared with the client. I see CBT as the orchestration of a series of relearning experiences for the client.

Instead of presenting supervisees with an infinite list of possible interventions, I have divided the possible CBT interventions into five categories. It is imperative that the supervisee indicates in which categories the interventions on which they want feedback fall, and that they specify the intervention.

Application of cognitive interventions

Competence is based on conducting the following aspects of the intervention correctly: link the intervention with problems and goals, link the intervention with case conceptualisation, explanation of the intervention to the client, practise in session following the correct steps of the intervention, giving the client homework to practise between sessions, and, finally, do an understanding check with the client.

Typical examples of competence:

- The *purpose* of the intervention is explained to the client (linking to formulation, problems, and goals).
- The *procedure* of the intervention is explained to the client.
- The *expected* outcome of the intervention is explained to the client.
- The therapist follows the recommended procedure and problem solves obstacles.
- When setting homework, the therapist ensures that in-session practice has taken place.

Typical examples of lacking competence:

- Not explaining the intervention properly: many novice therapists dive into change-directed interventions and "fix" things. The educational part of CBT is that clients become their own best therapist. Therefore, it is of the utmost importance to explain techniques and strategies so that the client can use them without the assistance of a therapist.

- The intervention is not linked with problems, goals, and formulation.
- The therapist does not follow the recommended procedure: for example, starts a behavioural experiment without having identified the beliefs that are to be tested, starts working with thought records, without having explained the cognitive model, etc.

Application of behavioural interventions

Competence is based on conducting the following aspects of the intervention correctly: linking the intervention with problems and goals, linking the intervention with case conceptualisation, explanation of the intervention to client, practise in session following the correct steps of the intervention, giving client homework to practise between sessions, and, finally, do an understanding check with the client.

Typical examples of competence:

- The *purpose* of the intervention is explained to the client (linking to formulation, problems, and goals).
- The *procedure* of the intervention is explained to the client.
- The *expected* outcome of the intervention is explained to the client.
- The therapist follows the recommended procedure and problem solves obstacles.
- When setting homework, the therapist ensures that in-session practice has taken place.

Typical examples of lacking competence:

- Not explaining the intervention properly: many inexperienced therapists dive into change-directed interventions and "fix" things. The educational part of CBT is that clients become their own best therapist. Therefore, it is of the utmost importance to explain techniques and strategies so that the client can use them without the assistance of a therapist.
- The intervention is not linked with problems, goals, and formulation.

- The therapist does not follow the recommended procedure: for example, starts exposure without having established a hierarchy, starts working with skills training without having a clear model of the skill, etc.

Application of environmental interventions

Competence is based on conducting the following aspects of the intervention correctly: linking the intervention with problems and goals, linking the intervention with case conceptualisation, explanation of the intervention to the client, practise in session following the correct steps of the intervention, giving client homework to practise between sessions, and, finally, do an understanding check with the client.

Typical examples of competence:

- The *purpose* of the intervention is explained to the client (linking to formulation, problems, and goals).
- The *procedure* of the intervention is explained to the client.
- The *expected* outcome of the intervention is explained to the client.
- The therapist follows the recommended procedure and problem solves obstacles.
- When setting homework, the therapist ensures that in-session practice has taken place.

Typical examples of lacking competence:

- Not explaining the intervention properly: many beginning therapists dive into change-directed interventions and "fix" things. The educational part of CBT is that clients become their own best therapist. Therefore, it is of the utmost importance to explain techniques and strategies so that the client can use them without the assistance of a therapist.
- The intervention is not linked with problems, goals, and formulation.
- The therapist does not follow the recommended procedure: for example, starts changing consequences of behaviour before a clear functional analysis has been developed, starts changing consequences without knowing exactly what the relevant "reinforcers" and "punishers" are.

Application of psycho-education

Competence is based on conducting the following aspects of the intervention correctly: linking the intervention with problems and goals, linking the intervention with case conceptualisation, explanation of the intervention to the client, practise in session following the correct steps of the intervention, giving the client homework to practise between sessions, and, finally, do an understanding check with the client.

Typical examples of competence:

- The therapist utilises elements of cognitive and behavioural underpinning of CBT to assist the client in making sense of the problems, understanding the need for specific therapeutic tasks, or explaining why certain things are challenging for the client.
- The therapist uses appropriate supporting materials, such as flipcharts, etc.
- The therapist explains and checks the client's understanding frequently.
- The therapist uses reinforcement theory and/or distorted thinking as explanation models.
- The therapist uses examples from the client's presentation to highlight and explain key points.

Typical examples of lacking competence:

- The therapist's explanation is too theoretical.
- The therapist's explanation is not linked with the client's idiosyncratic presentation.
- No understanding checks are undertaken.
- The therapist does not use underpinning theory of CBT, but theory from a different therapeutic modality.

Application of imagery based interventions

Competence is based on conducting the following aspects of the intervention correctly: linking the intervention with problems and goals, linking the intervention with case conceptualisation, explanation of the intervention to client, practise in session following the correct steps of the intervention, giving client homework to practise between sessions, and, finally, do an understanding check with the client.

Typical examples of competence:

- The *purpose* of the intervention is explained to the client (linking to formulation, problems, and goals).
- The *procedure* of the intervention is explained to the client.
- The *expected* outcome of the intervention is explained to the client.
- The therapist follows the recommended procedure and problem solves obstacles.
- When setting homework, the therapist ensures that in-session practice has taken place.

Typical examples of lacking competence:

- Not explaining the intervention properly: many novice therapists dive into change-directed interventions and "fix" things. The educational part of CBT is that clients become their own best therapist. Therefore, it is of the utmost importance to explain techniques and strategies so that the client can use them without the assistance of a therapist.
- The intervention is not linked with problems, goals, and formulation.
- The therapist does not follow the recommended procedure: for example, starts the imagery technique without having created the new image with the client.

Critical analysis of own therapeutic work

Competence is defined as the ability to apply the CBT competence scale in reviewing one's own therapeutic work. This deals with the supervisee's reflection on her/his therapeutic work, either by completing the competence feedback form or by commenting on their therapeutic interventions in a verbatim transcript. A key point is the supervisee's ability to identify roadblocks to therapeutic success as a result of their actions as a therapist.

Evidence of competence:

- The therapist recognises moments of lacking competence.
- The therapist is able to provide alternative interventions for moments of lacking competence.

Evidence of lacking competence:

- Therapist fails to recognise moments of lacking competence.

- No alternatives are suggested, or the alternatives are not an improvement.
- The therapist reacts very defensively or emotionally hurt when areas of lacking competence are highlighted.

Overcoming resistance

A competent therapist will be able to apply a range of motivation enhancement methods and adapt them to the motivational needs of the clients. This, again, is an important element of modern CBT. Interventions and techniques are presented to clients in ways that make them work for this specific client, not in a mass-produced, mechanistic manner. CBT is made to measure, not mass produced.

Ability to conceptualise client resistance in the stages of change model (Prochaska, DiClemente, & Norcross, 1992)

The competent supervisee is able to understand the client's lack of motivation in terms of the stages of change model and will use motivational interviewing strategies accordingly. This element is assessed through the supervisee's therapeutic interventions and through the explanation and underpinning of the interventions. In the explanation, the supervisee needs to be able to identify the client's motivational deficits (knowledge, self-esteem, self-efficacy, and/or concern).

Typical examples of competence:

- The therapist demonstrates, in written work about the progress of therapy, an understanding of the stages of change model.

Typical examples of lacking competence:

- The therapist labels client resistance to change in terms of personality traits.

Ability to adapt personal talking style in order to overcome client resistance

This is all about recognising which talking style to choose. Clients in precontemplation or contemplation are more in need of self-reflection, while clients in active change need information about strategies. Competence here is the match between client need and therapist response.

Excellent motivational interviewing can result in a low grade because the client was ready for change and gave clear indications of this.

Typical examples of competence:

- The therapist demonstrates flexibility when confronted with client resistance.
- The therapist adapts core strategies to client's stage of change.
- Precontemplation: eliciting self-motivational statements through reflective listening.
- Contemplation: tipping the balance through synthesising questions.
- Determination: assisting the client to make an informed choice by providing information about his/her problems (formulation) and potential interventions.

Typical examples of lacking competence:

- Sticking to the agenda no matter what.
- Not spotting the client's signs of resistance.
- Getting irritated with clients when they display resistance and showing this irritation.

Ability to adapt intervention planning in order to overcome client resistance

This is also about matching what the therapist suggests/does and the presentation of the client. Too often, novice therapists choose interventions in the beginning of therapy that cost rather a lot of effort from the client. This would be correct if the client is highly motivated, but will backfire with a reluctant and sceptical client. Competence here is to match the interventions suggested to the motivational state of the client.

Typical examples of competence:

- Adapt therapeutic interventions to the client's energy/motivational level.
- When confronted with therapeutic scepticism/resistance, the therapist's first focus is to get the client on board by:
  - helping the client to refocus on the goals;
  - helping the client to refocus on the "suffering" he/she wants to end with therapy.
  - explaining the intended effect of interventions and checking with the client how they think it might work for them.

Typical examples of lacking competence:

- Interventions are planned without giving any thought to client's level of motivation.
- Most difficult tasks are started on while client's motivation is still fragile.

Intervention planning

Intervention planning can be demonstrated in sessions *and* in reporting about sessions. During sessions, the therapist demonstrates careful preparation of interventions, linking the interventions with the formulation, and answering client's questions and concerns by using the formulation as a foundation. In reporting about the therapy, the clinician can demonstrate competence by outlining a treatment plan, carefully linked with essential elements of the formulation and presenting the chronology of interventions in an evidence-based and thought-out manner.

Putting complex assessment information together into a cohesive cognitive behavioural formulation that results in a detailed treatment plan

Competence here is defined as the ability to integrate the complex assessment information in a formulation that guides the treatment plan. A competent treatment plan outlines learning experiences that assist the client in going from problems to goals, while taking into account the mechanics described in the formulation.

Evidence of competence:

- The formulation presented by the therapist reflects the assessment information and describes clearly how the problem became established and how it is maintained.
- The treatment plan goes beyond the listing of interventions. It makes clear how *these* learning experiences will remove specific roadblocks so that the client can achieve the goals set.

Evidence of lacking competence:

- The assessment information is just listed, but not integrated in a comprehensive case formulation.
- The treatment plan consists of a list of interventions that are not linked to problems, goals, and formulation.

Ability to plan and execute interventions sequentially based on the formulation

Competence here is described as the ability to see the intervention/therapy as a sequence of orchestrated interventions (learning experiences) that enable the client to go from problems to goals.

Evidence of competence:

- The therapist demonstrates that the interventions are executed as planned.
- The therapist demonstrates the ability to overcome natural avoidance by clients (avoiding of exposure by anxious clients, avoiding of behavioural activation by clients with depression problems, etc.) and execute the planned interventions.

Evidence of lacking competence:

- The therapist is "distractable" by the client: for example, when planning behavioural activation with a depressed client, the greater part of a session is spent with cognitive restructuring because the client expressed some strong irrational beliefs.
- The therapist jumbles interventions together, lacks focus, and moves from one to the next without finishing any.

Evaluating treatment progress

Identifying roadblocks to therapeutic success in client behaviour, planning of the therapy, and environmental contingencies.

Signs of competence:

- The therapist monitors methodically client's response through treatment.
- The therapist demonstrates insight into the reasons for lacking success by adapting and enriching the formulation.

Ability to use evaluation instruments and, if need be, designing idiosyncratic therapy evaluation methods

Signs of competence:

- Therapist uses structured evaluation methods to evaluate client's response to treatment.

CBT competence tool

The feedback is based on (please tick at least one):

Tick	Type of presentation		Aim of the session	Tick
☐	Live supervision		Assessment	☐
☐	Video record of interview	Focused on	Psycho-education	☐
☐	Audio record of interview		Relapse prevention	☐
☐	Verbatim transcript of interview		Change-directed Interventions	☐
			1.	
			2.	
			3.	
			4.	
			Overcoming resistance	☐
			Intervention planning	☐

Introduction to client (when presenting to supervisor)

Please attach on a separate piece of paper, or present verbally, basic client information, identified problems, and associated SMART goals, formulation (hypothesis), and the phase of therapy (e.g., how many sessions the client has had with you).

Briefly describe or verbally outline the phase of treatment and the aims and goals of this session.

Feedback summary

Self feedback	Supervisor feedback
Good elements in this session:	Good elements in this session:
Skills development need apparent as a result of this session:	Skills development need apparent as a result of this session:

Rating scale

1. Skills execution at the *correct moment* counts for 50% of the mark. This is about matching client presentation with the CBT skills that were appropriate. For example, the therapist explaining the CBT model (psycho-education) in a competent manner is conducted at the correct moment after an initial brief assessment of the client's difficulties, but would be inappropriate at the beginning of the first session.
2. *Correct execution* of the skill counts for 50% of the mark. The CBT model might be explained in an elegant and concise manner or in a halting and not fluent manner. The way in which the skill is executed determines the mark for this element.
3. All these elements are rated on a three-point scale.

Insufficient evidence of competence in this specific element	Sufficient evidence of competence, but with mistakes made and room for improvement of performance	Sufficient evidence of competence with little room for improvement
1	2	3

4. *Responsivity* is the flexibility with which the therapist can adapt CBT skills to variations of client presentation. The base mark is

made up of skills execution at the right moment, and correct skills execution. The additional rating of responsivity can reflect working with complexity, for example, the trainee can demonstrate how CBT strategies are applied in the face of adversity and complexity. Responsivity is rated only when needed and can give extra marks, but does not form part of the basic mark and cannot result in a reduction in marks.

No responsivity demonstrated at all								Excellent responsivity demonstrated		
0	1	2	3	4	5	6	7	8	9	10
No extra marks added to the basic score						Add 10% to the basic		Add 20% to the basic score		Add 25% to the basic score

Terms

Was this skill needed in this session/report: Not all techniques and skills are required in each session or part of a session. Based on the information supplied about the client and the process of therapy *and* what actually happens in the session, the need for specific techniques can be identified.

Was the skill executed at the right moment? If the skill was needed, then the other columns can be completed. This column deals with the correct moment of executing the skill. For example, agenda setting done mid-way during the session might be technically correct, but done at the wrong moment.

Was the skill executed correctly? This column deals with the execution of the skill. An attempt at agenda setting might be done at the correct moment, but subsequently not correctly executed.

Responsivity: Deals with how well the student dealt with adverse circumstances. This will not be marked if the client behaves in a very collaborative manner and if no unforeseen issues are raised. This is marked when clients display in-session engagement difficulties, are oppositional, or when new problems come up unexpectedly, etc.

Skills group	Specific skills	Needed Yes/No	Timely 1/2/3	Correctly 1/2/3	Responsivity 0–10	Change needed to improve
Assessment For a pass: competent use of existing assessment tools and monitoring forms as well as designing idiosyncratic ones for specific situations; is able to translate historical and assessment data in cognitive behavoioural framework (BASIC-ID & SORCC).	Application of assessment tools. Application of monitoring methods. Conducting a historical analysis. Conducting a topographical analysis. Interviewing for a functional analysis. Presenting a CBT formulation to the client. Identifying specific and concrete therapy problems. Setting specific, measurable, achievable, realistic and transferrable goals. Application of report writing. Others, please specify.					

Skills group	Specific skills	Needed Yes/No	Timely 1/2/3	Correctly 1/2/3	Responsivity 0–10	Change needed to improve
Interviewing For a pass: ability to adapt interviewing and talking style to CBT therapeutic need of the moment.	Application of reflective listening. Application of effective summarising of session content. Application of concrete and specific questioning. Application of motivational interviewing. Application of Socratic questioning. Giving feedback to client(s). Eliciting feedback from client(s). Maintenance of a respectful attitude. Others, please specify. Eliciting relevant behaviours. Eliciting relevant cognitions. Eliciting relevant emotions. Eliciting relevant physical sensations. Eliciting relevant environmental factors.					

Skills group	Specific skills	Needed Yes/No	Timely 1/2/3	Correctly 1/2/3	Responsivity 0–10	Change needed to improve
Structuring sessions For a pass: is able to impose and maintain the structure of CBT on clients in an empathic manner and demonstrates good time management.	Application of agenda setting. Application of adhering to an agenda. Pacing in sessions. Time management in sessions. Reviewing and setting homework. Others, please specify. Homework reviewed. Homework set.					

Skills group	Specific skills	Needed Yes/No	Timely 1/2/3	Correctly 1/2/3	Responsivity 0–10	Change needed to improve
Change-focused interventions For a pass: is able to use a variety of CBT interventions to assist clients in working towards their goals.	Socratic dialogue. Daily thought records. Behavioural experiments. Application of psycho-education (including explaining interventions). Application of imagery-based interventions. Graded exposure: setting up a hierarchy. Graded exposure: executing a hierarchy. Flooding. *In vitro* exposure (reliving). Problem solving skills training. Communication skills training. Self-management training. Mindfulness training. Applied relaxation.					

The following apply to the written work accompanying the recording or trainee's verbal introduction and discussion.

Skills group	Specific skills	Was the skill needed in this session/report? Yes/No	Was the skill executed at the right moment? 1/2/3	Was the skill executed correctly? 1/2/3	Comments
Critical analysis of own therapeutic work.	Identifyingroadblocks to therapeutic success in actions as a therapist.				
For a pass: is able to apply CBT competence scale in reviewing own therapeutic work.	Ability to problem solve roadblocks to therapeutic success in actions as a therapist.				
Overcoming client resistance.	Ability to conceptualise client resistance in the stages of change model (Prochaska, Diclemente, & Norcross, 1992).				
For a pass: is able to apply a range of motivation enhancement methods and adapt them to the motivational needs of the clients.	Ability to adapt personal talking style in order to overcome client resistance. Ability to adapt the intervention planning in order to overcome client resistance.				
Intervention planning	Putting complex assessment assessment information together into a cohesive cognitive–behavioural formulation.				

Skills group	Specific skills	Was the skill needed in this session/report? Yes/No	Was the skill executed at the right moment? 1/2/3	Was the skill executed correctly? 1/2/3	Comments
Evaluating treatment progress	Ability to plan interventions sequentially based on the formulation. Identifying roadblocks to therapeutic success in client client behaviour, planning of the therapy and environmental contingencies. Ability to use evaluation instruments and, if need be, can design idiosyncratic therapy evaluation methods.				
	Totals				

Calculation of score	
A. Number of skills defined as required in this session.	
B. Total of scores of timely execution of skill.	
C. Totals of scores of correct execution of skills.	
D Total of the scores B and C.	
E. Number of times responsivity was required.	
F. Totals of added marks for responsivity.	
G. Add F and D.	
Final score: G–A	

REFERENCES

American Psychiatric Association (APA) (2000). *Diagnostic and Statistical Manual of Mental Disorders (DSM-IV-TR)*. Arlington, VA: American Psychiatric Association.

Bandura, A. (1969). *Principles of Behaviour Modification*. New York: Holt, Rinehart & Winston.

Bandura, A. (1986). *Social Foundation of Thought and Action: A Social Cognitive Theory*. Englewood Cliffs, NJ: Prentice Hall.

Barlow, D. H., & Craske, M. G. (1989). *Mastery of Your Anxiety and Panic (MAP)*. Albany, NY: Graywind.

Barlow, D. H., Allen, L. B., & Choate, M. L. (2004). Towards a unified treatment for emotional disorders. *Behavior Therapy, 35*: 205–230.

Beck, A. T. (1963). Thinking and depression. *Archives of General Psychiatry, 9*: 324–333.

Beck, A. T. (1967). *Depression: Clinical, Experimental, and Theoretical Aspects*. New York: Hoeber [republished as *Depression: Causes and Treatment*. Philadelphia: University of Pennsylvania Press].

Beck, A. T. (1976). *Cognitive Behaviour Therapy and the Emotional Disorders*. New York: International Universities Press.

Beck, A. T., Freeman, A., & Davis, D. T. (2007). *Cognitive Therapy of Personality Disorders*. New York: Guilford Press.

Beck, A. T., Rush, A. J., Shaw. B. F., & Emery, G. (1979). *Cognitive Therapy of Depression*. New York: Guilford Press.

Bennett-Levy, J. (2006) . Therapist skills: a cognitive model of their acquisition and refinement. *Behavioural and Cognitive Psychotherapy, 34*: 57–78.

Best, M., & Neuhauser, D. (2004). Ignaz Semmelweis and the birth of infection control. *Quality & Safety in Health Care, 13*: 233–234.

Blackburn, I. M., James, I. A., Milne, D. L., Baker, C., Standart, S., Garland, A., & Reichelt, K. (2001). The revised cognitive therapy scale (CTS-R): psychometric properties. *Behavioural and Cognitive Psychotherapy, 29*: 431–446.

Borg-Laufs, M. (2011). *Störungsübergreifendes Diagnostik-System für die Kinder- und Jugendlichenpsychotherapie (SDS-KJ)*. Tübingen: DGVT-Verlag.

Borkovec, T. D. (1994). The nature, functions, and origins of worry. In: G. C. L. Davey & F. Tallis (Eds.), *Worrying: Perspectives on Theory, Assessment and Treatment* (pp. 5–33). Oxford, UK: John Wiley & Sons.

Choy, Y., Fyer, A. J., & Lipsitz, J. D. (2007). Treatment of specific phobia in adults. *Clinical Psychology Review, 27*(3): 266–286.

Clark, D. M. (1996). Panic disorder: from theory to therapy. In: P. M. Salkovskis (Ed.), *Frontiers of Cognitive Therapy* (pp. 318–344). New York: Guilford Press.

Clark, D. M. (2004). Developing new treatments: on the interplay between theories, experimental science and clinical innovation. *Behaviour Research and Therapy, 42*: 10891104.

Clark, D. M., & Wells, A. (1995). A cognitive model of social phobia. In: R. Heimberg, M. Liebowitz, D.A. Hope, & F. R. Schneier (Eds.), *Social Phobia: Diagnosis, Assessment and Treatment* (pp. 69–93). New York: Guilford Press.

Davidson, K. (2007). *Cognitive Therapy for Personality Disorders*. London: Routledge.

Davis, D. M., & Hayes, J. A. (2011). What are the benefits of mindfulness? A practice review of psychotherapy-related research. *Psychotherapy, 48*(2): 198–208.

Denissen, K., & van Bilsen, H. (1987). Motivationele milieu therapie (Motivational milieu therapy). *Tijdschrift voor Psychotherapie, 13*(3): 128–138. Netherlands: Bohn Stafleu Van Loghum.

Department of Health (2008). *Improving Access to Psychological Therapies Implementation Plan: National Guidelines for Regional Delivery*. London: DoH.

Dimeff, L. A., & Marlatt, G. A. (1998). Preventing relapse and maintaining change in addictive behaviors. *Clinical Psychology: Science and Practice, 5*: 513–525.

Domjan, M. (2006). *The Principles of Learning and Behavior*. Belmont, CA: Thomson/Wadsworth.

Dugas, M. J., & Ladouceur, R. (2000). Treatment of GAD. Targeting intolerance of uncertainty in two types of worry. *Behavior Modification, 24*(5): 635–657.

D'Zurilla, T. J., & Nezu, A. M. (2007). *Problem Solving Therapy: A Positive Approach to Clinical Intervention*. New York: Springer.

Ehlers, A., & Clark, D. M. (2000). A cognitive model of posttraumatic stress disorder. *Behaviour Research and Therapy, 38*(4): 319–345.

Ellis, A. (1958). Rational psychotherapy. *Journal of General Psychology, 59*(1): 35–49.

Ellis, A. (1970). *The Essence of Rational Psychotherapy: A Comprehensive Approach to Treatment*. New York: Institute for Rational Living.

Ellis, A. (2004). *Rational Emotive Behavior Therapy: It Works for Me—It Can Work for You*. New York: Prometheus Books.

Eysenck, H. J. (1963). Behaviour therapy, extinction and relapse in neurosis. *British Journal of Psychiatry, 109*: 12–18 [doi: 10.1192/bjp.109.458.1].

Falloon, I. R. H. (2003). Family interventions for mental disorders: efficacy and effectiveness. *World Psychiatry, 2*(1): 20–28.

Falloon, I. R. H., Montero, I., Sungur, M., Mastroeni, A., Malm, U., Economou, M., Grawe, R., Harangozo, J., Mizuno, M., Murakami, M., Hager, B., Held, T., Veltro, F., & Gedye, R. (The OTP Collaborative Group) (2004). Implementation of evidence-based treatment for schizophrenic disorders: two-year outcome of an international field trial of optimal treatment. *World Psychiatry, 3*(2): 104–109.

Farmer, R. F., & Chapman, A. (2007). *Behavioral Interventions in Cognitive Behavior Therapy: Practical Guidance for Putting Theory into Action*. Washington, DC: American Psychological Association.

Festinger, L. (1956). *When Prophecy Fails: A Social and Psychological Study of A Modern Group that Predicted the Destruction of the World*, L. Festinger, H. Riecken, & S. Schachter (Eds.). New York: Harper-Torchbooks.

Festinger, L. (1957). *A Theory of Cognitive Dissonance*. Stanford, CA: Stanford University Press.

Foa, E. B., & Rothbaum, B. O. (1998). *Treating the Trauma of Rape: Cognitive Behavioral Therapy for PTSD*. New York: Guilford Press.

Foa, E. B., Steketee, G., & Groves, G. (1979). Use of behavioural therapy and imipramine in a case with severe OCD and depression. *Behavior Modification, 3*(3): 419–430.

Froggatt, W. (2001). *A Brief Introduction to Rational Emotive Behaviour Therapy*. New Zealand: REBT Institute.

Gambrill, E. D. (1977). *Behavior Modification: Handbook of Assessment, Intervention, and Evaluation*. San Francisco, CA: Jossey-Bass.

Giesen-Bloo, J., van Dyck, R., Spinhoven, P., van Tilburg, W., Dirksen, C., van Asselt, T., Kremers, I., Nadort, M., & Arntz, A. (2006). Outpatient psychotherapy for borderline personality disorder: a randomized trial of schema focused therapy versus transference focused therapy. *Archives of General Psychiatry, 63*(6): 649–658.

Glasser, W. (2003). *Warning: Psychiatry Can Be Hazardous to Your Mental Health*. New York: HarperCollins.

Goldfried, M. R., & Sprafkin, J. N. (1976). Behavioral personality assessment. In: J. T. Spence, R. C. Carson, & J. W. Thibaut (Eds.), *Behavioral Approaches to Therapy* (pp. 295–321). Morristown, NJ: General Learning Press.

Grove, W. M. (1987). The reliability of psychiatric diagnosis. In: C. G. Last, & M. Hersen (Eds.), *Issues in Diagnostic Research*. New York: Plenum Publishing Corp.

Harvey, A., Watkins, E., Mansell, W., & Shafran, R. (2004). *Cognitive Behavioural Processes Across Psychological Disorders: A Transdiagnostic Approach to Research and Treatment*. Oxford: Oxford University Press.

Hayes, S. C. (2004). Acceptance and commitment therapy, relational frame theory, and the third wave of behavior therapy. *Behavior Therapy, 35*: 639–665.

Hayes, S. C., Barnes-Holmes, D., & Roche, B. (Eds.) (2001). *Relational Frame Theory: A Post-Skinnerian Account of Human Language and Cognition*. New York: Plenum Press.

Hayes, S. C., Strosahl, K. D., & Wilson, K. G. (1999). *Acceptance and Commitment Therapy*. New York: Guilford Press.

Heimberg, R., Liebowitz, M., Hope, D. A., & Schneier, F. R. (Eds.) (1995). *Social Phobia: Diagnosis, Assessment and Treatment*. New York: Guilford Press.

Helzer, J. E., Clayton, P. J., Pambakian, R., Reich, T., Woodruff, R. Jr, Reveley, M. A. (1977). Reliability of psychiatric diagnosis: II. The test/retest reliability of diagnostic classification. *Archives of General Psychiatry, 34*(2): 136–141.

Hettema, J., Steele, J., & Miller, W. R. (2005). Motivational interviewing. *Annual Review of Clinical Psychology, 1*: 91–111.

Hillenbrand, C. (2006). *Einführung in die Pädagogik bei Verhaltensstörungen*. München.

Hyler, S., Williams, J., & Spitzer, R. (1982). Reliability in the DSM-III field trials. *Archives of General Psychiatry, 39*: 1275–1278.

Junge-Hoffmeister, J. (2006). Operante Verfahren. In: H.-U. Wittchen & J. Hoyer (Eds.), *Lehrbuch der Klinischen Psychologie und Psychotherapie* (Chapter 20, pp. 435–449). Heidelberg: Springer.

Kanfer, F. H., Reinecker, H., & Schmelzer, D. (2000). *Selbstmanagement-Therapie*. Berlin: Springer.

Kelly, G. (1955). *The Psychology of Personal Constructs, Volumes I & II*. New York: Norton [reprinted London: Routledge, 1991].

Kendal, P. C., & Braswell, L. B. (1985). *Cognitive Behavioural Modification with Impulsive Children*. New York: Guilford Press.

Kinderman, P. (2005). A psychological model of mental disorder. *Harvard Review of Psychiatry, 13*: 206–217.

Kinderman, P., & Tai, S. (2006). Clinical implications of a psychological model of mental disorder. *Behavioural and Cognitive Psychotherapy, 35*: 1–14.

Kingdon, D. G., & Turkington, D. (1991). The use of cognitive behaviour therapy with a normalising rationale in schizophrenia. *Journal of Nervous and Mental Disease, 179*: 207–211.

Kiresuk, T., & Sherman, R. (1968). Goal attainment scaling: a general method of evaluating comprehensive mental health programmes. *Community Mental Health Journal, 4*: 443–453.

Kirk, S. A., & Kutchins, H. (1988). Deliberate misdiagnosis in mental health practice. *Social Service Review, 62*: 225–237.

Kirk, S. A., & Kutchins, H. (1992). *The Selling of DSM: The Rhetoric of Science in Psychiatry*. Hawthorne, New York: Aldine de Gruyter.

Kuyken, W., Watkins, E., Holden, E., White, K., Taylor, R., Byford, S., Evans, A., Radford, S., Teasdale, J., & Dalgleish, T. (2010). How does mindfulness-based cognitive therapy work? *Behaviour Research and Therapy, 48*: 1012–1020.

Lazarus, A. A. (1973). Multimodal behavior therapy: treating the "BASIC ID." *Journal of Nervous and Mental Disease, 156*(6): 404–411.

Lazarus, A. A. (1989). *The Practice of Multimodal Therapy: Systematic, Comprehensive, and Effective Psychotherapy*. Baltimore, MD: Johns Hopkins University Press.

Lewin, K. (1935). *A Dynamic Theory of Personality*. New York: McGraw-Hill.

Lewin, K. (1936). *Principles of Topological Psychology*. New York: McGraw-Hill.

Lewin, K. (1948). *Resolving Social Conflicts; Selected Papers on Group Dynamics*, G. W. Lewin (Ed.). New York: Harper & Row.

Linehan, M. (1993). *Cognitive Behavioral Treatment For Borderline Personality Disorder*. New York: Guilford Press.

Linehan, M. M., Schmidt, H., Dimeff, L. A., Craft, J. C., Kanter, J., & Comtois, J. A. (1999). Dialectical behavior therapy for patients with borderline personality disorder and drug-dependence. *American Journal on Addictions, 8*(4): 279–292.

Lovaas, O. I. (1987). Behavioral treatment and normal educational and intellectual functioning in young autistic children. *Journal of Consultative Clinical Psychology, 55*(1): 3–9.

Mahoney, M. J. (1977). Reflections on the cognitive learning trend in psychotherapy. *American Psychologist, 32*: 5–13.

Marlatt, G. A., & Gordon, J. R. (Eds.) (1985). *Relapse Prevention: Maintenance Strategies in the Treatment of Addictive Behaviors*. New York: Guilford Press.

Miller, W. R., & Rollnick, S. (2002). *Motivational Interviewing: Preparing People for Change*. New York: Guilford Press.

Mowrer, O. H. (1950). *Learning Theory and Personality Dynamics*. New York: Ronald Press.

Narciss, S. (2006). Verhaltensanalyse und Verhaltensmodifikation auf der Basis lernpsychologischer Erkenntnisse. In: H.-U. Wittchen & J. Hoyer (Eds.), *Lehrbuch der Klinischen Psychologie und Psychotherapie* (pp. 383–395). Heidelberg: Springer.

National Institute for Health and Clinical Excellence (NICE). http://www.nice.org.uk/guidance/

Öst, L. G. (2008). Efficacy of the third wave of behavioral therapies: a systematic review and meta-analysis. *Behaviour Research and Therapy, 46*(3): 296–321.

Padesky, C. A. (1993). Socratic questioning: changing minds or guided discovery? *Congress of the European Association of Behavioural and Cognitive Therapies*, September, London.

Parker, G., & Hadzi-Pavlovic, D. (2001). A question of style: refining the dimensions of personality. *Journal of Personality Disorders, 15*(4): 300–318.

Premack, D. (1959). Towards empirical behavior laws: positive reinforcement. *Psychological Review, 66*: 219–233.

Prochaska, J. O., DiClemente, C. C., & Norcross, J. C. (1992). In search of how people change: applications to addictive behaviors. *American Psychologist, 47*(9): 1102–1114.

Rinck, M., & Becker, E. S. (2006). Lernpsychologische Grundlagen. In: H.-U. Wittchen & J. Hoyer (Eds.), *Lehrbuch der Klinischen Psychologie und Psychotherapie* (pp. 88–105). Heidelberg: Springer.

Roth, A., & Fonagy, P. (2004). *What Works for Whom?* New York: Guilford Press.

Roth, A. D., & Pilling, S. (2007). *The Competences Required To Deliver Effective Cognitive and Behavioural Therapy for People with Depression and with Anxiety Disorders*. London: DoH.

Salter, A. (1949). *Conditioned Reflex Therapy: The Direct Approach to the Reconstruction of Personality*. New York: Wellness Institute, 2002.

Segal, Z. V., Williams, J. M. G., & Teasdale, J. T. (2001). *Mindfulness-based Cognitive Therapy for Depression: A New Approach to Preventing Relapse.* New York: Guilford Press.

Skinner, B. F. (1938). *The Behavior of Organisms: An Experimental Analysis.* Cambridge, MA: B. F. Skinner Foundation.

Stolee, P., Rockwood, K., Fox, R. A., & Streiner, D. L. (1992). The use of goal attainment scaling in a geriatric care setting. *Journal of the American Geriatrics Society, 40*(6): 574–578.

Teasdale, J. D. (1977). Psychological treatment of phobias. In: N. Sutherland (Ed.), *Tutorial Essays in Psychology, Volume 1* (pp. 137–163). Hove: Lawrence Erlbaum.

Teasdale, J. D. (1983). Negative thinking in depression: cause, effect or reciprocal relationship. *Advances in Behaviour Research and Therapy, 5*(1): 3–25.

Teasdale, J. D. (1988). Cognitive vulnerability to persistent depression. *Cognition and Emotion, 2*: 247–274.

Teasdale, J. D., & Bancroft, J. (1977). Manipulation of thought content as a determinant of mood and corrugators electromyographic activity in depressed patients. *Journal of Abnormal Psychology, 86*, 235–241.

Teasdale, J. D., & Barnard, T. J. (1993). *Affect, Cognition and Change: Remodelling Depressive Thought*. Hove: Lawrence Erlbaum.

Teasdale, J. D., Segal, Z. V., Williams, J. M. G., Ridgeway, V. A., Soulsby, J. M., & Lau, M. A. (2000). Prevention of relapse/recurrence in major depression by mindfulness-based cognitive therapy. *Journal of Consulting and Clinical Psychology, 68*: 615–623.

Ullmann, L. P., & Krasner, L. (1975). *A Psychological Approach to Abnormal Behavior* (2nd edn). Englewood Cliffs, NJ: Prentice-Hall.

Van Bilsen, H., & Wilke, M. (1998). Drug and alcohol abuse in young people. In: P. J. Graham (Ed.), *Cognitive-Behaviour Therapy for Children and Families* (pp. 246–261). New York: Cambridge University Press.

Van Bilsen, H. P. (1985). Praktische problemen in de ambulante gedragstherapie bij heroïneverslaafden (Practical problems in the ambulatory behavior therapy among heroin addicts). *Gedragstherapie, 18*(1): 77–86.

Van Bilsen, H. P. (1986a). Heroin addiction: morals revisited. *Journal of Substance Abuse Treatment, 3*(4): 279–284.

Van Bilsen, H. P. (1986b). Moraliseren of normaliseren: een psychologische visie op de hulpverlening aan zogenaamd ongemotiveerde heroïneverslaafden in methadonprogrammas. (Moralization or normalization: a psychological view of the treatment of so-called unmotivated heroin addicts in methadone programs). *Tijdschrift voor Alcohol, Drugs en Andere Psychotrope Stoffen, 12*(5): 182–189.

Van Bilsen, H. P. (1991). Motivational interviewing: perspectives from the Netherlands, with particular emphasis on heroin dependent clients. In: W. R. Miller & S. Rollnick (Eds.), *Motivational Interviewing: Preparing People to Change Addictive Behaviour* (pp. 152–182). New York: Guilford Press.

Van Bilsen, H. P., & van Emst, A. J. (1989). Motivating drug users. In: G. Bennet (Ed.), *Treating Drug Abuse* (pp. 29–53). London: Routledge.

Van Bilsen, H. P. J. G. (1995). Motivation as a precondition and bridge between unmotivated client and overmotivated therapist. In: H. P. J. G. van Bilsen, P. C. Kendall, & J. Slavenburg (Eds.), *Behavioral Approaches for Children and Adolescents: Challenges for the Next Century*. New York: Plenum Press.

Veale, D. (2008). Behavioural activation for depression. *Advances in Psychiatric Treatment, 14*: 29–36.

Verheul, R. (2005). Clinical utility of dimensional models for personality pathology. *Journal of Personality Disorders, 19*: 283–302.

Watson, J. B., & Rayner, R. (1920). Conditioned emotional reactions. *Journal of Experimental Psychology, 3*(1): 1–14.

Weber, M. (1926). *Max Weber: A Biography*. New Brunswick: Transaction Books, 1988.

Wells, A. (1999). A cognitive model of generalized anxiety disorder. *Behavior Modification, 23*(4): 526–555.

Widiger, T. A. (1992). Categorical versus dimensional classification: implications from and for research. *Journal of Personality Disorders, 6*: 287–300.

Wolpe, J. (1964). *The Conditioning Therapies: The Challenge in Psychotherapy*. New York: Holt, Rinehart and Winston.

World Health Organisation (2001). *International Classification of Diseases and Related Health Problems (ICD-10)*. Geneva: WHO.

Young, J., Arntz, A., & Giesen-Bloo, J. (2006). Therapy adherence and competence scale. www.epp.unimaas.nl (accessed 1 May 2006).

Young, J. E., Klosko, J. S., & Weishaar, M. E. (2005). *Schemagerichte therapie; handbook voor therapeuten*. Houten: Bohn Stafleu van Loghum.

INDEX

For Product Safety Concerns and Information please contact our EU representative GPSR@taylorandfrancis.com
Taylor & Francis Verlag GmbH, Kaufingerstraße 24, 80331 München, Germany

www.ingramcontent.com/pod-product-compliance
Lightning Source LLC
Chambersburg PA
CBHW060741150926
51501CB00003B/66
9780367323813